OCCUPATIONS

A Selected List of Pamphlets

OCCUPATIONS

A Selected List of Pamphlets

By
GERTRUDE FORRESTER, Ed. D.

Director of Guidance, Public Schools,
Ridgefield Park, N. J.

Instructor, Summer Sessions,
Teachers College, Columbia University

THE H. W. WILSON COMPANY
NEW YORK   1946

Foreword

During recent years librarians have reported that literature on occupations is being called for with a high degree of frequency.

Books describing a single occupation or a group of occupations are numerous and are easily located in book lists. There is, however, another type of occupational literature that is more popular than books; namely pamphlets and brief monographs, each one describing a single occupation or occupational field. These pamphlets, for purposes of everyday vocational counseling, are more practical than books. They are less expensive; they give a terse resume of the requirements, conditions and rewards of an occupation; they can be discarded and cheaply replaced when they become obsolete. Because of these features pamphlets are the most popular form in which to store and convey information about occupations, and their number has become almost overwhelming.

In the early days of vocational guidance—from, say 1915 to 1925 —pamphlets were prepared chiefly by the bureaus of vocational guidance newly organized in school systems. Among the early series were those of Cincinnati, Indianapolis, Pittsburgh, and New Orleans; they were based on surveys generally local in character and were distributed free so long as the supply lasted.

As interest in vocational guidance spread, these locally produced pamphlets were unable to meet the demands existing in various parts of the country. Accordingly, in 1930 a commercial publisher (Institute for Research) courageously undertook to produce a pretentious series of pamphlets on occupations on a systematic plan and at uniform prices. The faith of this pioneer was justified. The pamphlets were widely sold. Soon other commercial firms entered the market with other series; until today there are nine firms that specialize in producing these pamphlets. Government has also entered the field, pamphlet series being produced by the U. S. Office of Education, the National Roster of Scientific and Specialized Personnel, and the Bureau of Labor Statistics.

A high point in the development of pamphlets in series was the inauguration of Occupational Abstracts in 1936 by the National Occupational Conference, operating under funds provided by the Carnegie Corporation. The series is continued by Occupational Index, Inc.

To the sources mentioned should be added the many professional and trade organizations which, while not publishing pamphlets in series or on a commercial basis, nevertheless add materially to the number of pamphlets available.

The average librarian, and even the trained vocational counselor, finds it difficult to keep abreast of these diverse publications. Some central index is imperative. As early as 1934 the publishers of this book issued a bibliography of pamphlets on occupations (*Occupations and Vocational Guidance* by Wilma Bennett). Since its last revision in 1938 the number of pamphlets and the number of sources have increased greatly. A completely new bibliography was required. This, Dr. Forrester has supplied in this volume. It goes without saying that her product is of supreme importance to vocational guidance and to American education. With this selected listing of titles, librarians can compile, with ease and economy, a set of pamphlets tailored to the needs of the community; counselors and teachers can make assignments to current occupational literature; and students can pursue their examination of occupational literature with relatively little help.

In addition to its immediately practical value, this compilation shows the wide fields covered by pamphlets about occupations; it should reveal the gaps now existing and should point the way to further steps which should be taken in the collection of information designed to assist the youth of this generation in finding their way through the occupational maze.

HARRY D. KITSON

Teachers College, Columbia University
December 1, 1945

Contents

PART I
Criteria Used in Compiling This Bibliography

This bibliography has been compiled in order to assist counselors, librarians, and teachers in locating occupational information in pamphlet form. Leaflets and pamphlets, evanescent in nature, often emanating from obscure sources, are likely to escape the most diligent collector of information about occupations. Often it is not until confronted with a question from a counselee that one feels the need for a pamphlet on a specific occupation.

Comprehensiveness. The first requisite of a bibliography of pamphlets on occupations is comprehensiveness. Effort has been made to have this list possess this characteristic for many sources have been explored. Existing lists were combed for names and addresses of publishers, and inquiries were then sent to 750 organizations that had been identified as publishers of occupational pamphlets.

Selectiveness. Second, to be effective, the bibliography should cite only monographs that follow accepted principles in the presentation of information. The pamphlets listed in this volume are those intended to help an individual in deciding whether the occupation described would be appropriate for him. Accordingly, in determining whether or not to include a given pamphlet, the compiler scrutinized each one to see whether the information touched the proper topics. The points that should be covered have been set forth by a committee of the National Vocational Guidance Association as follows:

OUTLINE FOR A PAMPHLET ON AN OCCUPATION [1]

- I   History of the occupation
- II   Importance of the occupation and its relation to society
- III   Number of workers engaged in occupation
- IV   Need for workers—trends
- V   Duties
- VI   Qualifications

[1] "Content of a Good Occupational Monograph—the Basic Outline." Revised by the Occupational Research Section of the National Vocational Guidance Association. *Occupations, the Vocational Guidance Magazine.* October, 1940. p. 20-3.

OUTLINE FOR A PAMPHLET ON OCCUPATION—*Continued*

Although not all of the pamphlets listed in this book follow this outline exactly, none was accepted that did not cover at least some of the major points. Many pamphlets published under the title of an occupation are not designed to give information about workers in the occupation (qualifications, requirements, and rewards); they are written to instruct one in the techniques of the occupation. An example of this type is a booklet entitled *Legal Stenographer.* Such pamphlets, prepared for use in vocational education and not for vocational guidance, were excluded from the bibliography.

Intensive search uncovered 1500 pamphlets that could be recommended as being reasonably adequate. The following criteria were used in selecting the pamphlets.

CRITERIA OF A GOOD OCCUPATIONAL PAMPHLET

Authenticity. The information given in a pamphlet must be correct. Accordingly, the source of each pamphlet was carefully considered and only those pamphlets were accepted which gave evidence that the writer was in possession of accurate information. The professional status of the author or organization sponsoring the publication serves as a helpful guide in determining whether the material is authoritative. Of the 1500 pamphlets here listed, 150 were issued by professional, trade, and national organizations. This evidences a warm interest in the vocational guidance of youth. The reader may confidently rely on pamphlets prepared by professional organizations with professional codes of ethics. It would be desirable to have more from such sources. They are objective, unbiased; they are generally based on sound statistical studies; and they constitute a valuable addition to vocational guidance literature.

Care was taken also to see if the information was authentic by scrutinizing the sources of quoted or paraphrased material, whether taken from printed matter, conferences, or interviews.

Objectivity. Another feature required is objectivity. The facts given should not be weighted in favor of a specific product or idea. The scientific approach should be manifest throughout: in the methods used in assembling the information; in the unbiased presentation; and in the obvious intent to serve, not special and limited interests, but the well-being of young people. A large number of the pamphlets present the advantages and disadvantages very impartially and conscientiously. All pamphlets were rejected that bore the unmistakable marks of propaganda.

Recency. Recency of information is another desideratum. The reader wishes to know the date of original publication and the dates of revision. He wishes to know whether the pamphlet includes the latest scientific knowledge and the latest returns of the U. S. Census. Perfect certainty on this point was not attainable in all cases since, unfortunately, some publishers of pamphlets do not insert the date when the information was gathered, or worse still, the dates of publication and revision are not given. In view of the frequent changes in occupational conditions, various publishers revise their pamphlets from time to time. It is hoped that all will adopt the practice of dating revisions.

When selecting pamphlets for purchase, the buyer will wish to note the date of copyright. A number of the pamphlets were published some time ago; the types of opportunities, salaries, and trends are out-dated. However, the requirements, traits, duties, qualifications, typical day's work, advantages and disadvantages of the type of work are fundamental and in many cases are better described in the older publications. For lists of approved schools the more recent pamphlets should be selected. The number of approved schools offering training in medical technology increased from 96 in 1936 to 136 in 1938. In the field of occupational therapy a 1941 pamphlet lists 6 approved schools for training while a 1945 publication lists 21 schools. Naturally, the reading lists in the more recent pamphlets have more value than the older ones.

Suitability. The librarian or counselor who is assembling the pamphlets is interested in their suitability. He wishes to know if they are appropriate to the age, interests, and understanding of the individuals who will use them. The annotations indicate any special groups for which the pamphlets were prepared.

Availability. To be useful a bibliography should list only publications that are currently available. The author has corresponded with all of the publishers listed and has assembled all of the materials indexed during the three months prior to publication of this bibliography. A few items which are temporarily out of print and were not available at the time of printing are so noted in the annotations. Pamphlets that have been withdrawn from circulation and cannot be purchased on the open market are not included in this list. An example is *Shipyard Diary of a Woman Welder* (Penguin Books Inc.). Again, the series of pamphlets published by several public school systems are not included since the supply is not great enough to meet any considerable demand. Pamphlets that are merely mimeographed or multilithed have, with few exceptions, not been included, since provision is not generally made for distributing them on a wide scale.

Information Not Found Elsewhere. For the most part recruiting bulletins of schools, colleges, and correspondence courses are not included. Exceptions have been made in the case of bulletins that contain information not otherwise available in inexpensive form or which contain exceptionally good illustrations. For the same reasons, some pamphlets have been included which describe industrial processes rather than kinds of work. In those cases the titles and annotations indicate the usefulness of the pamphlet.

Cost. While cost was not used as a criterion, care was exercised to include all free pamphlets that met the other requirements so that counselors and librarians might assemble a working library at least expense. The number of pamphlets listed that may be obtained free of cost is 265. Unfortunately they are the ones most likely to be out of print. The word "free" indicates that single copies are available without cost; frequently a charge is made for quantity orders. Also, because many pamphlets cost 75c and $1, some small books costing approximately one dollar are included.

References to Further Reading. A pamphlet which encourages further reading is more valuable for vocational guidance purposes than one which does not. The number of pamphlets containing annotated classified bibliographies is all too small. Those including references to vocational fiction; biographies of successful workers; and other printed information about conditions of work, qualifications, requirements, opportunities, and rewards are among those most highly recommended.

Style. An occupational pamphlet should be well written. The style should be interesting, clear, and concise. Some comments covering this point are included in the descriptions of the various series of publications.

Format. If several pamphlets contained approximately the same amount of information, the compiler selected those with the most attractive style, format, typography, and artistic appearance.

For further discussion of the features that should characterize an occupational pamphlet, the reader is referred to: "Distinguishing Marks of a Good Occupational Monograph" by the Occupational Research Committee of the National Vocational Guidance Association, published in *Occupations, the Vocational Guidance Magazine,* November, 1939.

Acknowledgement. For checking and correcting the titles and occupational code numbers, grateful acknowledgement is made to the Division of Occupational Analysis and Industrial Services, United States Employment Service, Department of Labor, Washington, D.C.

Especial thanks are extended for supplying the code numbers and terminology of titles from Edition III of the Supplement to the *Dictionary of Occupational Titles,* which is now in preparation.

PART II
How the Annotations Were Prepared

In the annotated bibliography (see Part VI, pages 66 to 229), the data given for each pamphlet include the title, author if known, publisher, date of publication, number of pages, and price. If five or more pamphlets of any publisher have been listed, the address is not given in the individual entries, but the series is described in Part IV. In case two or more copyright dates are given, the latest date is noted, followed by the words "revised edition." If the pamphlet is a reproduction of a typewritten manuscript, the word "mimeographed" is used even though the reproduction may have been made by the offset process, by photolithography or by photostat. That is, the word "mimeographed" distinguishes pamphlets that are in typewriter type from those that are in printing type.

The publications are of varying quality. The annotations aim to present in a few words the kind of information that may be found in each pamphlet, and to indicate any special group to which it may be addressed. If the pamphlet contains photographs or cuts showing workers engaged in typical kinds of work, the word "illustrated" is used in the annotation; in many cases the number of illustrations is given. Some pamphlets which describe industrial processes rather than kinds of work are included if the pictures are appropriate for bulletin board displays; in those instances, the annotations suggest this specific use of the pamphlet. Because the list of schools offering training in a specific vocation is frequently of interest, the annotations indicate the inclusion of this list.

The word "bibliography" in the annotation indicates that the pamphlet contains a reading list which refers the reader to other printed sources of occupational information. If the references relate solely to the technical aspects of the subject, the word "bibliography" does not appear. It is hoped that when some of the present pamphlets are revised, they will include more references to occupational literature.

Pamphlets recommended for first purchase in small libraries are marked with a star; and those especially recommended are marked with a double star.

PART III

Indexing and Filing Pamphlets on Occupations

Terminology and Classification. Many pamphlets were written before the publication of the *Dictionary of Occupational Titles* and hence do not use the standard vocational terminology. In this index, the name of the trade or profession is not used. Instead the name of the vocation is given in terms of the worker who follows it; thus, instead of photography, photographer; instead of law, lawyer. While this is a departure from the terminology used by the writers and publishers of some pamphlets, it conforms to the practice now advocated in vocational terminology. It is hoped that the reader will not be discommoded by this practice.

Certain pamphlets cover not merely the work of a single specialist but a group of workers. In these cases the general heading is used: Printing trades worker or Glass industry worker.

As in all indexing, questions of classification frequently arose; for example, whether to list music teacher under "Musician" or "Teacher." In such cases the titles and codes used in the *Dictionary of Occupational Titles* were adopted.

Questions About Filing Pamphlets. In the listing of titles of occupations (pages 66 to 229), an alphabetic arrangement is used. Many librarians claim that readers can find pamphlets more quickly and with less confusion in an alphabetically arranged file.

In describing a public library vocational information service, Grace O. Kelley discusses the filing of 3,600 pamphlets in a nine-drawer vertical file. She presents the following reasons for filing the occupational pamphlets alphabetically: [2]

(1) An alphabetical arrangement is easier to maintain and to operate than is a classified order. The latter requires not only familiarity with terminology but also a systematic knowledge of the whole field of occupations and calls for the constantly recurring decision as to where to place or to look for each pamphlet or subject in relation to all other material. The alphabetical order requires mainly a knowledge of consistent and up-to-date terminology, not of relationships.

(2) An alphabetical arrangement is easier to use by both laymen and librarians. When inquirers are left alone to use the files the great majority would be helpless before a classified order.

(3) Classified groupings require an alphabetical subject index to guide one to the specific occupations desired. Such indexes are found in the few libraries

[2] Kelley, Grace O. "A Large Public Library Prepares for Postwar Vocational Information Service." *Library Journal.* October 1, 1944. p. 804-7.

which have classified catalogs and in some of the printed bibliographies where subjects are classified. Where indexes are lacking it is hard to find concrete information quickly. But a specific alphabetical arrangement needs no index; it serves as a kind of index itself.

(4) Any code arrangement is affected by future developments in its subject field, even to a point where relationships within the whole field may be changed. Simple expansion does not always suffice since insertions may seriously dislocate related groupings. An alphabetical arrangement under specific topic takes care of new subjects usually by insertion, or by retiring an old subject if a newer one supersedes it.

(5) An argument favoring an alphabetical order comes from the way in which requests are received in the public library. The majority of these are for a single occupation, sometimes for several occupations totally unrelated to one another, often from the point of view of the varied interests or equipment of the inquirer. The individual is seldom interested in surveying, or even conscious of the existence of, a whole related field or of the relationships within a large inclusive field. The great majority of the inquiries seem to be met through an alphabetical order.

Some collections of occupational pamphlets are filed according to the classification system used in the *Dictionary of Occupational Titles*. In describing this method of filing in the reference library of vocational literature at Alabama College, Rochelle Rodd Gachet concludes: [3]

The use of the code system of the *Dictionary of Occupational Titles* gives to students and counselors familiarity with the terms in use in the working world and encourages the use of nomenclature now employed in the offices of the U. S. Employment Service, which may become standard in all placement work. . . The *Dictionary* offers for the first time a common language in referring to jobs, and because of its present wide use its universality of acceptance as a classification structure is not improbable. . . As the issuing of supplements to the *Dictionary* is planned as a continuing project, a library using these classifications has its research work done for it, so to speak, and is assured of permanency and flexibility in the classification plan.

Another description of filing occupational pamphlets according to this system is entitled: "A Plan for Filing Unbound Occupational Information Based on the *Dictionary of Occupational Titles*." [4] Providing for a vertical file of 276 occupational titles, it is a numerical system based on a subject classification, following the arrangement of titles and codes used in the *Dictionary*.

This plan was recommended by the Guidance Bureau of the New York State Department of Education to the public schools of the State. So many libraries outside of the State of New York have adopted this plan that materials have been made available commercially from the

[3] Gachet, Rochelle Rodd. "Filing Occupational Information for Women." *Occupations, the Vocational Guidance Magazine.* March, 1944. p. 354-7.

[4] Handville, Raymond. "A Plan for Filing Unbound Occupational Information Based on the *Dictionary of Occupational Titles*." The Chronicle Press, Port Byron, N. Y. 1944. 16p. 50c.

Chronicle Press, Port Byron, N.Y. These include a booklet of perforated gummed guide labels containing clearly printed code numbers and titles used in the file.

For many years, the author has used the classification system of 27 headings and 135 divisions suggested in *Methods of Vocational Guidance*.[5] In her counseling office about two hundred young people have assisted, over a period of time, in filing and replacing clippings and pamphlets. While it takes a few minutes to become orientated to the plan, most young people become acquainted with it in a surprisingly short time. This plan is in some respects similar to that of the *Dictionary of Occupational Titles*. According to both classification systems, the medical occupations would be grouped together, the types of engineering would be assembled in one place, the various sciences would be in adjoining folders, and the several kinds of agricultural occupations would follow one another.

Many users of occupational pamphlets agree that if an enquirer is to go to a vertical file and find quickly a pamphlet on a specific occupation the alphabetic arrangement is simplest. However, if the counselor wishes to use the file to present a panoramic view of the world of work, to extend young people's horizons, to sharpen their curiosity, or to make them aware of related occupations of which they are unaware, the classified system is recommended.

Filing the Pamphlets. The pamphlets are indexed alphabetically by occupational title in the annotated bibliography (pages 66 to 229). An alphabetic file may be set up following the same arrangement. Many libraries may have the set of seventy-five file folders printed with an alphabetic list of occupations distributed by the Science Research Associates, Chicago, Ill. If so, the following titles may be added to the set so that some folders will not be too cumbersome:

Air conditioning	Nursing
Beauty culture	Occupational therapy
Clerical work	Optometry
Chiropody	Osteopathy
Civil engineering	Pharmacy
Dentistry	Physical education
Dietetics	Physical therapy
Electrical engineering	Public health work
Mathematics	Truck gardening
Medical laboratory technology	Undertaking and funeral directing
Medical record librarianship	Veterinary medicine
Mechanical engineering	X-ray technology
Medicine	

[5] Forrester, Gertrude. *Methods of Vocational Guidance.* D. C. Heath and Co. 1944. p. 423-8. $3.00.

For the convenience of users who may wish to arrange their occupational files according to the *Dictionary of Occupational Titles,* the *Dictionary* code numbers have been added to this list. The title at the head of each group of entries is the title under which the occupation is defined in the *Dictionary.* Opposite the title, at the right-hand side of the same line, is the code number. This "base" title is the one by which the occupation is most commonly known, or the one which is considered most descriptive of the occupation. Other titles by which the occupation may be designated are given in their proper alphabetical order in the list with a "see" reference to the "base" title.

The file folders may be arranged in numerical order according to the assigned code numbers. The structure of the U. S. Employment Service Occupational Classification, as set forth in the *Dictionary of Occupational Titles,* is given below. The codes have been assigned in such a manner as to form related groups of occupations, arranged in major groups, divisions, and subdivisions.

MAJOR OCCUPATIONAL GROUPS AND DIVISIONS

0. Professional and managerial occupations
0—0 through 0—3	Professional occupations
0—4 through 0—6	Semiprofessional occupations
0—7 through 0—9	Managerial and official occupations

1. Clerical and sales occupations
1—0 through 1—4	Clerical and kindred occupations
1—5 through 1—9	Sales and kindred occupations

2. Service occupations
2—0	Domestic service occupations
2—2 through 2—5	Personal service occupations
2—6	Protective service occupations
2—8 through 2—9	Building service workers and porters

3. Agricultural, fishery, forestry, and kindred occupations
3—0 through 3—4	Agricultural, horticultural, and kindred occupations
3—8	Fishery occupations
3—9	Forestry (except logging) and hunting and trapping occupations

4. ⎫
5. ⎬ Skilled occupations

6. ⎫
7. ⎬ Semiskilled occupations

8. ⎫
9. ⎬ Unskilled occupations

Although the *Dictionary* defines 21,653 job titles, not all of the occupations listed here are included in it; for example: mathematician, explorer, politician, scientist, penologist, pharmacologist, criminologist, nutritionist, probation officer, and television industry worker. For those titles a code number has not been determined. So that each title in this list would have a numerical designation for purposes of numercial filing, the author has assigned a residual or temporary code number (those ending with the last digit 9); for example, "explorer" has been given the code number 0-39.79 which is the residual code for the grouping embracing "natural scientists." The code numbers which are not official end with the digit 9; the user may assign as many of these residual codes as necessary when a given situation necessitates it.

Also, code numbers for general terms are not given in the *Dictionary*. A general term is a common title by which several specific jobs or occupations in one or more types of work may be designated. Since these general terms embrace not one but several different jobs, it is impossible to allocate them to specific groups within the group arrangement. Examples of general terms are Civil Service worker, Museum worker, and Ocean liner worker. For filing purposes, the author has designated the first three digits of the appropriate occupational code groups.

Some titles defined in the *Dictionary*, particularly "grouping titles" are not given a code number in the *Dictionary*. A "grouping title" is an uncoded, arbitrary title under which are grouped a number of titles that cannot be assigned a single code solely on the basis of occupational information, but that can be assigned any one of several codes when external factors, such as industry worked in or product worked on, are considered. When feasible, the range of code numbers is noted after the title; for example, fishery occupations: 3-38 to 3-89.

If a librarian arranges the folders alphabetically according to the titles at the left-hand side of the folder label, the code numbers at the right-hand side may be referred to in order to extract folders on related groups of occupations.

The space required for the 1500 pamphlets listed in this bibliography is a three-drawer vertical file, whether they are arranged according to the alphabet or another system. The 3600 occupational pamphlets in the Jamaica Public Library, New York City, occupy a nine-drawer vertical file. In other words, one drawer of a filing cabinet will house 400 pamphlets on the average.

PART IV

How to Use the Annotated Bibliography

In the Classroom. After the pamphlets have been selected, purchased, and filed, plans for promoting their use should be put into effect. Two purposes should be in mind. One is to stimulate youth to read about occupations so as to obtain an overview of the occupations in which people engage, and a general idea of what is required and what is offered in the various fields of work. The other aim is to encourage young people to narrow their choice of occupations, to select three or four which they are considering favorably and make an intensive study of the requirements, opportunities, and trends. As young people find information about occupations, they are urged to compare the qualifications required for success in these occupations with those which they possess or can acquire.

After the individual has narrowed his choice to two or three vocations, he should investigate one which appears to be suitable. After analyzing the occupation, he should be assisted in appraising his physical capacities, his intellectual grasp, his economic resources, and his tastes, so as to rule out any occupation in which he would not be successful and happy.

For credit in social studies, English, citizenship, or as a basis for club and group discussions, each student may be asked to submit a written report on an occupation he has investigated. Directions for carrying on such an investigation may be found in *I Find My Vocation.*[6] An outline found useful by the author in directing the occupational study of students in grades nine through twelve is reproduced below.[7]

Detailed Outline for Student's Report on Investigation of an Occupation

1. Title page. Title; name of student, class, teacher; date.

2. Table of contents.

3. HISTORY, development, and probable future trends of the occupation.

4. DUTIES of worker. Tasks performed by a person in this occupation. Outline of a typical day's work. Working conditions.

[6] Kitson, H. D. *I Find My Vocation.* McGraw-Hill Book Company. Revised edition. 1946. 227p.

[7] Forrester, Gertrude. *Methods of Vocational Guidance.* D. C. Heath and Company. 1944. p. 226-7.

5. REQUIREMENTS of the worker for entering and succeeding in the occupation. Education and training necessary. Where secured. Entrance requirements of those schools. High school courses that are essential for that occupation. School courses that are recommended as desirable. School courses that are recommended as preparation for a college course that offers training for this occupation. Union organization and requirements. Licenses required. Examinations required. Civil Service requirements.

6. QUALIFICATIONS of the worker. Personal qualities desirable. Character traits, personality traits, physical qualifications necessary. Hobbies that are especially relevant to this occupation.

7. ECONOMIC DEMAND. Number of workers in the occupation according to the U. S. Census report. Number of workers in your state. In your city. Number of men workers in this occupation. Of women. Number of workers ten and twenty years ago. Is the occupation growing in importance? Is the field crowded? Is work seasonal? Is work in this field necessary in times of depression? In times of war? Is work geographically limited? Average salary. Of men. Of women. Of beginning workers. Of experienced workers.

8. OPPORTUNITIES for placement. For experience. For apprenticeship. For advancement. Related occupations to which one might seek promotion. Opportunities for honorary, monetary or social rewards. Opportunities for profit sharing, bonuses, annuity or retirement provisions, unemployment insurance, sick benefits, vacations, discounts on goods purchased from the employer. Opportunities for home life, cultural growth, recreation, and participation in community affairs. What service useful to society does the worker perform?

9. ADVANTAGES of the occupation. What workers in this occupation like best about it.

10. DISADVANTAGES and special problems. What workers in this occupation like least about it.

11. Report of a BIOGRAPHY OF A SUCCESSFUL WORKER in this occupation. Abstracts of books and magazine articles written by modern Americans who faced conditions somewhat like those which modern youth will encounter. An occupational ladder.

12. Report of a PERSONAL INTERVIEW with a worker in this occupation.

13. Additional information.

14. NEWSPAPER CLIPPINGS. Typed or pen-written excerpts from books and magazines. Pictures.

15. PERSONAL CONCLUSION.

16. BIBLIOGRAPHY. References for future reading. Literature consulted in making this report.

For preparation of such a report young people are referred to the collections of occupational books and pamphlets. Since many of the pamphlets follow somewhat the same outline in presenting the information, they will be found to be a satisfactory source of reference.

To acquaint pupils with sources of information regarding occupations, and to help them in acquiring skill in locating, using, and organizing information from printed sources, the ingenious teacher will also encourage students to (1) compile reading lists from indexes and bibliographies; (2) compile lists of recommended books and pamphlets which can be affixed to bulletin boards; (3) procure additions to the pamphlet file; (4) prepare posters, displays, and exhibits designed to stimulate the study of the occupational books and pamphlets.

The Counselor. One of the principles of vocational guidance is that the counselor or teacher does not determine for the pupil what occupation he shall enter, but he refers him to sources of information upon which he can base his choice. In individual counseling an adviser wishes to have within reach a file of occupational pamphlets, so he may refer to a specific section for information and in order to point out the sources of information to the counselee. For example, the counselor will wish to refer to the pamphlets for lists of approved schools, regulations concerning apprenticeship, and other data which will assist the counselee in planning wisely his educational program. Since the library is the logical depository for reading materials which are to be circulated, the youth should be informed that he may draw out a pamphlet from the library occupational file for two weeks, or whatever happens to be the circulation period.

The Librarian. The librarian's interest in occupational pamphlets is to provide enquirers with readings on specific vocations. If the inquiry is for "medical occupations" or for "scientific occupations," for example, there would be an opportunity to show a section of a classified file as a panoramic view of occupations in that field.

The librarian is also interested in ways of attracting attention to recent vocational materials. The library is the hub of the occupational information wheel. But since the habit of research grows slowly, it is not enough that a library possess authentic up-to-date books and pamphlets; youth must be directed to them and trained in their use. Hence the need for bibliographies, leaflets, annotated book lists, posters, reviews, bulletin board displays, exhibits, and other means designed to encourage interest in reading. These devices mark an active coordinated program of occupational information which requires the cooperation of the classroom teacher, the librarian, and the counselor.

PART V

Pamphlets Published in Series, Arranged According to Publisher of Series

BALTIMORE DEPARTMENT OF EDUCATION, DIVISION OF VOCATIONAL EDUCATION, VOCATIONAL GUIDANCE, Baltimore, Md.

Your Future Series. 10c each.

The twenty-three pamphlets in this series were prepared by instructors and administrators in the city school system. They are intended for distribution to youth who are selecting courses of study in the vocational schools in Baltimore. Consequently, they contain some local information.

The topics covered include a description of work, education and training required, personal qualifications, opportunities for promotion, remuneration, sources of employment, advantages, and disadvantages. The reading references are carefully selected.

Between 6 and 12 pages in length, size 6 by 9 inches, each pamphlet contains an appropriate cover illustration. Some titles from this series that are listed in the annotated bibliography contain information not available from many other sources; for examples see sign painter, telephone operator, and cosmetologist.

The accountant. 1942
The auto mechanic. 1942
A career in life insurance. 1941
The civil engineer. 1940
The cosmetologist. 1941
The dentist. 1943
The electrical engineer. 1944
The electrician. 1941
The lawyer. 1944
The librarian's work. 1944
The machinist. 1942
The mechanical engineer. 1939

The nurse. 1943
The office worker. 1941
The pharmacist. 1941
The physician. 1944
The printer. 1943
The plumber. 1942
Retail store occupations. 1941
The secretary and stenographer. 1943
The sign painter. 1942
The social worker. 1941
The telephone operator. 1943

BELLMAN PUBLISHING COMPANY, 6 Park Street, Boston 8, Mass.

Vocational and Professional Monographs. 50c and 75c each. $25 for series of 75.

The sixty-three monographs in this series follow a uniform outline in providing information about the following basic points:

1. Origin, history and development of the vocation or profession.
2. Personal qualifications needed for entering the vocation or profession.
3. Scholastic training required for engaging in the vocation or profession.
4. Complete analysis of all employment possibilities.
5. Remuneration received.
6. Chances for advancement.
7. Frank statement of advantages and disadvantages.
8. Possibilities for both men and women engaging in the vocation or profession.
9. Professional associations and publications.

Published during the years 1940 to 1945, each pamphlet is bound in heavy gray or red covers, and averages about 24 pages in length. The first fifteen monographs were multilithed but later issues have been printed. The size is 6 by 9 inches.

Written by experts in each field, these monographs contain more technical information than some of the other publications. The history, development, and contribution to society of the occupation are unusually well presented. Some monographs contain considerable information about the industry and too few details about the conditions of work, requirements, and qualifications. However, up-to-date information is given about schools for further training, tuition, length of course, and description of the various subjects included in the training sequence.

In each monograph a page is devoted to a biography of the author and the titles on the back cover are followed by the names and positions of the authors. The names of outstanding people who are well known in their fields of work establish confidence in the reliability of the text.

It is hoped that in the revised editions, the table of contents will contain page numbers for ease of reference because this series will be included in the best vocational libraries.

1. Library work. 1945
2. Journalism. 1940
3. Business administration. 1940
4. Medicine. 1940
5. Hotel business. 1940
6. Music. 1940
7. Accounting. 1940
8. Forestry. 1940
9. Dentistry. 1940
10. Direct mail advertising. 1940
11. Agriculture. 1940
12. Teaching. 1940
13. Beauty culture. 1940
14. Engineering. 1940
15. Cooking. 1940
16. Costume design. 1942
17. Occupational therapy. 1941
18. Religion. 1945
19. Social work. 1941
20. Osteopathy. 1942

21. Law. 1945
22. Retailing. 1945
23. Mining engineering. 1945
24. Advertising. 1941
25. Office machines. 1941
26. The iron and steel industry. 1941
27. The Navy, Coast Guard, and Merchant Marine. 1941
28. Mechanical engineering. 1941
29. Adult education. 1941
30. The telegraph industry. 1941
31. Interior decoration. 1941
32. Electrical manufacturing. 1941
33. Metallurgy. 1941
34. Air conditioning. 1941
35. The petroleum industry. 1941
36. Fine and applied arts. 1941
37. Restaurant business. 1941
38. Chiropody. 1941
39. Modeling. 1941
40. Management engineering. 1941
41. Nursing. 1941
42. The pulp and paper industry. 1941
43. The railroad industry. 1941
44. The program side of radio. 1941
45. The government service. 1941
46. The meat packing industry. 1944
47. The drug and cosmetic industry. 1944
48. Chemical engineering. 1944
49. The paint, varnish and lacquer industry. 1945
50. Secretarial science. 1945
51. Pharmacy. 1945
52. The motion picture industry. 1945
53. Banking. 1945
54. Planning jobs and jobs in planning. 1945
55. Record photography in industry. 1945
56. Patent law as a profession. 1945
57. Girl scouting as a profession. 1945
58. Public relations. 1945
59. Casualty insurance. 1945
60. Cartography. 1946
61. Optometry. 1946
62. Portrait and commercial photography. 1946
63. Publishing. 1946

THE CHRONICLE, Port Byron, N. Y.

Guideposts to Occupational Information. 5c each; 10 copies or more 3c each.

These are reprints of occupational briefs prepared by the Guidance Bureau of the New York State Department of Education for free distribution to the New York schools. These 3 by 12 inch leaflets contain brief discussions of qualifications, preparation, working conditions, and trends. Lists of colleges and private trade schools in New York state make these reprints especially useful in New York and neighboring states. The bibliographies are exceptionally well prepared and consist of references to occupational information. The following are listed in the annotated bibliography:

Aircraft instrument manufacture. 1943
Aviation mechanic. No date
Clinical laboratory technician. No date
Dental assistant. No date
Dental hygienist. No date
Manufacture of surgical and dental instruments and equipment. 1943
Optical instrument and fire control instrument manufacture. 1943
Practical nurse. 1943
Registered professional nurse. 1943
Women in aircraft production. 1943
X-ray technician. No date

COMMONWEALTH BOOK COMPANY, INC., 80 East Jackson Boulevard, Chicago 4, Ill.

Commonwealth Vocational Guidance Monographs. Single copies 75c; any combination of 25 monographs $12.75; 50 titles $24.50; complete set of 75 monographs $35.

These seventy-five monographs have been edited by Miss Anne S. Davis, former Vocational Guidance Director of the Chicago Public Schools. All of the monographs follow the outline for occupational studies set up by the National Vocational Guidance Association (referred to in the annotations as NVGA). This outline includes the following:

1. Foreword
2. History of occupation
3. Importance and trend of occupation
4. Duties
5. Qualifications
6. Education
7. Training
8. Line of promotion
9. Earnings
10. Hours
11. Regularity of employment
12. Health and accident hazards
13. Organizations
14. Employment agencies
15. Related occupations
16. Conclusion
17. Bibliography
18. Suggested projects and topics for discussion

Adhering to the above outline, practically all of the information has a bearing on occupational information; very little irrelevant material is included. Careful research is evident.

The material is mimeographed but is attractively set up, is very legible, and the monographs are bound in stiff orange-colored printed folders with the occupational title printed on the left hand side. As the mimeographed materials become exhausted, an offset printing process is being substituted. Varying in length from 20 to 32 pages, the monographs are 9 by 11 inches in size.

Supplements to many of the monographs were issued in 1939. They were intended for purchase by users whose sets were bought prior to 1939. Current purchase of these monographs includes the supplementary materials which contain the statement: "This supplement is correlative to the original monograph and contains additional information as revealed by recent research." Each supplement, containing from 6 to 10 pages, presents information on the same topics as the original monograph and usually contains a bibliography of related books and magazines.

Many of the trades are covered in this series, such as bricklaying, painting, plastering, plumbing, welding, watchmaking, dressmaking, baking, barbering, and tailoring. Also many mechanical fields are included such as electrical industry, mechanical dentistry, automotive mechanics, and air conditioning. Considerable information is presented as a result of interviews with workers in the various fields and with union organizations.

Suggested projects and topics for class discussion are included in each monograph.

Series A

1. My lifework. 1939
2. Air conditioning. 1938
3. Auto and garage service. 1938
4. Baking. 1938
5. Barbering. 1938
6. Beauty culture. 1937
7. Chain store management. 1939
8. Chiropody. 1938
9. Restaurant management. 1936
10. Circulating library management. 1936
11. Dressmaking and alterations. 1936
12. Jewelry designing and engraving. 1936
13. Mechanical dentistry. 1939
14. Mortician. 1939
15. Office machine operation. 1939
16. Personnel management. 1939
17. Laboratory technician. 1938
18. Postal service. 1936
19. Printing salesmanship. 1938
20. Photography. 1936
21. Radio and television. 1936
22. Retail meat dealer. 1939
23. Social service. 1938
24. Secretaryship. 1936
25. Watchmaking and repairing. 1939

Series B

1. Retail merchandising. 1936
2. Airplane mechanics. 1936
3. Cleaning and dyeing. 1936
4. Market gardening and truck farming. 1936
5. Automotive mechanics (diesel engine). 1936
6. Railroading (commercial). 1936
7. Railroading (mechanical). 1936
8. Stock raising. 1936
9. Welding. 1936
10. Tool and die maker. 1936
11. Machine shop mechanics. 1936

12. Landscape gardening and tree surgery. 1936
13. Nursery and flower growing. 1936
14. Laundry business. 1936
15. Carpentry and millwork. 1938
16. Drafting and designing. 1936
17. Poultry raising. 1936
18. Bee keeping. 1936
19. Dairying. 1936
20. Hostess. 1936
21. Dietician. 1936
22. Hotel industry. 1936
23. Mining (coal and iron). 1936
24. Mining (petroleum and metals). 1936
25. Confectioner. 1936

Series C

1. Advertising. 1938
2. Bricklayer. 1938
3. Corsetier. 1938
4. Electrician. 1938
5. Forestry. 1938
6. Interior decorator. 1938
7. Lithographer. 1938
8. Millinery. 1938
9. Nursing. 1938
10. Optometry. 1938
11. Painter. 1938
12. Physical education. 1938
13. Plasterer. 1938
14. Plumber. 1938
15. Printer. 1938
16. Real estate and insurance. 1938
17. Shoemaking and repairing. 1938
18. Silversmith. 1938
19. Tailoring. 1938
20. Telegraphy. 1938
21. Telephony. 1938
22. Theatre. 1938
23. Travel bureau. 1938
24. Warehouse and storage. 1938
25. X-ray technician. 1938

HINDS, HAYDEN AND ELDREDGE, INC., 105 5th Ave., New York 3, N. Y.

Picture Fact Books.   School edition, net price 80c each.

This series of small books, formerly published by Harper & Brothers, presents facts about vocations in photographs, pictorial charts, and explanatory captions.   The text supplements the pictures, giving information about the number of workers in the vocation, training and education required, chances of advancement, salaries, and trends.

Containing many charts and photographs, these 56-page books, 7 by 9 inches in size, are attractive in format.   The numerous pictographs contribute to the interest.   Sentence structure and vocabulary are adapted to pupils of junior high school age while the photographs and pictographs will appeal to older students.   The value of this series is to orient the reader to varied fields of work rather than to present detailed information.   It is most useful as introductory or supplementary vocational material for younger students of grade 6 to 10 level of reading difficulty.

Air workers today. 1942	News workers. 1939
Doctors at work. 1941	Nurses at work. 1939
Farm workers. 1940	Office workers. 1940
Household workers. 1941	Radio workers. 1940
Library workers. 1940	Railroad workers. 1941
Machinists at work. 1941	Retail sales workers. 1941
Movie workers. 1939	Textile workers. 1939

THE INSTITUTE FOR RESEARCH, 537 South Dearborn Street, Chicago 5, Ill.

Careers Research Monographs.   Each group $3.75 (except Group A which is $5.25) ; 5 or more groups in one order 10% discount; 10 or more 20% discount; 26 or more 30% discount.

These one hundred forty-two monographs present detailed information about each career presented.   The monographs follow, in general, a uniform outline.   In addition to nature of work, personal qualifications, training, educational requirements, opportunities, earnings, attractive and unattractive features, many monographs contain either a list of schools offering specialized training or the name and address of a professional association from which a list of recommended schools may be obtained.   They also give lists of organizations or professional societies, trade journals and periodicals, and suggested readings.

Considerable general information and historical background material are included.   A description of a typical day's work constitutes a useful feature of each monograph.   Many charts and tables are used.

Bound in heavy brown paper covers, they average about 24 pages in length and contain several half-tone illustrations. The information is not condensed, since the authors are not crowded for space. The pages, size 8½ by 11 inches, contain two columns of clearly printed type, averaging about 700 words. In other words, 24 pages are equivalent to twice that amount if published in ordinary book form. The style is clear, interesting, factual, and non-technical.

Titles listed in Part VI of this bibliography with the date of the latest copyright, are the following:

GROUP A

1. Selecting a career. 1931
2. Civil engineering as a career. 1941
3. Biological work as a career. 1946
4. Accountancy as a career. 1941
5. Interior decoration as a career. 1936
6. Physical education as a career. 1940
7. Law as a career. 1944

GROUP B

8. Librarianship as a career. 1941
9. Publishing as a career. 1936
10. Dentistry as a career. 1939
11. Music as a career. 1939
12. Architecture as a career. 1939

GROUP C

13. Landscape architecture as a career. 1938
14. Commercial and industrial art as a career. 1944
15. Careers in geology. 1939
16. Chemistry and chemical engineering as careers. 1939
17. Advertising as a career. 1936

GROUP D

18. The diplomatic service as a career. 1939
19. Journalism as a career. 1944
20. General agriculture as a career. 1930
21. Horticulture as a career. 1946
22. Animal husbandry as a career. 1939

GROUP E

23. Forestry as a career. 1940
24. Home economics as a career. 1940
25. Nursing as a career. 1940
26. Medicine as a career. 1940
27. Optometry as a career. 1937

GROUP F

28. Osteopathy as a career. 1940
29. Hospital management as a career. 1940
30. Investment banking as a career. 1946
31. Banking as a career. 1940
32. Manufacturing as a career. 1941

GROUP G

33. Salesmanship as a career. 1940
34. Hotel management as a career. 1938
35. Personnel work in commerce and industry as a career. 1939
36. Mechanical engineering as a career. 1939
37. Electrical engineering as a career. 1936

GROUP H

38. Acoustical engineering as a career. 1940
39. Aviation as a career. 1946
40. Careers in life insurance. 1940
41. Hospital dietetics as a career. 1939
42. Criminological work as a career. 1941

GROUP I

43. Social work as a career. 1939
44. Pharmacy as a career. 1946
45. Statistical work—careers. 1940
46. Clay working as a career. 1946
47. Photography as a career. 1941

GROUP J

48. Merchandising as a career. 1939
49. Dramatic art as a career. 1936
50. Recreation leadership as a career. 1941
51. Consular and foreign trade services as careers. 1936
52. Teaching as a career. 1946

Titles listed in Part VI—*Continued*

GROUP V

108. Office management as a career. 1945
109. Physical therapy as a career. 1941
110. Eye, ear, nose, and throat specialists—careers. 1941
111. Careers in fire and casualty insurance. 1941
112. Textile designing as a career. 1944

GROUP W

113. Careers in electrical wiring and electrical contracting. 1941
114. Careers in plumbing and plumbing contracting. 1941
115. Careers as a bookkeeper. 1941
116. Psychiatry as a career. 1941
117. Men's furnishings store operation as a career. 1945

GROUP X

118. Editorial work as a career. 1941
119. Arts and crafts—careers. 1945
120. Careers resulting from rural electrification. 1941
121. Radio-music store operation as a career. 1945
122. Career as an aviation mechanic. 1941

GROUP Y

123. Careers in the United States army. 1942
124. Careers in the naval services of the United States. 1942
125. Careers in the F. B. I. 1942

126. Clerical careers in government service. 1942
127. Careers for women in factory work. 1942

GROUP Z

128. Flying careers in the United States air forces. 1942
129. Careers in the armored force. 1942
130. A career in the United States Marine corps. 1943
131. A career in the United States Coast Guard. 1943
132. Careers in the United States merchant marine. 1942

GROUP SR

SR 5. A career as a medical records librarian. 1943
SR 6. Ground careers in the United States army air corps. 1943
SR13. Careers in the American Red Cross. 1945
SR14. Career as an X-ray technician. 1945
SR15. Careers in the United States Employment Service. 1945

GROUP AA

133. Careers for women as advertising copy writers. 1944
134. Careers for women in advertising art. 1944
135. Careers for women in office work. 1944
136. Careers for women in public relations work. 1944
137. Careers for women with the air lines. 1941

MADEMOISELLE—The Magazine for Smart Young Women, 122 East 24th Street, New York 17, N.Y.

Vocational Materials Available from Jobs and Futures Department of Mademoiselle. 10c each.

This series consists of reprints of charts and articles which have appeared in *Mademoiselle*, prepared by the Jobs and Futures Department of the magazine. Written in sprightly style, these four-page articles are intended to arouse interest in the vocation, rather than to present factual information. Attractive illustrations are included. Many of the articles include bibliographies and are useful in supplying introductory information to girls in junior and senior high school.

The charts present brief information in tabulated form and are useful for bulletin board use.

CHARTS: (10c each)

Civil Service jobs—May, 1944

Arts jobs—October, 1944

Medical jobs—May, 1945

Food jobs—October, 1945

LISTS: (free)

Occupational therapy schools—December, 1943

Physical therapy schools—December, 1943

Journalism schools—October, 1944

Colleges with radio courses—October, 1944

Home economics-journalism schools—March, 1945

Radio audition readings—April, 1945

Medical records librarian schools—May, 1945

Television bibliography — September, 1945

ARTICLES: (10c each)

Gift of healing (therapy)—December, 1943

An apple for the teacher (high-school teaching)—February, 1944

Trouble shooters (industrial counseling)—March, 1944

Globalingo (language jobs)—April, 1944

Working in Washington (Government jobs)—May, 1944

Take your medicine now (medicine) —June, 1944

The warm heart (social work)—September, 1944

Girl reporter (journalism)—October, 1944

Radio script writing—October, 1944

World wondering (geography)—November, 1944

Lady of the house (housing and planning)—January, 1945

Everybody's business (vocational guidance)—February, 1945

Cooking with words (home economics-journalism)—March, 1945

Blind date with mike (radio auditions) —April, 1945

Groundwork for a career (value of work experience)—May, 1945

Jobs and futures in book publishing—June, 1945

Jobs and futures in television—September, 1945

Redesign for living (industrial design applied to home management)—October, 1945

Start picking up pins (fashion)—October, 1945

MORGAN-DILLON & COMPANY, 4616 North Clark Street, Chicago 40, Ill.

Success Vocational Information Monographs. 32c each; 10 or more monographs in one order, 30c each.

The sixty monographs in this series were prepared by teachers and associated research persons of the Social Science Department, Joliet Township High School, Joliet, Ill., under the direction of Chloris Shade. To check the accuracy of the information, manuscripts were submitted for review and criticism to leading authorities in the vocation and to educational committees of national organizations. Many quotations are included from publications of professional associations.

A uniform outline is followed covering: history, duties, opportunities, qualifications and training required, salaries, advantages and disadvantages for the worker, number of workers in the field, list of schools providing training, suggestions to the pupil for further study, and bibliography. In many cases, the classified bibliography lists biographies and vocational fiction. Codes of ethics also are included in this series.

The monographs in this series are 5 by 8 inches in size and average 25 pages in length. Charts, diagrams, and tables are frequently included. The fifty-five monographs originally published in 1937 were revised in 1940-1944.

1. Mechanical drafting. 1940
2. Pattern making. 1940
3. Machine shop mechanics. 1939
4. Electric arc welding. 1940
5. Architectural drafting. 1939
6. Carpentry. 1940
7. Cabinet making. 1940
8. Plumbing. 1940
9. Electrical installation. 1940
10. Air-conditioning. 1939
11. The compositor, the pressman, 1940
12. Petroleum (mining and refining). 1940
13. Department store work. 1940
14. Salesmanship. 1940
15. The grocery store. 1940
16. The florist shop. 1939
17. Insurance. 1940
18. Laundry industry. 1940
19. Cleaning and dyeing. 1940
20. Bookkeeping. 1939
21. Accounting. 1939
22. Office machine operation. 1939
23. Secretarial work. 1939
24. Aviation. 1939
25. Auto mechanics and garage management. 1939
26. Diesel engineering. 1939
27. Trucking and bus service. 1939
28. Telephone and telegraph service. 1939
29. Radio and television. 1940
30. Commercial art. 1939
31. Industrial design. 1940
32. Costume design. 1939
33. Interior decoration. 1939
34. Architecture. 1940
35. Landscape gardening. 1940
36. Photography. 1939
37. Medicine. 1939
38. Dentistry. 1940
39. Medical technology. 1940
40. Nursing. 1939
41. Biological work. 1940
42. Chemistry in industry. 1939
43. Physical education. 1940
44. Home economics in industry. 1939
45. Journalism. 1939
46. Police and fire protection. 1939
47. Civil service. 1940
48. Foreign service. 1940
49. Beauty parlor work. 1939
50. Restaurant and tea room work. 1940
51. General farming. 1940
52. Stock raising. 1939
53. Dairying. 1940
54. Market gardening and truck farming. 1939
55. Forestry. 1940
56. Osteopathy. 1942
57. Social work. 1940
58. City and county management. 1940
60. Law. 1940
65. Pharmacy. 1940

NATIONAL FEDERATION OF BUSINESS AND PROFESSIONAL WOMEN'S CLUBS, INC., 1819 Broadway, New York 23, N.Y.

Vocations for Women. Reprints published prior to 1944, 10c each; published 1944 to date, 15c each.

A collection of articles on occupations reprinted from the *Independent Woman,* magazine of the National Federation of Business and Professional Women's Clubs, Inc. A regular feature of the magazine, many of the articles are written by outstanding women who are well qualified to discuss their own or related occupations.

Illustrations, photographs, and brief biographical sketches of prominent women are included in these 3 to 4 page reprints. They are decidedly inspirational in tone. Although the disadvantages of each career are discussed briefly, the approach is intended to arouse interest, to create confidence, and to encourage further investigation. Timely information on requirements, opportunities, salaries, and the changing outlook in work for women are considered in each article. These reprints are more useful in supplying introductory information, however, rather than complete factual data. The material is presented in an interesting manner and appeals to girls in junior and senior high schools.

Careers on the labor front. 1942	Office management. 1940
Department store work. 1941	Penology. 1940
Designing. 1940	Personnel work. 1941
Home demonstration work. 1941	Psychiatry. 1942
Insurance. 1941	Public relations. 1941
Laundries. 1945	Recreation. 1944
Music teaching. 1941	Retailing. 1944
Nursery education. 1942	Statistical work. No date.

NATIONAL ROSTER OF SCIENTIFIC AND SPECIALIZED PERSONNEL. UNITED STATES DEPARTMENT OF LABOR. Washington 25, D.C.

Descriptions of Professions Series. Free.

These descriptions constitute a concise source of information about types of work in the professions and related fields. Considerable factual information is presented, much of it in outline form. A uniform outline is followed for each description: occupational titles and code numbers, occupational summary, major branches, functional specialization, professional licensure and affiliations and Civil Service ratings, educational and experience qualifications, related occupations and fields, and sources of employment. Printed on light cardboard and folded, 5 by 8 inches, for convenient filing as cards, the descriptions vary in length from 2 to 6 pages.

Helpful information is given concerning the educational and experience qualifications required. No data is given about schools for training, however; and wages, personal qualifications, opportunities, and trends are not discussed.

Sixty-one titles were published in 1944 and 1945; twenty more are in preparation.

DESCRIPTIONS OF PROFESSIONAL FIELDS

AGRICULTURAL AND BIOLOGICAL SCIENCES

Agronomy
Anatomy
Animal, dairy and poultry sciences
Bacteriology
Botany
Dental hygienists
Dietician
Entomology
Forestry and range management
Genetics
Horticulture
Medical laboratory technician
Medical pathology
Medical physiology
Nutrition research
Optomotrists
Parasitology
Pharmacology
Plant pathology and plant physiology
Veterinarians
X-ray technician
Zoology including fish and wildlife management

ENGINEERING

Aeronautical engineering
Agricultural engineering
Ceramic engineering
Chemical engineering
Civil engineering
Electrical engineering (including radio and communications engineering)
Fire protection engineering
Industrial engineering
Marine engineering
Mechanical engineering

Metallurgy, metallurgical engineering and mineral technology
Mining engineering
Naval architecture
Petroleum and natural gas engineering
Safety engineering

PHYSICAL SCIENCES

Astronomy (including astrophysics)
Chemistry
Geology
Geophysics
Mathematics
Meteorology
Oceanography
Physics

SOCIAL SCIENCES

Actuarial science
Anthropology
Economics
Geography
Historian
Library science
Psychology
Social work
Sociology
Speech pathology
Statistics

OTHER

Accounting
Architecture
Foreign languages
Landscape architecture
Personnel Administration

DESCRIPTIONS IN PREPARATION

Advertising agent
Architectural engineer
County agent
Dentist
Educator (college teacher of pro-
    fessional education)
High school teacher
Home economist
Lawyer
Occupational therapist
Osteopath

Pharmacists
Planners
Political scientist
Physical educator
Physical therapist
Physician
Public relations man
Purchasing agent
Registered nurse
Reporter and editor

Handbooks of Description of Specialized Fields. Order from Supt. of Documents, Washington 25, D.C.

The National Roster has prepared a series of mimeographed handbooks, describing in considerable detail the specialized work performed in various fields of science. Each handbook contains information under the following headings: occupational summary, related fields, functional activities, fields of specialization, educational qualifications, and related nonprofessional occupations. There is no discussion concerning salaries or employment prospects.

Varying in length from 7 to 140 pages, the handbooks are primarily for the use of the Roster's staff in classification and placement work, but a limited number are available for free distribution to government agencies, large libraries, and educational organizations. They are not available to individuals.

Prepared in 1945, the handbooks are especially useful to placement officers. The titles named below are included in the annotated bibliography. Twelve additional titles are in preparation.

Agricultural engineering. 1944. 5c
Agronomy and soil sciences. 1945. 5c
Animal, dairy and poultry husbandry and dairy products technology. 1945. 10c.
Bacteriology. 1945. 5c
Civil engineering. 1945. 10c
Ceramic technology and engineering. 1944. 5c

Chemistry and chemical engineering. 1944. 30c
Entomology. 1945. 10c
Forestry. 1945. 5c
Geology. 1945. 10c
Horticulture. 1945. 5c
Industrial engineering and business management. 1945. 10c
Plant pathology. 1945. 5c
Zoology and parasitology. 1945. 10c

HANDBOOKS IN PREPARATION

Accounting
Economics
Electrical engineering
Geophysics
Home economics
Mechanical engineering

Metallurgy and mining engineering
Meteorology
Personnel administration
Physics
Professional education
Public administration

Occupational Briefs. Order from Supt. of Documents, Washington 25, D.C. 5c each.

Fifty-three Occupational Briefs were prepared by the National Roster for the War Department for use in connection with the United States Armed Forces Institute courses and the War Department's other educational and counseling programs.

In carrying out its wartime mission of mobilizing technical and professional people for war industry, the armed services, and government, the National Roster found little precise information available which could be used in defining and classifying professional workers and professional jobs. To supply this lack, the Roster, working with professional societies, prepared occupational briefs describing the work done in different branches of a profession, fields of specialization, or special competence in subject matter and in function. Information includes occupational summary, earnings, outlook, qualifications, and training.

This series cannot be obtained from the National Roster. They may be purchased from the Superintendent of Documents at five cents a copy. The following titles are available:

Accountant

Advertising manager

Agricultural and biogolical scientist (general survey)

Animal, dairy and poultry scientist

Architect

Bacteriologist

Botanist, plant pathologist and plant physiologist

Catholic clergyman

Chemist

Counselor, vocational guidance

Dentist

Dietitian

Economist

Engineers (general survey)

Engineer, aeronautical

Engineer, automotive

Engineer, chemical

Engineer, civil

Engineer, electrical

Engineer, industrial

Engineer, mechanical

Engineer, metallurgical

Engineer, mining

Foreign language specialist

Forester

Geologist

Geophysicist

Horticulturist, agronomist and soil scientist

Lawyer

Librarian

Medical laboratory technician

Meteorologist

Musician and music teacher

Nurse, registered

Optometrist

Personnel worker

Pharmacist

Physical educator

Physician

Physicist

Protestant clergyman

Psychiatrist

Psychologist

Rabbi

Reporter and editor

Social worker

Sociologist

Statistician

Teacher, high school

Teacher, vocational schools

Veterinarian

Writer

Zoologist, entomologist, and parasitologist

OCCUPATIONAL INDEX, INC., New York University, Washington Square, New York 3, N.Y.

Appraisals and Abstracts of Available Literature on Various Occupations. 25c; 10 or more copies 15c each.

This series was prepared originally under the direction of the National Occupational Conference with a grant provided by the Carnegie Foundation. Information gathered from available literature on a specific occupation is summarized under the following headings: Nature of work, abilities and preparation required, rewards, number and distribution of workers, probable future trends, advantages and disadvantages, a list of organizations from which current information may be obtained, bibliography, and an outline to be used in filling in local data. Each pamphlet also contains a survey and appraisal of the literature. References especially recommended are marked with an asterisk.

Published between 1936 and 1939, the pamphlets vary in length from 6 to 12 pages and are 7 by 10 inches in size. Good research methods are employed. The texts of the abstracts contain many numerical references to titles in the bibliography in such a way as to encourage further reading. The reading references are unusually well selected and carefully annotated. The appraisal of the printed literature is one of the outstanding features of this series.

Many of these studies have been revised and published in the series of Occupational Abstracts. Titles of the original series included in this bibliography are as follows:

City and county management as an occupation. 1937

Dental hygiene as an occupation. 1936

Dietetics as an occupation. 1938

Occupations in aviation. 1937

Occupation of the baker. 1938

Occupation of the barber. 1937

Occupation of the blacksmith. 1938

Occupation of the bricklayer. 1938

Occupation of the carpenter. 1938

Occupation of the dental mechanic. 1938

Occupation of the dentist. 1939

Occupation of the electric lineman. 1939

Occupation of the letter carrier. 1936

Occupation of the sheet metal worker. 1938

Occupation of the welder. 1938

Painting as an occupation. 1936

Pharmacy as an occupation. 1937

Photography as an occupation. 1937

Occupational Abstracts. 25c each; 10 or more copies 15c each.

These are concise six-page abstracts of available literature on a wide range of occupations. Under the editorship of Robert Hoppock, the abstracts are prepared by a number of authors who "summarize what has appeared in print about the occupations described." The topics generally summarized are types of work, postwar prospects, number and distribution of workers, duties, qualifications, preparation, methods of entering, advancement, earnings, regularity of employment, health and accident hazards, organizations, advantages, disadvantages, sources of further information, and an annotated bibliography.

Published in a variety of colors, the leaflets measure 3½ by 8½ inches. Although the information presented is brief, it is to the point. No irrelevant material about the technical aspects of the subject is included. The summaries are presented in a dignified style; there are no over-statements or rash generalities. The reading references are unusually well selected, carefully annotated, and can be depended upon. This series is worth buying for the bibliographies alone if one is encouraging youth to read about the workaday world. Because of the quantity price, purchase of the entire series is recommended.

Accountant. 1944	Lawyer. 1945
Air conditioning engineer. 1944	Landscape architect. 1944
Architect. 1944	Linotype operator. 1944
Automobile salesman. 1944	Medical laboratory technologist. 1945
Banker. 1945	Medicine. 1945
Beekeeping. 1945	Motion picture actor. 1945
Boilermaking. 1945	Music. 1941
Book illustration. 1944	Nursing. 1945
Bookkeeper. 1945	Occupational therapy. 1944
Building contractor. 1944	Office machine operator. 1941
Bus and truck driver. 1944	Patternmaker. 1944
Butcher. 1944	Physical therapy. 1945
Cabinetmaker. 1944	Plasterer. 1944
Ceramic engineer. 1946	Plastics. 1944
Children's librarian. 1943	Police officer. 1945
City fireman. 1945	Public health nursing. 1944
Detective. 1944	Radio service. 1944
Diesel engineer. 1945	Real estate. 1944
Dressmaker. 1945	Rural teacher. 1944
Electronics. 1944	Social work. 1945
Farming. 1941	Starting your own business. 1941
Free-lance writer. 1944	Stenographic work. 1945
Funeral director. 1945	Taxi driver. 1945
Gasoline filling stations. 1944	Teaching. 1945
Guidance and personnel services. 1945	Television worker. 1944
Industrial chemist. 1941	Veterans' counselor. 1945
Insurance salesman. 1945	Veterinarian. 1945
Interior decorator. 1944	Vocational rehabilitation. 1944
Journalist. 1945	Window display. 1940

THE QUARRIE CORPORATION, 35 East Wacker Drive, Chicago 1, Ill.

Vocational Monographs (Quarrie Reference Library). 29 monographs formerly priced at 35c each or $7.50 a set; currently available at $1 a set.

This series was prepared specifically for users of the *World Book Encyclopedia* and was intended to encourage the young student to explore a variety of occupational fields. Each monograph contains references to be found in the *Encyclopedia*. However, these are supplemented by lists of book for advanced reading and sources of free and inexpensive literature. Suggestions for leisure time activities related to the occupation constitute a helpful feature of this series.

Each monograph discusses the general nature of work in a particular field, with a brief discussion of the specific occupations within it. The personal qualifications that are desirable are analyzed and the behavior characteristics of one who may expect to progress in the field are listed. These are to assist the parent in appraising his child's interests. Other topics covered are opportunities, training required, income possibilities, advantages, and disadvantages. Each provides an outline for informational reading, a list of technical publications for further reading, and suggests leisure time activities of an exploratory nature.

The twenty-nine monographs, varying in length from 6 to 20 pages, are planographed and bound in a loose-leaf paper cover. The series is supplemented by *An Occupational Guidance Record* for the use of the parent in summarizing the interests, behaviors, and abilities of the youth.

Because the monographs are currently available at the low price of $1.00 for the set, they are listed in Part VI of this bibliography.

1. Accounting. 1942
2. Advertising. 1944
3. Agriculture. 1938
4. Architecture. 1942
5. Aviation. 1942
6. Banking and investments. 1944
7. Chemistry. 1944
8. Civil engineering. 1944
9. Commercial art and industrial design. 1938
10. Dentistry. 1943
11. Dressmaking and costume design. 1942
12. Electrical engineering. 1942
13. Government service. 1942
14. Home economics. 1944
15. Insurance. 1944
16. Journalism—writing for print. 1945
17. Law. 1942
18. Librarianship. 1944
19. Mechanical engineering. 1938
20. Medicine. 1943
21. Merchandising. 1943
22. Music. 1944
23. Nursing. 1938
24. Office, clerical and secretarial work. 1943
25. Radio. 1942
26. Real estate. 1944
28. Science. 1944
29. Social work. 1944
30. Teaching. 1938

ROCHESTER INSTITUTE OF TECHNOLOGY, Rochester 8, N.Y.

The Vocational Guidance Series. 1944. 10c each.

The ten pamphlets were written to give information to prospective students about fields of work for which the Institute offers technical training. Authors of the pamphlets are members of the faculty at the Institute.

Information is given about the various branches of the vocation, the duties performed by persons employed, requirements for employment, wages, salaries, security, promotions, advantages and disadvantages of employment in that field. An illuminating feature of each pamphlet is a job chart prepared to aid students in visualizing the kinds of beginning jobs in the field as well as the kinds of jobs to which successful persons may be promoted. At the bottom of the chart are listed the training or beginning jobs. Above these are listed the intermediate jobs, related and supplementary jobs to which persons with demonstrated ability, maturity, and experience may be promoted. The terminal jobs at the top of the chart are those toward which college training is specifically directed. The related jobs, named at the side of the charts, are those for which the curriculum does not specifically train but which are attained by demonstrating special aptitudes and by profiting by experience and self-training.

The pamphlets are attractively bound in heavy paper covers of various colors. Size 6 by 9 inches, they average about 24 pages. Considerable pertinent information is clearly presented. Revised in 1944, this series contains useful and up-to-date information.

1. If you are considering retailing. 1944
2. If you are considering photography. 1944
3. If you are considering industrial chemistry. 1944
4. If you are considering applied art. 1944
5. If you are considering costume design. 1944
6. If you are considering a career in the mechanical field. 1944
7. If you are considering a career in the electrical field. 1945
8. If you are considering food administration. 1944
10. If you are considering a career in publishing and printing. 1944
11. If you are considering interior decoration. 1944

ROW, PETERSON AND COMPANY, Evanston, Ill.

The Way of Life Series. List price 96c each; net price to schools and libraries 56c each.

Of the thirty-five books in this series, twenty-nine are included in this bibliography. According to the brochure accompanying the books, each one tells the story of some "way of life" in an occupation, an industry, a profession, a social phase, or a historical period. Information is presented in the form of a story, conversation, or a personally conducted tour. In some cases, the reader follows the members of a staff as they go about their work.

The books average 64 pages in length and have a stiff binding, 6 by 9 inches, with a cover illustration appropriate to the content of the individual volume. Approximately 50 photographs are included in each book.

These books constitute interesting reading and may serve as an introduction to the study of more factual material. Some young people who will not be interested in a statistical monograph will be more easily attracted to the pictures of people engaged in typical kinds of work and the explanatory captions.

Very little information about qualifications and training is included, but the advantages and disadvantages of the work are woven into the conversations and interviews. There is no index or table of contents as these books obviously were intended as stories rather than reference books. Intended for pupils of grades 7 to 12, they will be found most useful for pupils of 5th to 10th grade level of reading difficulty.

Animal kingdom—way of life in a zoo. 1941

At your service—way of life in a hotel. 1941

Before your eyes—way of life in a museum. 1941

Black land—way of life in the coal fields. 1941

Blue highway—way of life on an ocean liner. 1940

Captains of the sky—way of life of a military aviator. 1942

Doctor Jad—way of life of a physician. 1941

Golden harvest—way of life in the tobacco industry. 1941

Green kingdom—way of life of a forest ranger. 1940

Here comes tomorrow—the chemurgic way of life. 1942

Keep 'em flying—way of life of an aviation mechanic. 1942

Nose for news—way of life of a reporter. 1941

One in a thousand—way of life on the road to Hollywood. 1941

Riders in scarlet—way of life of the Mounties. 1941

Rolling stones—way of life of a civil engineer. 1942

Roughneck—way of life in the oil fields. 1941

Sandhog—way of life of the tunnel builders. 1941

Shoppers' special—way of life in a department store. 1941

Stone and steel—way of life in a penitentiary. 1941

Streamliner—way of life on a passenger train. 1941

Talking shadows—way of life in Hollywood. 1942

Talking wires—way of life in the telegraph industry. 1942

They guard the gates—way of life on the American borders. 1941

Timber!—way of life in the lumber camps. 1942

To the colors—way of life of an army officer. 1942

Trail of the trefoil—way of life of a girl scout. 1941

Treasure shelves—way of life in a library. 1941

Warriors of the sea—way of life in the U. S. Navy. 1942

White gold—way of life in the cotton kingdom. 1941

SCIENCE RESEARCH ASSOCIATES, 228 South Wabash Avenue, Chicago 4, Ill.

The American Job Series of Occupational Monographs. 60c each; 4 or more at 55c each; 10 or more at 45c each; 30 at 40c each.

The twenty-eight monographs of this series that are listed in this bibliography are "designed to provide the essential information a young person needs in considering a field of work as a possible life career." They describe the history of the vocation, kinds of work, training, wages and earnings, and opportunities. Authors of the monographs are, for the most part, persons engaged in the occupation.

Averaging 48 to 56 pages in length, size 6 by 9 inches, the pamphlets are convenient to handle. The earlier issues contain line drawings but the later pamphlets are profusely illustrated with informative photographs. About half of the titles have been revised since 1944 to bring information up to date. The vocabulary and style are adapted to the teen-age group to whom the material apparently is addressed. The format of the monographs is attractive; most of the covers carry a two-color photograph.

1. Opportunities for statistical workers. 1944
4. Jobs in rural journalism. 1945
5. Teaching as a career. 1944
6. Employment trends in the printing trades. 1945
7. How to choose a career. 1940
8. Highway jobs. 1944
9. Advertising as an occupation. 1944
11. Clerical occupations. 1945
12. Occupations in radio. 1945
13. Jobs in the foundry. 1944
14. Household workers. 1940
15. Horticulture. 1944
18. Opportunities in farming. 1941
19. How to get THE job. 1944

20. The fields of personnel work. 1945
21. Careers in forestry. 1945
23. Jobs in rural service. 1945
24. Photography as a vocation. 1941
25. A job in banking. 1941
26. Occupations in rubber. 1942
27. Jobs in the machine shop. 1945
29. Careers in wildlife management. 1942
30. A career in engineering. 1942
32. Careers in labor relations. 1943
33. Jobs in the aircraft industry. 1943
34. Instrument makers. 1943
35. Careers in public health. 1943
37. Your future in chemistry. 1943

Occupational Briefs. 15c; 50 or more copies, 10c each.

From four to seven briefs are published each month. The brief leaflets, four pages in length, are planographed. Measuring 8 by 11 inches, they usually contain two illustrations and an annotated bibliography of six or eight references. Information given on each occupation includes job descriptions, a survey of present opportunities, the training needed, working conditions, future outlook, advantages, and disadvantages. Many briefs are available on titles not discussed in other pamphlets.

(1944 SERIES)

51. Electronics workers
52. Public administration workers
53. Vocational rehabilitation workers
54. Personnel workers
55. Brick and stone masons
56. Carpenters

57. Building maintenance workers
58. Architects
59. Interior decorators and window display workers
60. Florists, nurserymen, landscapers
61. Foresters
62. Occupational and physical therapy

63. Laboratory technicians
64. Home economics workers
65. Classroom teachers
66. College professors
67. Auto sales and service workers
68. Aviation
69. Shoemakers
70. Food store workers
71. Book store and rental library workers
72. Agents and collectors
73. Executives

(1945 Series)

74. Commercial travelers
75. House-to-house canvassers and miscellaneous sales jobs
76. Purchasing agents and merchandise buyers
77. Variety store workers
78. Paint and varnish workers
79. Plastics and synthetics workers
80. Paper and pulp workers
81. Textile workers
82. Furniture workers
83. Clothing manufacturing workers
84. Leather workers
85. Transportation equipment workers
86. Tobacco workers
87. Non-ferrous metal workers
88. Public relations and publicity workers
89. Editors and reporters

90. Recreation workers
91. Clergymen and religious workers
92. Diplomatic service and foreign trade workers
93. Laundry workers
94. Cleaning and dyeing workers
95. Household workers
96. Barbers and beauticians
97. Tailors and dressmakers
98. Practical nurses
99. Morticians
100. Postal workers
101. Pharmacists
102. Public utility workers
103. Stationary engineers
104. Psychologists
105. Plasterers
106. Politicians
107. Consumer cooperative workers
108. County extension workers
109. Painters
110. Bookbinders
111. Hotel workers
112. Dentists
113. Fur farmers
114. Optometrists
115. Librarians
116. Local transportation workers
117. Television workers
118. Cannery workers
119. Meat packing workers
120. Motion picture workers
121. Free-lance writers
122. Air conditioning workers

Occupational Reprints. 15c; 50 or more copies, 10c each.

These are reprints and abstracts of current leaflets, addresses, and magazine articles, described as "important vocational material from publications not readily available." The articles are reprinted from a wide variety of sources. Many of them are general discussions and written with a popular appeal; they contain a limited amount of information concerning conditions of work, requirements, opportunities, and rewards. Some of these two-to-four page reprints are available for occupations on which no other monographs are available, such as chemical editor, male nurse, and aviation dispatcher.

Beginning in September 1945, the monthly issues of Occupational Reprints are known as Guidance Reprints and treat professional aspects of vocational and educational guidance.

The Occupational Reprints listed in this bibliography are as follows:

OCCUPATIONAL REPRINTS

10. Machinist—a basic trade
11. Salesman—what makes a good industrial salesman?
14. Accounting—women in accountancy
16. Business and management—wanted: building managers
19. Chemist—the chemical secretary
22. Women doctors
24. Dental hygienist
26. Preparing for music careers
27. Welding in a steel mill
28. The U. S. foreign service
30. Success in photography
32. The public accountant
35. Why I want my boy to be a farmer
36. Background for purchasing
38. The power engineer
39. The aviation dispatcher
41. Getting a job with Uncle Sam
42. Salt of the earth
46. The mortician
50. Opportunities for men nurses
51. Radio manufacturing
53. Forestry
55. The cartoonist
59. Job trends in the plastics industry
62. Are you going to be a druggist?
64. Job opportunities in journalism
66. Careers for the home economist
67. The marine engineer and the naval architect
71. Beginning jobs in business
73. The buyer
77. Cleaning and pressing jobs
79. Jobs in machine shops
81. Jobs in barber shops and beauty shops
89. The garment worker
96. Fashion designing
101. Planning a career in the paper industry
102. How to be an opera singer
110. Anesthesia—a career for the graduate nurse
112. So, you want to be a petroleum engineer
114. The nurse in industry
117. Occupational therapy as a vocation
118. Banking—a career and an opportunity
121. Sky mail clerk
128. Airline passenger agents—their training and duties
132. White collar jobs
134. Opportunities for women in transportation
136. Mathmagicians
137. Career in photography
145. Career in teaching
146. Jobs for young workers in welding occupations
149. Passing the book
159. The home economist—her day
161. Archaeology as a career for women
163. Chemical editing
167. Consider social work
168. A letter to G. I. Joe
169. Men of the mold loft
170. Patent work as a field for chemists
171. Selling fine chemicals
172. Photo retouching as a career
174. Opportunities for chemists in literature service work
175. Jobs in geography
177. Our veterans need more nurses
176. Post-war demands for women in foreign service
179. The outlook for motion pictures
180. Qualifications of an industrial training director
182. The role of women in banking

GUIDANCE REPRINTS

190. Susan Brown: wants to make music her life career

UNITED STATES DEPARTMENT OF COMMERCE. BUREAU OF FOREIGN AND DOMESTIC COMMERCE.

Industrial Series. 1945. Order from the Supt. of Documents, Washington 25, D.C.

This series consists of twenty publications giving instructions on how to establish various small businesses. Between 150 and 200 pages in length, each booklet is intended as a practical guide to experienced skilled persons who are considering starting their own businesses. Considerable technical information is included, with sugestions concerning shop management, equipment, operating costs, and methods of conducting the business. Some information is given about the qualifications, requirements, and nature of the work.

Establishing and operating a beauty shop
Establishing and operating a building contracting business
Establishing and operating a dry cleaning business
Establishing and operating a grocery store
Establishing and operating a hardware store
Establishing and operating a heating and plumbing business
Establishing and operating a laundry
Establishing and operating a metal working shop, No. 16
Establishing and operating a painting and decorating contracting business
Establishing and operating a real estate and insurance brokerage business
Establishing and operating a restaurant
Establishing and operating a retail bakery
Establishing and operating a service station
Establishing and operating a shoe repair business, No. 17
Establishing and operating a small sawmill business, No. 20
Establishing and operating a variety and general merchandise store
Establishing and operating an apparel store
Establishing and operating an automobile repair shop
Establishing and operating an electrical appliance and radio shop
Establishing and operating your own business, No. 19

UNITED STATES DEPARTMENT OF LABOR. Washington 25, D.C.

Labor Market Information for United States Employment Service Counseling—Industry Series. 1945. Free.

This series of mimeographed statements has been prepared to provide current background information on the major industries. Each statement contains a brief description of the nature and location of the industry; the industrial processes and occupational structure; wages, hours, conditions of work, union affiliation; training; employment prospects; and bibliography. Many of them contain charts showing distribution of workers by occupational groups or by states.

Prepared for use of the United States Employment Service, the statements are helpful to all counselors who aim to keep abreast of realistic labor market information. The distribution is restricted to school and adult counselors, research and vocational guidance organizations, government agencies, and high school, college and university libraries.

STATEMENTS NOW AVAILABLE

Series No.	Industry	Series No.	Industry
12–1	Bituminous coal mining	33–1	Basic iron and steel
15–1	Construction	33–2	Iron and steel foundries
20–1	Slaughtering and meat packing	35–1	Aluminum and magnesium
22–1	Cotton textiles	36–1	Radio and radar equipment
22–2	Woolen and worsted textiles	39–1	Plastics products
24–1	Logging camps and lumber mills	40–1	Railroads
28–1	Plastic materials	41–1	Street railway and motor bus transportation
28–2	Chemicals		
28–3	Synthetic rubber	42–1	Trucking
29–2	Petroleum extraction and refining	43–1	Air transportation
		44–1	Merchant marine
32–1	Glass		

STATEMENTS IN PREPARATION

Series No.	Industry	Series No.	Industry
20–2	Bakeries	60–1	Banks and trust companies
27–1	Printing	64–1	Insurance
30–1	Rubber tires	70–1	Hotels
34–1	Railroad equipment	72–1	Laundries and dry cleaners
34–2	Aircraft	73–1	Advertising
34–3	Shipbuilding	73–1	Radio and television communication
35–1	Automobile dealers		
38–1	Automobiles	76–1	Electric and radio appliance sales and services
46–1	Telephone and telegraph		
48–1	Gas and electric utilities	78–1	Motion picture theaters
51–1	Distribution of petroleum products	94–1	Government
		94–2	Federal civil service
53–1	Department stores	94–3	State civil service
53–2	Chain stores	94–4	Municipal civil service
58–1	Restaurants	94–5	Postal service
59–1	Automobile services		

UNITED STATES DEPARTMENT OF LABOR. BUREAU OF LABOR STATISTICS.

Occupational Outlook Division Series. 10c each. Order from Supt. of Documents, Washington 25, D.C.

This series has been prepared by the Occupational Outlook Division which is organized to make studies of nationwide trends in employment in the various occupations and to evaluate the outlook in terms of employment, earnings, and working conditions.

The general outline of the pamphlets in the series includes the following topics of information: summary, nature of the occupation, status of the occupation before and during the war, employment prospects, education and training, hours, earnings, and working conditions. Statements are substantiated by graphs, charts, and statistics prepared by the Bureau of Labor Statistics.

The studies appear first as articles in the *Monthly Labor Review* and later are reprinted as bulletins, approximately 20 pages long and 6 by 9 inches in size.

Architect. (In preparation)
Automobile mechanic. 1945
Civilian aviation. 1945
Diesel-engine mechanics. 1945
Foundry occupations. 1945

Hosiery industry. 1945
Physicians. 1945
Radio repairman. (In preparation)
Welder. 1945

UNITED STATES DEPARTMENT OF LABOR. DIVISION OF OCCUPATIONAL ANALYSIS.

Individual Job Descriptions. Order from Supt. of Documents, Washington 25, D.C.

The titles in this series are not included in the annotated bibliography but they are listed here for the information of employment interviewers. They are useful in placement work if employment opportunities in the specific jobs are available locally.

Published between 1943 and 1945, each leaflet is 4 to 10 pages in length and printed on stiff paper 5 by 8 inches. The composite descriptions are based upon analyses of the individual job in a number of different establishments in various industries. There is included in each, a list of industries in which each job has been found to occur. Information is presented according to a general outline: job summary, employment variables, occupational tests, significant job factors, sources of workers, applicable job family, work performed, equipment and definitions, training briefs, trainee-selection factors, physical demands, working conditions, and industries.

Single copies of free items may be requested from the Division of Occupational Analysis, U. S. Department of Labor. Items for which there is a charge must be purchased from the Supt. of Documents, Washington 25, D. C. Price, 5 cents a copy, or $1.50 for 100 identical copies.

DICTIONARY CODE NO.	JOB DESCRIPTION
5–80.130	Aircraft-engine mechanic. 5c
5–80.120	Aircraft mechanic. 5c
5–03.010	Airplane coverer. 5c
4–33.916	Airplane woodworker I. Free
6–99.011	Armature winder I. Free
6–99.011	Armature winder II. Free
4–01.100	Baker I. Free
5–92.302	Bessemer-converter blower. 5c
4–86.010	Blacksmith II. Free
4–91.311	Blast-furnace blower. 5c
5–25.610	Boatbuilder, wood. Free
4–83.100	Boilermaker I. 5c
5–17.350.	Boilermaker, loftsman. Free
6–84.160.	Bolter and reamer. Free
4–49.010	Bookbinder. Free
4–78.041	Boring-mill operator. Free
6–84.410	Bucker-up III. Free
4–32.100	Cabinetmaker I. Free
7–05.620	Cable-hangar man. Free
4–27.811	Canvas worker, II. Free
5–25.110	Carpenter I. Free
5–25.640	Carpenter, fairing. Free
5–25.640	Carpenter, ship. Free
4–33.361	Carver, hand I. Free
4–78.920	Chipper III. Free
6–78.925	Chipper, metal. Free
0–46.01	Clothes designer. Free
4–56.010	Coke burner. 5c
4–44.010	Compositor I. Free
4–38.010	Cooper II. Free
4–80.080	Coppersmith II. Free
4–82.010	Coremaker I. Free
5–88.030	Crane rigger. Free
4–78.511	Cylindrical-grinder operator I. Free
4–76.010	Die maker II. Free
5–89.011	Diver. Free
5–92.422	Dock master. Free
6–84.150	Driller VI. Free
4–86.110	Drop-hammer operator II. Free
4–86.170	Drop-hammer operator IV. 5c

DICTIONARY CODE NO.	JOB DESCRIPTION
5–83.031	Electric-refrigerator serviceman. 5c
4–97.910	Electrician, airplane I. Free
4–97.210	Electrician, ship. Free
4–97.220	Electrician, shop. Free
4–78.011	Engine-lathe operator I. Free
5–80.350	Engine tester. 5c
4–73.510	Engraver I. Free
5–03.030	Fabric worker I. 5c
4–91.445	First helper II. 5c
6–85.215	Flame-cutter operator. Free
6–78.293	Flange-facing-machine operator. Free
6–88.742	Flanging-press operator. Free
6–78.632	Floor assembler. Free
5–17.060	Form builder I. 5c
4–86.130	Four - column - hydraulic - press operator. Free
4–91.571	Furnace tender, coke or coal. Free
4–91.571	Furnace tender, oil or gas. Free
4–86.020	Furnaceman XII. Free
4–21.010	Furrier II. Free
5–83.032	Gas-refrigerator serviceman. 5c
4–78.132	Gear-hobber operator I. Free
5–77.010	Glazier II. 5c
4–84.085	Grating installer. Free
4–86.120	Hammersmith. Free
5–30.020	Hangerman. Free
4–88.081	Heat treater II. Free
4–87.010	Heater III. 5c
6–88.732	Heater, forge. Free
4–78.042	Horizontal-boring and milling machine operator. Free
4–95.051	Hot bender III. Free
4–78.671	Inspecttor (machine shop). Free
5–83.972	Instrument man IV. 5c
4–78.512	Internal-grinder operator. Free

Dictionary Code No.	Job Description
4–78.043	Jig-boring-machine operator. Free
5–25.650	Joiner VI. Free
5–03.554	Landing-gear assembler. 5c
4–80.022	Lay-out man (aircraft mfg.). 5c
4–83.200	Lay-out man (boilermaking). Free
4–75.140	Lay-out man (machine shop). Free
5–05.530	Lay-out man (ship & boat bldg. & rep.). Free
4–33.912	Lay-out man (woodworking). Free
5–17.210	Loftsman II. Free
4–75.010	Machinist II. Free
4–75.150	Machinist, outside. Free
6–88.733	Mangle-roll operator. Free
4–07.100	Miller III. Free
4–33.914	Millman. Free
5–78.100	Millwright. Free
5–17.240	Mock-up assembler. 5c
4–81.010	Molder, bench. Free
4–81.020	Molder, finish. Free
4–52.735	Oxygen-plant operator. Free
7–05.510	Packer. Free
5–27.010	Painter I. Free
5–28.100	Paperhanger I. Free
5–28.100	Paperhanger II. Free
5–17.248	Patternmaker XI. 5c
5–17.010	Patternmaker, metal. Free
5–17.020	Patternmaker, wood. Free
0–56.11	Photographer, commercial. Free
5–30.030	Pipe assemblyman. Free
6–95.056	Pipe bender, machine. Free
5–33.110	Pipe coverer II. Free
5–30.010	Pipe fitter I. 5c
5–30.015	Pipe fitter II. Free
6–78.671	Pipe tester. Free
4–78.071	Planer operator II. Free
4–33.461	Planer operator IV. Free
5–17.250	Plaster-pattern caster. Free
6–78.071	Plate-edge-planer operator. Free
4–74.010	Plater I. Free
5–77.040	Plexiglas former. 5c
5–30.210	Plumber I. Free

Dictionary Code No.	Job Discription
5–30.260	Plumber II. Free
5–03.562	Plumber, aircraft. Free
6–88.664	Power-shear operator I. Free
5–03.562	Propeller-installation assembler. 5c
6–88.623	Punch-press operator II. Free
5–05.620	Radford straightener. Free
5–76.020	Railroad-car inspector. Free
4–91.441	Reverberatory-furnace operator. Free
6–88.667	Ripshear operator. Free
6–84.430	Rivet heater. Free
4–33.411	Router operator I. Free
5–25.230	Scaffold builder, wooden. Free
4–78.061	Shaper operator I. Free
4–88.622	Sheet-metal installer. Free
4–80.020	Sheet-metal lay-out man I. Free
4–80.060	Sheet-metal worker, Aircraft II. 5c
4–80.010	Sheet-metal worker II. Free
4–88.622	Sheet-metal worker III. Free
4–84.012	Shipfitter. Free
5–05.570	Ship rigger. Free
4–94.201	Spinner IV. 5c
6–84.115	Steel erector II. Free
5–05.620	Straightener V. Free
4–78.513	Surface-grinder operator. Free
5–51.520	System operator. Free
4–26.101	Tailor I. Free
4–84.110	Tank tester I. Free
4–59.501	Tanner. Free
5–17.260	Template maker, wire. Free
4–91.572	Tilting-furnace operator. Free
0–48.41	Tool designer. Free
5–84.110	Tool-grinder operator. Free
4–76.210	Tool maker. 5c
4–78.021	Turret-lathe operator. Free
4–85.080	Unionmelt operator. Free
4–35.720	Upholsterer II. Free
4–78.022	Vertical-turret-lathe operator. Free

DICTIONARY CODE No.	JOB DESCRIPTION	DICTIONARY CODE No.	JOB DESCRIPTION
4–85.030	Welder, acetylene. Free	6–85.080	Welder, tack. Free
4–85.020	Welder, arc. Free	4–85.020	Welding tester I. Free
4–85.040	Welder, combination. Free	5–05.610	Wood calker I. Free
6–85.060	Welder, spot. Free	5–05.610	Wood calker II. Free

Industry Composition Patterns. (Former title: Industry Manning Tables). Free.

The titles in this series are not included in the annotated bibliography but are listed here for the information of employment interviewers. They are useful in the placement of experienced workers if employment opportunities in that industry are available locally.

For single industries, the patterns provide (1) information on the occupations found in the industry, (2) percentage distribution of workers in these occupations, (3) distribution of workers according to training time required to reach normal production, and (4) manpower utilization practices.

This series is useful during the reconversion period in the placement of workers in a new industry and in recruiting additional workers. They assist in guiding workers into the fields in which the greatest number of workers is employed.

Free single copies are available from the Division of Occupational Analysis.

Aircraft assembly
  a. Metal aircraft
  b. Wooden aircraft
Aircraft parts
Aluminum and magnesium sand casting
Ball and roller bearings
Bituminous coal mining
Blast furnaces
Canning and preserving
Communications equipment
Cotton textiles
Fabricated plastic products
Fabricated structural steel
Footwear
Forgings
Grain and feed milling
Gray iron jobbing foundries
Machine tool accessories
Machine tools
Military tank assembly
Motor truck transportation
Nonferrous die casting
Nonferrous metal foundries

Paint and varnish
Paper and fiber containers
  a. Fiberboard and corrugated containers
  b. Folding and set-up containers
  c. Tubular containers
Petroleum refining
  a. Aviation gasoline refining
  b. Complete refining process
  c. Lubricating oil refining
Photolithography
Planing mills
Precision optical elements
Pulp, paper, and paper products
Quartz crystal oscillator plate
Screw machine products
Ship repair and conversion yards
Slaughtering and meat packing
Smokeless powder
Southern sawmills
Small naval combat craft
Steel foundries
Victory and liberty shipbuilding
Wooden goods

Interviewing Aids. Free.

These interviewing aids are not included in the annotated bibliography as they are useful only to the employment interviewer. They present in outline form the employment variables which should be considered in taking applications and employer orders, such as type of work performed, kinds of materials used, type of training, skills required, and health hazards. They are printed on 5 by 8 inch cards, usually on one side only.

Free single copies are available from the Division of Occupational Analysis.

Dictionary Code No.	Job Discription
6–87.110	Annealer
5–09.420	Artificial-limb assembler
5–09.430	Artificial-limb maker II
0–01.60	Auditor
5–81.510	Automobile-body repairman, metal
5–81.410	Automobile-generator repairman
5–81.010	Automobile mechanic
5–81.610	Automobile mechanic, motor I
5–81.530	Automobile-radiator man
6–33.211	Band-ripsaw operator
6–78.611	Band-sawing-machine operator
6–33.212	Band-scroll-saw operator
6–78.025	Barrel chamberer
4–78.211	Barrel reamer
4–78.214	Barrel rifler I
4–93.772	Barrel straightener
4–19.201	Beamer III
4–61.681	Bed laster
6–77.710	Bench grinder
5–74.020	Blaster I
6–14.173	Boarding-machine operator
4–83.400	Boiler-shop mechanic
6–83.130	Boiler tester
1–01.02	Bookkeeper II
1–01.03	Bookkeeper III
1–02.01	Bookkeeping-machine operator I
1–02.02	Bookkeeping-machine operator II
1–02.03	Bookkeeping-machine operator III
6–78.041	Boring-machine operator, automatic

Dictionary Code No.	Job Discription
6–33.412	Boring-machine operator, multiple spindle
6–94.206	Brake operator, hand
6–94.207	Brake operator, machine II
5–24.110	Bricklayer I
5–24.010	Bricklayer II
5–24.130	Bricklayer, refractory brick
5–24.020	Bricklayer, sewer
6–78.051	Broaching-machine operator
6–77.020	Buffer I
7–23.030	Bulldozer operator I
6–94.221	Bumper operator I
4–32.100	Cabinetmaker I
1–25.13	Calculating-machine operator
6–18.220	Card grinder
5–25.110	Carpenter I
5–25.150	Carpenter, finish
5–25.830	Carpenter, maintenance
5–25.230	Carpenter, rough II
1–01.52	Cashier I
1–01.53	Cashier II
6–82.920	Casting inspector
5–73.050	Caterpillar-crane operator
5–26.100	Cement finisher II
6–78.511	Centerless-grinder operator
6–91.181	Charging-machine operator I
6–98.010	Chassis assembler II
6–98.030	Check inspector
6–82.910	Chipper, foundry
4–61.171	Cobbler, sole
4–61.172	Cobbler, upper
4–44.010	Compositor I
2–26.32	Cook V
4–09.212	Cook VI
6–82.120	Core-oven tender
6–82.060	Core paster

DICTIONARY CODE NO.	JOB DESCRIPTION
5–76.110	Cotton classer
6–91.051	Cupola charger I
6–91.052	Cupola charger II
4–91.351	Cupola tender
6–27.054	Cutter, machine I
6–87.210	Cyanide-furnace operator
6–49.410	Cylinder-press feeder
4–48.101	Cylinder-press man
7–03.542	Detail assembler I
7–00.938	Detail-electrical assembler
5–75.410	Diamond driller
4–76.030	Die cleaner and polisher
4–76.120	Die setter I
6–78.512	Disk-grinder operator
6–78.610	Do-all-saw operator
5–75.020	Driller, machine II
6–86.110	Drop-hammer operator I
5–73.010	Electric-bridge-crane operator
5–73.040	Electric-gantry-crane operator
5–73.020	Electric-monorail-crane operator
4–97.930	Electrical inspector II
4–97.420	Electrical repairman I
4–97.010	Electrician I
0–88.24	Engineer V
0–88.21	Engineer, chief, marine
3–15.01	Farm hand, berry
3–12.10	Farm hand, cotton
3–14.10	Farm hand, dairy
3–15.21	Farm hand, fruit
3–16.10	Farm hand, general
3–11.10	Farm hand, grain
3–17.10	Farm hand, livestock
3–18.10	Farm hand, poultry
3–13.01	Farm hand, sugar beet
3–13.51	Farm hand, tobacco
3–19.10	Farm hand, vegetable
3–35.10	Farm mechanic
5–16.710	Finisher (furniture)
7–70.040	Fireman, stationary boiler
4–83.300	Fit-up man
6–87.142	Flame-annealing-machine adjuster
6–85.240	Flame-cutting-machine operator
6–94.208	Folding-machine operator VII
4–86.125	Forging-press operator I

DICTIONARY CODE NO.	JOB DESCRIPTION
6–94.215	Forming-machine operator IV
6–78.613	Friction-sawing-machine operator
6–88.081	Furnaceman VIII
6–36.050	Furniture assembler
6–74.110	Galvanizer
6–56.010	Gas producer man
4–78.131	Gear-generator operator I
6–78.133	Gear-generator operator II
6–78.134	Gear-hobber operator II
4–78.133	Gear-milling-machine operator I
6–78.135	Gear-milling-machine operator II
4–78.134	Gear-sharper operator I
6–78.136	Gear-shaper operator II
7–85.010	Greaser III
4–87.220	Hardener II
4–87.910	Hardness inspector
4–78.411	Honing-machine operator
5–25.160	Hardwood-floor layer
5–73.520	Hoisting engineer II
5–73.510	Hoistman I
5–72.050	Hot-mill engineer
6–54.038	Inspector I (ammunition)
4–61.861	Inspector (boot and shoe)
4–75.160	Job setter II
6–33.462	Jointer operator III
4–88.624	Joggle-press operator I
6–78.413	Lapping-machine operator I
6–90.712	Leacher II
6–62.160	Leather worker II
5–08.070	Lens grinder
5–53.420	Lineman IV
5–73.060	Locomotive-crane operator
5–17.245	Loftsman II
4–15.030	Loom changer
4–16.010	Loom fixer
7–83.326	Machine adjuster III
5–83.324	Machine fixer III
6–81.010	Machine molder, jarring
4–81.050	Machine molder, squeeze
6–81.020	Machine molder, stripping plate
5–83.621	Maintenance man, factory or mill
6–78.031	Milling-machine operator, automatic
5–78.100	Millwright

Dictionary Code No.	Job Description
5–21.010	Miner I
7–32.371	Miner IV
4–81.020	Molder, finish
6–82.950	Molder helper III
6–33.464	Molder operator III
6–78.081	Multiple-spindle-drill-press operator
4–48.050	Offset-press man
7–16.550	Paint-touch-up man
5–27.010	Painter I
7–16.210	Painter, spray I
4–27.431	Pattern cutter II
4–27.432	Patternmaker IV
6–54.020	Pellet-press operator I
6–95.058	Pipe-threading-machine operator
6–49.420	Platen-press feeder I
6–49.430	Platen-press feeder II
4–74.010	Plater I
6–77.060	Polisher II
5–73.210	Power-shovel operator
6–78.111	Profiling-machine operator II
6–78.112	Profiling-machine operator III
4–88.012	Pulpit-man II
7–72.510	Pumpman I
6–87.220	Quenching-machine operator
6–94.226	Radial-router operator
5–72.310	Refrigerating engineer
6–95.080	Riveter, aircraft
4–84.060	Riveter, pneumatic II
4–88.021	Roller I
6–88.024	Roller operator V
4–88.291	Roll polisher
6–94.227	Router operator III
6–94.204	Rotary-shear operator II
6–82.710	Sandblast-or-shotblast-tumbler operator
6–78.145	Screw-machine operator, automatic I
6–78.144	Screw-machine operator semi-automatic
6–33.364	Shaper operator II
6–78.673	Shell inspector
6–88.215	Sheet-aluminum inspector

Dictionary Code No.	Job Description
6–94.202	Sheet-metal-fabricating-machine operator
5–03.820	Sheet-metal inspector I
6–78.676	Sheet-metal inspector II
6–94.222	Sheet-metal lay-out man II
5–92.301	Sheet roller I
4–88.025	Sheet roller II
1–34.13	Shipping clerk I
6–78.083	Single-spindle-drill-press operator
1–78.012	Speed-lathe operator
6–95.001	Solderer I
6–52.446	Solvent-recovery man
6–84.910	Steel-plate calker
5–72.010	Stationary engineer
4–45.210	Stereotyper
5–24.210	Stonemason
7–16.610	Striper, hand I
4–84.010	Structural-steel worker
7–02.321	Subassembler I
6–88.036	Tableman III
4–59.501	Tanner
6–78.143	Thread-milling-machine operator
5–22.010	Timberman I
5–25.260	Timberman II
4–88.023	Tin roller, hot mill
4–76.220	Tool inspector
4–76.210	Tool maker
7–36.510	Tractor operator
6–88.717	Trimming-press operator II
6–95.053	Tube-bending-machine operator I
4–35.720	Upholsterer II
6–27.060	Upholstery-and-trim cutter
6–98.260	Wax impregnator
4–15.020	Weaver IV
6–85.010	Welder, bar
6–85.020	Welder, butt
6–85.030	Welder, flash
6–85.100	Welder, roller seam
6–85.070	Welder, thermite
4–33.363	Wood turner
5–99.010	Yardmaster I

Job Family Series. Order from Supt. of Documents, Washington 25, D.C.

The titles in this series are not included in the annotated bibliography but are listed here for the information of employment interviewers. *Job families* pamphlets list groups of occupations which are related to selected base occupations, or to key occupations in selected industries. In some cases information is given about training requirements and physical demands. These job relationships are established on the basis of similarities in the work performed; tools, equipment, materials, and work-aids utilized; knowledge required; and the mental and physical worker-characteristics required for successful job performance. Job families techniques are useful in personnel recruitment, selection, counseling, training, or transfer of workers since they identify: (1) The kinds of workers that may be used efficiently and with a minimum of retraining to fill specific jobs, (2) the kinds of jobs in which workers can be most efficiently employed when work in which they have had experience and training is not available, and (3) fields of work in which transferability among jobs is possible.

The Occupational "O" Series lists job groups which constitute good sources of workers to fill specified base occupations. The Industrial "I" Series are of two kinds: (1) Lists of job-groups from each of which a specified key job in a particular industry can be filled, and (2) lists of job-groups in specified industries from each of which workers can effectively be upgraded or transferred to a specified key job in the same industry.

The Army "A" Series would be helpful to employment interviewers who are placing men who have had experience in the specific Army occupations.

Single copies of the free leaflets are available from the Division of Occupational Analysis, U. S. Department of Labor. Items for which there is a charge must be purchased from the Supt. of Documents, Washington 25, D. C.

ARMY "A" SERIES

A-9	Aerial engineer. Free
A-8	Aerial gunner. Free
A-2	Armorer flight chief. Free
A-18	Artillery mechanic. Free
A-10	Baker, all-round. Free
A-6	Bombardier. Free
A-1	Bombsight mechanic. Free
A-20	Camoufleur. Free
A-5	Communications sergeant. Free
A-11	Cook, all-round. Free
A-7	Crew chief, balloon. Free
A-4	Helium gas worker. Free
A-12	Navigation clerk. Free
A-13	Parachute rigger. Free
A-21	Photographers, military. Free
A-3	Propeller repairman. Free
A-19	Radio operators and mechanics, military. Free
A-15	Range sergeant. Free
A-14	Reclamation man. Free
A-16	Truck driver, army. Free
A-17	Vocational examiner. Free

Occupational "O" Series

O-68 Aircraft engine mechanic. Free
O-80 Aircraft instrument mechanic. Free
O-89 Aircraft mechanic. 10c
O-32 Airplane woodworker. 5c
O-49 Armorer. Free
O-25 Assemblers, heavy work. Free
O-77 Automobile mechanics, all-round. Free
O-35 Barrel straightener. Free
O-36 Blacksmith and tool dresser. Free
O-35 Boatbuilder, wood. Free
O-12 Boilermaker. 10c
O-26 Bricklayer. Free
O-59 Cabinetmaker I. Free
O-62 Carpenter, ship. Free
O-88 Clock and watch repairman. 10c
O-73 Crane rigger. Free
O-40 Die setter. Free
O-39 Drop-hammer operator. 5c
O-38 Electric-arc-furnace operator. 5c
O-48 Electric-motor repairman. Free
O-34 Electrician, ship. 5c
O-41 Electrician, airplane. Free
O-30 Electroplater. Free
O-3 Engine-lathe operator. 10c
O-58 Forming-press operator II. Free
O-76 Foundry molders and core-makers, hand. Free
O-37 Heat treater, all round. 10c
O-72 Heavy fabric workers, all round. Free
O-22 Hosiery knitters, full-fashioned. Free
O-47 Hydraulic-control and fuel-and-oil units assemblers. 5c
O-55 Inspectors, small-arms, ammunition. Free
O-53 Instrument maker II. Free
O-43 Job setter II. Free
O-85 Locomotive engineers, steam. Free
O-4 Loftsman II. Free
O-23 Mechanical draftsmen. 5c
O-50 Mechanical inspectors. 5c
O-51 Machine adjuster, primer assembly. Free
O-57 Machine operators, small-arms ammunition. Free
O-11 Machinist II. Free
O-67 Machinist, bench. Free
O-54 Machinist, marine. Free
O-42 Machinist, marine gas-engine. Free
O-66 Major assemblers, aircraft. Free
O-82 Marine engineers. Free
O-52 Metal chippers and calkers, pneumatic hammer. Free
O-75 Milling-machine operator II. Free
O-78 Millwright. Free
O-87 Milk processing occupations, all-round. 10c
O-86 Miners, all-round. 15c
O-65 Painter I. Free
O-13 Patternmaker, wood. 10c
O-45 Pipe fitter, marine. Free
O-64 Plaster patternmaker, all-round. Free
O-79 Plexiglas former. Free
O-71 Pneumatic riveters, aircraft. Free
O-9 Power-shovel operator. 5c
O-1 Precision-lens grinder. Free
O-70 Radio mechanic. Free
O-20 Roller. Free
O-31 Screw-machine operator, automatic. 10c
O-63 Sheet-metal lay-out man, Free
O-81 Sheet-metal workers, all-round. Free
O-10 Shipfitter. Free
O-60 Ship rigger. Free
O-69 Still operator, chemical. Free
O-17 Stone carver. Free
O-21 Stone-lathe operator. Free
O-28 Stonemason. 5c
O-84 Synthetic-rubber monomer occupations. 10c
O-46 Tool, die, fixture, gage, and jig makers. Free
O-44 Tool-grinder operator. Free
O-29 Tool or machine designers Free

OCCUPATIONS "O"—*Continued*

O-8 Tractor operator. Free
O-56 Weavers. Free
O-83 Welder, acetylene. Free
O-74 Welder, arc. Free

INDUSTRIAL "I" SERIES

I-65 Airframe industry—related jobs. 20c
I-40 Airframe manufacturing — upgrading suggestions. 35c
I-50 Aluminum production — related jobs. 15c
I-58 Aluminum production—upgrading suggestions. 10c
I-7 Aluminum ware manufacturing. Free
I-51 Ammunition manufacturing. 15c
I-29 Automobile manufacturing. 20c
I-55 Beverage industries. Free
I-6 Boilermaking. 10c
I-18 Boot and shoe manufacturing. 20c
I-15 Building construction. 20c
I-41 Cane-sugar refining. 15c
I-71 Canning and preserving industry. 15c
I-70 Dress manufacturing. 10c
I-43 Drug preparations and related products. 10c
I-60 Electrical equipment industry. 15c
I-37 Fiber and paper container manufacturing. 10c
I-64 Foundry industry. 10c
I-23 Fur goods manufacturing. 10c
I-48 Furniture manufacturing, metal. 10c
I-16 Glass and glass products manufacturing. Free
I-46 Glue and gelatin manufacturing. 15c
I-26 Hat manufacturing. 20c
I-33 Heating equipment manufacturing. Free
I-1 Hosiery manufacturing, silk. Free
I-34 Iron and steel—related occupations in other industries. Free
I-31 Iron and steel—upgrading suggestions. Free
I-44 Jewelry manufacturing. 10c
I-32 Leather products manufacturing. 15c

I-49 Locomotive and car building and repair. 15c
I-45 Logging and sawmill—related jobs. 10c
I-59 Logging and sawmill—upgrading suggestions. 10c
I-38 Machine tool manufacturing—upgrading suggestions. 10c
I-53 Magnesium production — related jobs. 10c
I-54 Magnesium production—upgrading suggestions. 10c
I-56 Miscellaneous manufacturing activities, including:
Amusement machine manufacturing. Free
Decorative feather and artificial flower fabrication. Free
Mirror and picture frame manufacturing. Free
Musical instrument manufacturing. Free
Sign and advertising display manufacturing. Free
Toy and game manufacturing. Free
I-69 Paper and pulp production. 10c
I-61 Precision instrument manufacturing. 20c
I-22 Printing and publishing. 20c
I-10 Quarrying. 10c
I-52 Radio equipment, parts and tube manufacturing—upgrading suggestions. 15c
I-8 Radio manufacturing — related jobs. 10c
I-5 Refrigerator and refrigerating and icemaking equipment manufacturing. 15c
I-14 Rubber products manufacturing. 10c
I-62 Ship and boat building and repair. 15c
I-42 Shipbuilding-upgrading suggestions. 25c
I-9 Silverware manufacturing. Free
I-63 Slaughtering and meat packing industry. 15c
I-12 Stoneworking. Free
I-30 Structural and ornamental metal work. 10c
I-57 Textile goods, and fabric products manufacturing, miscellaneous, including:
Carpets, rugs, and pads. Free
Curtains, draperies, and bedspreads. Free

OCCUPATIONS "I"—*Continued*

    Fancy fabrics such as lace and lace goods. Free
    Pleating, stitching, tucking and embroidery. Free
    Trimmings and art needlework. Free

I–28 Textile printing. 10c

I–47 Textiles and knit goods, except hosiery, silk. 10c

I–35 Tin can and tinware manufacturing. Free

I–66 Veneer and plywood manufacturing. 10c

I–39 Wooden box manufacturing. 15c

I–24 Woodworking general. 20c

I–36 Woolen and worsted manufacturing. 20c

National Job Descriptions. $1-$1.25 a volume. Order from Supt. of Documents, Washington 25, D.C.

Bound volumes contain occupational information describing work performed for sixteen major industries. Job descriptions are based upon analysis of each job in a number of establishments. As an example of the content of these volumes, *Job Descriptions for Office Occupations* includes for ninety occupations a job summary, description of work performed, employment variables, and relation to other jobs under the headings: promotion to, promotion from, transfer to and from, and other relationships.

5. Bakery products industry. 1939
6. Cleaning, dyeing, and pressing industry. 1938
7. Construction industry. 1936
8. Confectionery industry. 1939
9. Cotton textile industry. 1935
10. Domestic service and personal service. 1939
11. Garment manufacturing industry. 1939
12. Hotels and restaurants. 1939
13. Industrial service and maintenance occupations. 1939
14. Job foundries. 1938
15. Job machine shops. 1938
16. Laundry industry. 1937
17. Lumber and lumber products industries. 1939
18. Retail trade. 1938
19. Automobile manufacturing industry. 1935
20. Office occupations. 1945

UNITED STATES DEPARTMENT OF LABOR. NATIONAL ROSTER OF SCIENTIFIC AND SPECIALIZED PERSONNEL. *See* National Roster of Scientific and Specialized Personnel.

UNITED STATES DEPARTMENT OF LABOR. WOMEN'S BUREAU.

The Outlook for Women in Occupations in the Medical Services. 10c each. Order from Supt. of Documents, Washington 25, D.C.

This series, written by Marguerite Zapoleon with the assistance of Elsie Katcher of the Bureau's Research Division, has been prepared to present the postwar outlook for women. It discusses the changes that have taken place during the war and the effect of these changes on the postwar supply of and demand for women in particular occupational fields. It describes the prewar situation, the wartime changes, and the postwar outlook for women in occupations in the field of medical services, in which women in 1940 composed almost two thirds of the workers.

Each pamphlet presents the minimum requirements for entrance to an approved school for training, for completion of approved courses, for membership in professional associations, and for beginning Federal Civil Service positions. Prepared in 1945, this series contains up-to-date information and useful bibliographies.

The pamphlets vary in length from 10 to 60 pages and are 6 by 9½ inches in size. They have a uniform cover at the top of which is a design symbolic of medical and other health services.

1. Physical therapists. 1945
2. Occupational therapists. 1945
3. Professional nurses. 1945
4. Medical laboratory technicians. 1945
5. Practical nurses and hospital attendants. 1945
6. Medical record librarians. 1945
7. Women physicians. 1945
8. X-ray technicians. 1945
10. Dental hygienists. 1945

UNITED STATES OFFICE OF EDUCATION.

Guidance Leaflets. 5c each. Order from Supt. of Documents, Washington 25, D.C.

This series of leaflets on professional careers has been prepared by Walter J. Greenleaf, Specialist in Occupational Information and Guidance, U. S. Office of Education. According to the introduction, these leaflets are designed for the use of students in high schools and colleges, orientation classes, guidance committees, counselors, teachers, and parents.

Information concerning each profession consists of a historical survey, description of occupation, opportunities, compensation, training, and selected list of references. The discussion of training includes what preliminary education is required, where training is offered, length of training, student budgets, tuition rates, and expenses.

Varying in length from 6 to 24 pages, these 6 by 9 inch leaflets are attractive in format. The front cover of each contains a woodcut symbolic of the career. Four of the nineteen leaflets have been revised since 1940; the need for revision of others is apparent, since the number of schools offering professional training has increased.

The historical surveys are presented in an interesting manner and summaries of research studies, such as state examination requirements, make these five-cent leaflets a useful addition to the occupational library.

5. Law. 1932	15. Nursing. 1932
6. Medicine. 1941	16. Forestry. 1932
7. Dentistry. 1932	17. Music. 1934
8. Journalism. 1932	18. Veterinary medicine. 1940
9. Librarianship. 1932	19. Chemistry and chemical engineering. 1932
10. Architecture. 1932	
11. Civil engineering. 1932	20. Art. 1932
12. Electrical engineering. 1932	21. Home economics. 1932
13. Mechanical engineering. 1934	22. Optometry. 1934
14. Pharmacy. 1945	23. Osteopathy. 1945

UNITED STATES WAR DEPARTMENT.

Occupational Briefs. 5c each. Order from Superintendent of Documents, Washington 25, D.C.

The fifty-three Occupational Briefs were prepared by the National Roster of Scientific and Specialized Personnel for the War Department. They were used in connection with the United States Armed Forces Institute courses and the War Department's other educational and counseling programs. The information given includes occupational summary, earnings, outlook, qualifications, and training.

Copies cannot be obtained from the National Roster but may be purchased from the Superintendent of Documents at five cents each. The following titles are available:

Accountant
Advertising manager
Agricultural and biological scientist
Animal, dairy and poultry scientist
Architect
Bacteriologist
Botanist, plant pathologist and plant physiologist
Catholic clergyman
Chemist
Counselor, vocational guidance
Dentist
Dietitian
Economist
Engineers (general survey)
Engineer, aeronautical
Engineer, automotive
Engineer, chemical
Engineer, civil
Engineer, electrical

Engineer, industrial
Engineer, mechanical
Engineer, metallurgical
Engineer, mining
Foreign language specialist
Forester
Geologist
Geophysicist
Horticulturist, agronomist and soil scientist
Lawyer
Librarian
Medical laboratory technician
Meteorologist
Musician and music teacher
Nurse, registered
Optometrist
Personnel worker
Pharmacist
Physical educator

Physician
Physicist
Protestant clergyman
Psychiatrist
Psychologist
Rabbi
Reporter and editor
Social worker

Sociologist
Statistician
Teacher, high school
Teacher, vocational schools
Veterinarian
Writer
Zoologist, entomologist, and parasitologist

VOCATIONAL GUIDANCE MANUALS, INC., 45 W. 45th Street, New York 19, N.Y.

Vocational Guidance Manuals. $1-$1.25 each.

The first eight titles in this series are announced for 1946 publication. At this writing they are not available for examination.

The announcement states that they are designed to give pertinent facts about the desirable and undesirable features of various vocations. Bibliographies, lists of schools, names of trade papers, and other helpful information will be included. Bound in paper leatherette, the average length is 96 pages.

Opportunities in acting
Opportunities in architecture
Opportunities in free-lance writing
Opportunities in interior decoration

Opportunities in journalism
Opportunities in motion pictures
Opportunities in public relations
Opportunities in radio

WESTERN PERSONNEL SERVICE, 130 Raymond Avenue, Pasadena 1, Calif.

Occupational Briefs. 1941-1944. 25c each.

The ten pamphlets in this series are based on intensive research. By reason of the strategic location of the sponsoring organization, the six pamphlets on specialties within the motion picture industry contain information not found elsewhere.

Printed on white paper, the pamphlets are 5½ by 8½ inches in size and average from 10 to 15 pages in length. Most of the pamphlets describe the nature of the work, requirements, earnings, opportunities, and outlook.

The Western Personnel Service is a research institute for western colleges and universities, serving as a clearing house of information about occupations and student personnel work. The earlier briefs are reported to be out of print. Those annotated in this bibliography are the following:

The carrier traffic manager. 1945
Law enforcement. 1945
Motion picture cartooning. 1941
Motion picture editing. 1941
Motion picture laboratory technicians. No date

Motion picture photography. 1944
Motion picture research. 1941
Motion picture sound technicians. 1944
Pipe line traffic management. 1944
Social anthropology. 1945

In Preparation

Foreign service
Foreign trade
Housing

Personnel work
Psychology and psychiatry

XAVIER UNIVERSITY, Washington and Pine Streets, New Orleans 18, La.

Occupational Opportunities. Twenty-five monographs in a display box, $9.

These studies in the occupational opportunities for Negroes have been prepared by the Research Department of Xavier University for the information of prospective students.

The material is mimeographed but is attractively bound in stiff green-colored printed folders, 9½ by 11½ inches, with the occupational title printed on the left hand side.

All of them include a discussion of the employment outlook for Negro youth and information about the schools offering training to Negroes.

1. The situation and the challenge. 1937
2. An essential part of education. 1937
3. What vocation. 1937
4. How to choose a vocation. 1937
5. A survey of the field. 1937
6. The Negro physician. 1937
7. The trained nurse. 1937
8. Pharmacy. 1937
9. Architecture and engineering. 1937
10. The social worker. 1937
11. Education as a field of work. 1937
12. Journalism. 1937
13. Life insurance. 1938
14. Music as a vocation. 1938
15. Civil service. 1938
16. The Negro in business. 1938
17. Dentistry. 1938
18. Physical education. 1938
19. Chemistry. 1938
20. The agricultural expert: the veterinarian. 1938
21. Librarianship. 1938
22. Home economics. 1938
23. Radio and aviation. 1938
    tions. 1938
25. Skilled artisans. 1938

CANADIAN SERIES

The pamphlets in the Canadian Series have not been listed in Part VI.

BRITISH COLUMBIA. DEPARTMENT OF EDUCATION, Textbook Branch, Victoria, B.C.

Vocational Information Series. 10c each.

Each of the seven pamphlets is an occupational study of one of the important industrial fields in British Columbia. The studies give a general picture of the industry and information about working conditions, training, and compensation of individual jobs.

The pamphlets vary in length from 10 to 31 pages and are firmly bound with suitable covers. The cost is ten cents per copy.

Agriculture. 1939
Communication. 1940
Fishing. 1939
Forest industries. 1939

Manufacturing. 1940
Mining. 1939
Transportation. 1940

CANADIAN LEGION EDUCATIONAL SERVICES, 27 Goulburn Avenue, Ottawa, Ont.

Let's Consider Jobs Series. Occupational Manuals.

Each of the thirty manuals describes Canadian occupations and is prepared for the use of the Canadian Armed Forces. Canadian schools and institutions may obtain them at cost from the Canadian Federal and Provincial Departments of Government. They are not available to the general public nor to individuals.

Information is presented under the following headings: history of the field, nature of the work, qualifications required, training for the occupation, opportunities for employment in the field, possibilities of advancement, and compensation. Canadian organizations and professional associations are listed. References for further reading are included.

A handbook entitled *How to Choose Your Post-War Job* accompanies the series.

1. Homemaking
2. Agriculture, including fur farming
3. Agricultural industries
4. Forestry and logging
5. Forest products industries
6. Prospecting, mining and smelting
7. Transportation—land, sea and air
8. Communication—telegraph, telephone, radio, mail
9. Building trades
10. Fishing, fisheries products and marketing
11. Machinists
12. Automotive repairing and garages
13. Stenography, typewriting and clerical work
14. Steel construction, riveting, welding and flame cutting
15. Education and teaching
16. Meals and lodgings
17. Textile industries
18. Clothing industries
19. Retail trade distribution
20. Salesmanship
21. Civil service, public administration
22. Barbering and beauty culture
23. Plumbing, pipe-fitting, sheet metalwork and tinsmithing
24. Foundry work—moulders and core makers
25. Shoe repairing
26. Meat packing, marketing and butchering
27. Baking and catering
28. Electrical work
29. Printing trades
30. Patternmaking
31. Domestic service
32. Laundering, pressing, cleaning and dyeing
33. Law
34. Professional health services—medicine, dentistry, nursing, pharmacy, and public health
35. Boiler making
36. Blacksmithing
37. Commercial art and advertising
38. Accountancy and bookkeeping

39. Social services
40. Engineering—chemical, civil, metallurgical, mechanical, architectural, etc.
41. Journalism
42. Scientific agricultural and veterinary services
43. Librarianship
44. Photography
45. Household science
46. Stationary engineering
47. Police and fire services
48. Undertaking and embalming
49. Pottery work—brick and tile, clay and glass
50. Personnel work

ONTARIO SECONDARY SCHOOL TEACHERS' FEDERATION, Toronto District.

Occupational Monographs. 10c each. Order from Sir Isaac Pitman and Sons, 381-3 Church Street, Toronto 2, Canada.

Prepared by the Research Committee of the Toronto District of the Ontario Secondary School Teachers' Federation, each booklet includes the following information: history and importance, trends, nature of the work involved, qualifications, training required, working conditions, remuneration, opportunities for promotion, advantages, disadvantages, and bibliography.

The booklets contain approximately six pages each and include no illustrations. The cost is 10 cents per single copy; 5 cents for quantity orders.

At the present writing, twelve monographs are available; others are announced for later publication.

1. Accountant
2. Interior decorator
3. Telephone operator
4. Electrical engineer
5. Street car operator and bus driver
6. Dentist
7. Office machine operator
8. Auto mechanic
9. Stenographer
10. Life insurance salesman
11. Machinist
12. Electrician

TORONTO, UNIVERSITY OF. ONTARIO COLLEGE OF EDUCATION, VOCATIONAL GUIDANCE CENTRE, 371 Bloor Street West, Toronto 5, Ont.

Vocational Guidance Centre Occupational Information Monographs. 7c each.

These monographs present information about workers in Canada and are equally useful in all provinces of the Dominion. The monographs start with a short definition of the occupational title and give information under the following headings: history and importance, nature of the work, working conditions, qualifications necessary for entry and success, preparation needed, opportunities for advancement, remuneration, advantages, disadvantages, how to get started in or towards the occupation, related occupations, further reading. Provision is made so that special information concerning the occupation in a particular area may be added.

Four pages in length, containing from 2,500 to 3,500 words, they are printed on heavy, coated stock, since this paper tends to resist dirt. One picture is used in each monograph. Special prices are quoted for large quantity orders.

Accountant. 1945	Musician. 1945
Architect. 1945	Nurse. 1945
Bookkeeper. 1945	Patternmaker. 1945
Commercial artist. 1944	Physician. 1944
Dentist. 1945	Printer. 1945
Engineer, professional. 1945	Social worker. 1944
Home economist. 1945	Stenographer. 1944
Librarian. 1944	Teacher. 1944

In Preparation

Airline stewardess	Mechanical draftsman
Baker	Occupational therapist
Beautician	Optometrist
Chemist	Pharmacist
Clergyman	Plumber
Cook	Physiotherapist
Lawyer	Tailor
Machinist	Watchmaker

PART VI

Annotated Bibliography

A. Pamphlets Listed by Occupations

— ACCOUNTANT   0-01.

Accountancy. Bentley, H. C. The Bentley School of Accounting and Finance, 921 Boylston St., Boston 15, Mass. No date. 12p. Free
> Discussion of accountancy under the following divisions of practice: constructive, inspective, budgeting, tax accounting, and recordative (general and cost accounting). The Certified Public Accountant law is briefly described, showing the difference between the commercial accountant and public accountant. Factors are given which should be considered before one attempts to enter the public accounting profession.

Accountancy. Pace Institute, 225 Broadway, New York 7, N.Y. 1945. 40p. Free
> Includes a statement regarding the character of services rendered by certified public accountants and the qualities required for success.

* Accountancy as a career. Institute for Research. 1941. 19p. 75c
> Duties, qualifications, training, typical day's work, salaries, attractive and unattractive sides. Describes opportunities in institutions, governmental bodies, teaching, legal work, and specialized business. Two illustrations.

**Accountancy as a career field—a handbook of vocational information. Spaulding, George A. National Council of Business Schools, 839 17th St., N.W., Washington 6, D.C. 1944. 14p. 10c
> Duties, earnings, qualifications and preparation. Discusses the private and public practice of accountancy and lists fourteen positions in modern business where training in accounting is an asset.

* Accountant. Prepared for the War Department by the National Roster. Supt. of Documents, Washington 25, D.C. 1945. 17p. 5c
> Occupational brief containing summary, earnings, outlook, qualifications, and training.

* Accountant. Revised edition. Occupational Index. 1944. 6p. 25c
> Occupational abstract. Duties, qualifications, preparation, entrance and advancement, compensation, number and distribution of workers, advantages, disadvantages, and postwar prospects. Bibliography.

Accountants, bookkeepers, and cashiers. Science Research Associates. 1943. 4p. Planographed. 15c
> Occupational brief number 6. Two illustrations. Annotated bibiography.

Accounting. Lockwood, Jeremiah, and Rankin, Calvin. Bellman Publishing Co. 1940. 39p. Vari-typed. 50c
> Types of work performed by accountants, qualifications, training, opportunities, and trends. List of schools offering from 20 to 75 semester credits in accounting courses. Bibliography.

Accounting. Revised edition. Quarrie Corporation. 1942. 7p. Planographed. 10c
> Vocational monograph number 1.

* Accounting. Shade, Chloris, ed. 2nd edition revised. Morgan-Dillon & Co. 1939. 22p. 32c
> Description of work in private, public, and Governmental accounting. Duties, qualifications, training, conditions of work, opportunities, and trends. Bibliography.

* Cost accounting as a career. Institute for Research. 1940. 24p. 75c
> Importance of cost accounting, personal qualifications, opportunities, rewards, and requirements for membership in the National Association of Cost Accountants. Description of work in the public accounting field, in government positions, and in the cost accounting department. The latter includes the timekeeper, labor distribution record clerk, payroll records clerk, social security records clerk and distribution cost clerk. One illustration.

Description of profession of accounting. National Roster. 1945. 4p. Free
> See p. 34 for description of series.

Handbook of descriptions of specialized fields in accounting. National Roster. 1946
> In preparation.

Regulation and practice of accountancy. Beights, David M. University of Florida, Bureau of Economic and Business Research, Gainesville, Fla. 1944. 4p. 10c
> Development, scope and variety of accounting work. Duties of public accountant and of private accountant are preceded by a discussion of the legal distinction. Regulation of public accounting by law and by organizations such as the American Institute of Accountants, the American Accounting Association, and the National Association of Cost Accountants.

Women in accountancy. Science Research Associates. No date. 2p. Planographed. 15c
> Occupational reprint number 14
> *See also* Bookkeeper; Public accountant

ACOUSTICIAN   0-39.55
* Acoustical engineering as a career. Institute for Research. 1940. 16p. 75c
> History and development of work, its relation to electrical engineering, personal qualifications, preparation, opportunities, salaries, methods of obtaining a position, advantages and disadvantages, and list of six schools which offer courses in architectural acoustics. Description of other aspects of acoustical engineering such as sound insulation of buildings, noise quieting in offices and factories, radio, talking pictures, and research. One illustration.

ACTOR AND ACTRESS   0-02.

Dramatic art as a career. Institute for Research. 1936. 20p. 75c
> Qualifications, preparation, opportunities, methods of securing a position, advantages, and disadvantages. Also information about playwrighting and dramatic criticism.

* Motion picture actor. Revised edition. Occupational Index. 1945. 6p. 25c
> Occupational abstract. Duties, abilities, preparation, entrance and advancement, earnings, number and distribution of workers, advantages, and disadvantages. Annotated bibliography.

One in a thousand—the way of life on the road to Hollywood. Robertson, Marian. Row, Peterson and Co. 1941. 64p. 96c
> Describes experiences in the department of a talent scout. See p. 41 for description of series. Thirty-six illustrations.

ACTUARIAL STATISTICIAN. *See* Statistician

ADVERTISING AGENT   0-81.

* Advertising. Davis, Anne S., ed. Commonwealth Book Co. 1938. 29p. Mimeographed. 75c
> Information presented according to the NVGA outline. See p. 26 for description of series. Includes description of duties in a small retail store, retail department store, retail chain store, manufacturing concern, mail order house, newspaper, magazine, and radio. Bibliography.

Advertising. Revised edition. Quarrie Corporation. 1944. 13p. Planographed. 10c
> Vocational monograph number 2.

* Advertising. Smith, Herbert H. Bellman Publishing Co. 1941. 20p. 50c
> Description of work in creating the advertising copy, illustrating the advertisements, and selling the advertisements. List of twenty-four schools of advertising. Bibliography.

Advertising as a career. Institute for Research. 1936. 20p. 75c
> Describes work in various advertising media such as newspaper, national magazine, radio, outdoor advertising, direct mail advertising, business and trade publications, and dealers' helps. Qualifications, preparation, earnings, advantages, and disadvantages. Includes duties of advertising manager, advertising agency and association advertising work. One illustration. Bibliography.

Advertising as a career. O'Dea, Mark. Revised edition. Printers' Ink Publishing Company, 205 E. 42nd St., New York 17, N.Y. 1945. 138p. 50c
> Some of the topics included are preparation in high school and college, qualifications, writing ability, experience, salaries, and opportunities.

Advertising as an occupation. Davis, Edwin W. Science Research Associates. 1944. 50p. 60c
> Table of contents: history of advertising, role of advertising in business, advertising jobs, who are these advertising people, breaking into advertising, and what about the future. Includes table showing number of men and women engaged in each of thirty advertising positions in 1930. Twelve illustrations. Annotated bibliography.

Advertising manager. Prepared for the War Department by the National Roster. Supt. of Documents, Washington 25, D.C. 1945. 5c

> Occupational brief containing summary, earnings, outlook, qualifications, and training.

* Careers for women as advertising copy writers. Institute for Research. 1944. 24p. 75c

> Describes activities of a copy writer in a small retail store, large department store, advertising agency, and mail order house. Includes qualifications, opportunities, training, salaries, attractive and unattractive features. Three illustrations. Bibliography.

Description of profession of advertising agent. National Roster. 1946. Free

> In preparation. See p. 34 for description of series.

Direct mail advertising. Hoke, Henry Reed. Bellman Publishing Co. 1940. 27p. Vari-typed. 50c

> Brief descriptions of positions in direct mail advertising. Qualifications, compensation, and opportunities. Bibliography.

ADVERTISING ARTIST. *See* Artist

AERONAUTICAL ENGINEER 0-19.03

Aeronautical engineer. Prepared for the War Department by the National Roster. Supt. of Documents, Washington 25, D.C. 1945. 5c

> Occupational brief containing summary, earnings, outlook, qualifications, and training.

Description of the profession of aeronautical engineering. National Roster. 1945. 4p. Free

> See p. 34 for description of series.

See also Engineer

AGRICULTURAL AGENT, COUNTY 0-12.20

Description of profession of county agent. National Roster. 1946. Free

> In preparation. See p. 34 for description of series.

County extension workers. Science Research Associates. 1945. 4p. 15c

> Occupational brief number 108. Two illustrations. Annotated bibliography.

AGRICULTURAL ENGINEER 0-16.; 0-17.; 0-19.

Agricultural engineering as a professional career. American Society of Agricultural Engineers, St. Joseph, Mich. No date. 11p. Free

> Description of divisions of agricultural engineering: farm power and machinery, farm structures, rural electrification, and soil and water control and conservation. Opportunities, earnings, training, and a suggested four-year list of courses recommended by the Committee on Curriculums, American Society of Agricultural Engineers.

AGRICULTURAL ENGINEER—*Continued*
Description of the profession of agricultural engineering. National
Roster. 1945. 4p. Free
See p. 34 for description of series.

**Handbook of descriptions of specialized fields in agricultural engi-
neering. National Roster. Supt. of Documents, Washington 25,
D.C. 1944. 5p. 5c
Occupational summary, related fields, functional activities, fields of specialization, and related occupations.

See also Engineer

AGRICULTURAL SPECIALIST   0-68.
The agricultural expert and the veterinarian. Corcoran. J. P.
Xavier University. 1938. 18p. 50c
Describes the work of the specialist in soil, grains, horticulture, animal
husbandry, and the veterinarian. Addressed to Negro youth. Bibliography.

* Jobs in rural service. Chapman, Paul. Science Research Associates. 1945. 50p. 60c
Discussion of rural service workers under the headings of agricultural
education workers, scientists and technicians, industrial and commercial
workers, regulatory service employees, and members of agricultural professions. Fourteen illustrations. Annotated bibliography.

* Teaching vocational agriculture as a career. Michigan State College,
East Lansing, Mich. 1945. 16p. Free
Discussion of duties, requirements, training, and opportunities. Twelve
illustrations.

See also Agricultural agent, County; Agronomist

AGRONOMIST   0-39.54
Description of the profession of agronomy. National Roster. 1945.
4p. Free
See p. 34 for description of series.

**Handbook of descriptions of specialized fields in agronomy and soil
science. National Roster. Supt. of Documents, Washington 25,
D.C. 1945. 10p. 5c
Describes the work of soil conservation, soil technology, soil science,
and crop science. Includes occupational summary, related fields, functional
activities, and fields of specialization.

Horticulturist, agronomist and soil scientist. Prepared for the War
Department by the National Roster. Supt. of Documents, Washington 25, D.C. 1945. 13p. 5c
Occupational brief containing summary, earnings, outlook, qualifications,
and training.

AIR CONDITIONING ENGINEER   0-19.01
* Air conditioning. Davis, Anne S., ed. Revised edition. Commonwealth Book Co. 1938. 22p. Mimeographed. 75c
Information presented according to the NVGA outline. See p. 26 for
description of series. Includes duties of the designing engineer, research
engineer, construction engineer, and stationary engineer.

* Air conditioning engineer. Revised edition. Occupational Index. 1944. 6p. 25c
    Occupational abstract. Duties, abilities, preparation, entrance and advancement, compensation, advantages, disadvantages, and future trend of employment. Annotated bibliography.

    See also Engineer

AIR CONDITIONING INDUSTRY WORKER 5-83.941

* Air conditioning. Schaefer, John T. Bellman Publishing Co. 1941. 20p. 50c
    Includes description of work in management, sales, engineering, installation and service. Qualifications, compensation, and list of schools offering training.

Air conditioning. Shade, Chloris, ed. 2nd edition revised. Morgan-Dillon & Co. 1939. 24p. 32c
    Duties, qualifications, and training of air conditioning engineers. Also duties, skills and knowledge needed by the skilled mechanics in the installation and servicing of air conditioning equipment. Bibliography.

Air conditioning as a career. Institute for Research. 1935. 16p. 75c
    Temporarily out of print.

Air conditioning workers. Science Research Associates. 1945. 4p. 15c
    Occupational brief number 122. Description of types of jobs, requirements, number of workers, earnings, and future prospects. Two illustrations. Annotated bibliography.

AIR TRANSPORTATION WORKER 0-41.; 5-49.; 5-80.

Air transportation jobs and you. United Air Lines. 1944. 20p. Free
    Illustrated manual of information to accompany a slidefilm showing the various workers and the basic qualifications for employment.

Air workers today. Keliher, Alice, ed. Hinds, Hayden and Eldredge, Inc. 1942. 56p. 80c
    Discussion of workers on the ground, in the airlines, in civil air services of the U. S. Government, and in the Armed Forces. See p. 28 for description of Picture Fact Books.

Aircraft makers. Science Research Associates. 1943. 4p. Planographed. 15c
    Occupational brief number 16. Two illustrations. Annotated bibliography.

Airline engineering. Air-Age Education Research, 100 E. 42nd St., New York 17, N.Y. 1945. 17p. 10c
    Profusely illustrated booklet showing workers engineering the flagship fleet and engineering the air freighter.

An appraisal and abstract of available literature on occupations in aviation. Spiegler, Samuel. Occupational Index. 1937. 12p. 25c
    Information concerning the pilot, navigator, radio operator, air stewardess, meteorologist, dispatcher, airways keeper, engine mechanic, airplane mechanic, instrument technician, parachute rigger, engineer, test pilot, and traffic agent. Annotated bibliography of twenty-six items.

AIR TRANSPORTATION WORKER—*Continued*

Aviation. Quarrie Corporation. 1942. 13p. Planographed. 10c
Vocational monograph number 5.

* Aviation. Shade, Chloris, ed. 2nd edition revised. Morgan-Dillon
& Co. 1939. 24p. 32c
Discussion of progress in scheduled air transportation. Duties and
qualifications for flying occupations, plane-maintenance and airport-main-
tenance jobs, manufacturing, Government, and teaching positions. Training,
working conditions, earnings, and trends. Classified bibliography.

The aviation dispatcher. Science Research Associates. No date.
2p. Planographed. 15c
Occupational reprint number 39. One illustration.

Aviation handbook for junior and senior high schools. Wheatley,
William A., and Mertes, Ray O. United Air Lines. No date.
52p. 15c
Included in this booklet of information about aviation are occupational
data concerning the airline pilot, stewardess, and the airport meteorologist.
Profusely illustrated.

Aviation jobs. Science Research Associates. 1943. 4p. Planographed. 15c
Occupation brief number 68. Two illustrations. Annotated bibliography.

CAA estimates postwar employment in aviation. Civil Aeronautics
Administration, Dept. of Commerce, Washington 25, D.C. 1945.
5p. Mimeographed. Free
Includes estimate of employment in industrial flying, crop dusting, hunt-
ing of animal pests, power communication and oil line inspection, aerial
photography, light-weight air freight transport, airline transportation, airport service, and air traffic control and maintenance.

* Careers for women with the air lines. Institute for Research. 1944.
24p. 75c
Basic requirements, training, benefits, salaries, and trends. Describes
duties on a typical flight of a stewardess. Information about station positions, traffic positions, dispatcher, meteorologist, teletype operator, and radio
telephone operator. Six illustrations.

Careers in aeronautics (non-flying). Institute for Research. 1937.
29p. 75c
Major divisions of aeronautics. Qualifications, opportunities, and types
of positions with scheduled airlines, municipal airports, Federal airways and
weather stations, and aeronautics manufacturing plants. Five illustrations.

**An educational guide in air transportation. Hinkel, Ralph, and
Baron, Leo. Transcontinental and Western Air, Inc., Kansas
City 6, Mo. 1944. 140p. 75c
Function, qualifications, desirable training, and vocational description
are presented for each of fifty-two positions. Includes engineering pilot,
flight control clerk, meteorologist, radio technician, airline mechanic, traffic
representative, and airline hostess. Thirty-one excellent illustrations. Bibliography.

**Employment opportunities in aviation occupations, Part I. Bureau of Labor Statistics. U. S. Dept. of Labor. Supt. of Documents, Washington 25, D.C. 1945. 36p. 10c
   Reprint from the Monthly Labor Review presenting the postwar employment outlook.

**Employment opportunities in aviation occupations, Part II. Bureau of Labor Statistics. U. S. Dept. of Labor. Supt. of Documents, Washington 25, D.C. 1946. 10c
   Presents duties, qualifications, earnings, and working conditions.

* Jobs in the aircraft industry. Helbing, Albert T. Science Research Associates. 1943. 50p. 60c
   Description of jobs, working conditions, qualifications, training, and future outlook. Twenty-six illustrations. Bibliography.

Opportunities for youth in air transportation. Air-Age Education Research, 100 E. 42nd St., New York 17, N.Y. 1944. 28p. 25c
   Description of work, qualifications, training, and suggested preparatory courses for each of the following jobs: persuading people to travel by air, reserving space and selling tickets, maintaining the air liner, determining flight conditions, dispatching the air liner, flying the air liner, serving passengers in flight, calling all airports and air liners, keeping track of the business, and working in the offices. Illustrated.

The outlook for domestic air transport. Williams, Ernest W. National Planning Association, 800 21st St., N.W., Washington 6, D.C. 1943. 30p. 25c
   Background information for the counselor concerning basic characteristics of air transport, recent technical trends and prospects, effects of the war, traffic potentialities, problems and obstacles to be overcome, and the place of air transport in the political and international scene.

Radio and aviation. Corcoran, J. P. Xavier University. 1938. 16p. 50c
   Addressed to Negro youth, description of work and opportunities. Bibliography.

There's a future for you in air transportation. American Airlines Inc., 100 E. 42nd St., New York 17, N.Y. 1945. 18p. Free
   Description of positions available in air transportation and the qualifications. Includes reservations agent, operations agent, stewardess, radiotelephone operator, stock clerk, ground service man, mechanic, instrument mechanic, machinist, sheet metal worker, welder, radio mechanic, and paint sprayer.

Women in aircraft production. The Chronicle. 1943. 6p. 5c
   Guidepost to occupational information number 41. Bibliography.

Your future in the age of flight. United Air Lines. 1945. 4p. Free
   Description of new opportunities and more exacting requirements for workers. Illustrated.

AIRLINE PASSENGER AGENT. *See* Passenger agent

AIRLINE STEWARDESS. *See* Airplane hostess

AIRPLANE HOSTESS   2-25.37
Greetings on our 15th anniversary from your United stewardess.
United Air Lines. 1945. 12p. Free
Illustrated booklet giving qualifications.

AIRPLANE MECHANIC   5-80.100
Airplane mechanics. Davis, Anne S., ed. Commonwealth Book
Co. 1936 with 1939 supplement. 24p. Mimeographed. 75c
Information presented according to the NVGA outline. See p. 26 for
description of series. Includes license requirements.

Aviation maintenance. Air-Age Education Research, 100 E. 42nd
St., New York 17, N.Y. 1944. 16p. 10c
Opportunities for youth in airline maintenance are illustrated and described, such as: dispatch office, fleet service, base inspection, airplane overhaul, engine disassembly and overhaul, engine build-up, accessories overhaul,
instrument overhaul, and radio overhaul.

The aviation mechanic. The Chronicle. No date. 6p. 5c
Guidepost to occupational information number 1. Bibliography.

* Career as an aviation mechanic. Institute for Research. 1941.
24p. 75c
Describes work of various types of mechanics such as hangar service
mechanic, airport ground serviceman, parachute rigger, airline overhaul base
mechanic, and airline radio maintenance mechanic. Certification requirements. Five illustrations.

* Ground careers in the U. S. Army air corps. Institute for Research.
1943. 32p. 75c
Information about eight types of technicians directly concerned with the
maintenance of aircraft and fifteen types of ground technicians concerned
with various phases of Air Corps operation. Seven illustrations.

Keep 'em flying—the way of life of an aviation mechanic. Williams,
Henry L. Row, Peterson and Co. 1942. 64p. 96c
See p. 41 for description of series. Thirty-two illustrations.

AIRPLANE PILOT   0-41.10
Aviation as a career. Revised edition. Institute for Research. 1946.
32p. 75c
In press.

Captains of the sky—the way of life of a military aviator. Munday,
Albert H. Row, Peterson and Co. 1942. 64p. 96c
Includes qualifications and training. See p. 41 for description of series.
Thirty-four illustrations.

Flying careers in the United States Air Forces. Institute for Research. 1942. 38p. 75c
History and organization of the Army Air Force. Discussion of work
in the Army, Naval, and Coast Guard aviation. Seven illustrations. Bibliography.

See also Air transportation worker

AIRPORT MANAGER. See Airport superintendent

AIRPORT SUPERINTENDENT   0-98.81
Airport management. Civil Aeronautics Administration, U. S. Dept.
of Commerce. Supt. of Documents, Washington 25, D.C. 1944.
32p. 10c

    Intended to aid airport owners and operators in establishing more efficient methods of airport management, operation, and maintenance. Includes duties, qualifications, responsibilities, and income.

ALUMINUM INDUSTRY WORKER
4, 6, 8-94.800 through 8-94.849
Aluminum and magnesium. Labor market information for USES
counseling—Industry Series. U. S. Dept. of Labor, Washington
25, D.C. 1945. 6p. Mimeographed. Free

    Statement including a description of the nature and location of the industry, training, conditions of work, and employment prospects. Bibliography.

ANATOMIST   0-39.41
Description of the profession of anatomy. National Roster. 1945.
2p. Free

    See p. 34 for description of series.

ANESTHETIST   0-26.20
Anesthesia a career for the graduate nurse. Science Research Associates. No date. 15c

    Occupational reprint number 110. One illustration.

* Anesthesiology a specialized field for professional registered nurses.
American Association of Nurse Anesthetists, 18 E. Division St.,
Chicago 10, Ill. 1945. 6p. Free

    Development of the work, qualifications, training, and opportunities.
Includes points to consider in choosing a school for training. Illustrated.

* Careers in anesthesia. Institute for Research. 1945. 24p. 75c

    Describes functions of the medical anesthesiologist and the nurse
anesthetist. Development and technical progress, typical day's work, educational standards, opportunities, attractive and unattractive features. Requirements for certification and recommended requirements for admission
to schools of anesthesia. Two illustrations.

ANIMAL FARMER   3-07.
* Animal husbandry as a career. Institute for Research. 1939. 15p.
75c

    Types of positions, salaries, training, advantages and disadvantages. Opportunities in production of beef cattle, dairy cattle, sheep, hogs, horses and
mules, goats, and poultry. Two illustrations.

Cattle farmer. Science Research Associates. 1943. 4p. Planographed. 15c

    Occupational brief number 33. Two illustrations. Annotated bibliography.

Fur farmers. Science Research Associates. 1945. 4p. Planographed. 15c

    Occupational brief number 113. Two illustrations. Annotated bibliography.

ANIMAL FARMER—*Continued*

Rabbit raising as a small business. Bureau of Foreign and Domestic Commerce, Washington 25, D.C. 1945. 2p. Free
> Reprint from *Domestic Commerce* describing the raising of rabbits for meat, fur, and angora wool. Bibliography.

Stock raising. Davis, Anne S., ed. Commonwealth Book Co. 1936 with 1939 supplement. 29p. Mimeographed. 75c
> Information presented according to the NVGA outline. See p. 26 for description of series. Includes a chart illustration of expansion in production of cattle, sheep, hogs, and horses.

* Stock raising. Shade, Chloris, ed. 2nd edition revised. Morgan-Dillon Co. 1939. 24p. 32c
> Nature of workers engaged in the specialized types of stock raising. Nature of work, qualifications, and training. Bibliography.

See also Wildlife worker

ANIMAL HUSBANDMAN   0-68.01

Animal, dairy and poultry scientist. Prepared for the War Department by the National Roster. Supt. of Documents, Washington 25, D.C. 1945. 5c
> Occupational brief containing summary, earnings, outlook, qualifications, and training.

Description of the professional fields in the animal, dairy and poultry sciences. National Roster. 1945. 4p. Free
> See p. 34 for description of series.

ANTHROPOLOGIST   0-39.11

Description of the profession of anthropology. National Roster. 1945. 3p. Free
> See p. 34 for description of series.

ARCHAELOGIST   0-39.12

Archaeology as a career for women. Science Research Associates. 1944. 2p. 15c
> Occupational reprint number 161. One illustration.

Description of the profession of anthropology. National Roster. 1945. 3p. Free
> See p. 34 for description of series.

ARCHITECT   0-03.10

* Architect. Revised edition. Occupational Index. 1944. 6p. 25c
> Occupational abstract. Duties, abilities, preparation, entrance and advancement, compensation, distribution of workers, geographical distribution, advantages, disadvantages, and postwar prospects. Annotated bibliography.

Architect. Prepared for the War Department by the National Roster. Supt. of Documents, Washington 25, D.C. 1945. 5c
> Occupational brief containing summary, earnings, outlook, qualifications, and training.

Architects. Science Research Associates. 1943. 4p. Planographed.
15c
> Occupational brief number 58. Two illustrations. Annotated bibliography.

Architecture. Greenleaf, Walter J. U. S. Office of Education.
Supt. of Documents, Washington 25, D.C. 1932. 9p. 5c
> Guidance leaflet number 10. Qualifications, training, opportunities, and compensation. Bibliography.

Architecture. Revised edition. Quarrie Corporation. 1942. 10p.
Planographed. 10c
> Vocational monograph number 4.

* Architecture. Shade, Chloris, ed. 2nd edition revised. Morgan-
Dillon & Co. 1940. 24p. 32c
> Nature of work, qualifications, training, conditions of work, and opportunities. List of member and non-member schools of the Association of Collegiate Schools of Architecture. Bibliography.

Architecture, a profession and a career. American Institute of
Architects, 1741 New York Ave., N.W., Washington 6, D.C.
1945. 57p. 50c; 25c to schools and libraries
> Twenty-one members of the profession describe the duties, functions, and professional training of the architect. Includes a list of thirty-seven member schools of the Association of Collegiate Schools of Architecture.

Architecture and engineering. Corcoran, J. P. Xavier University.
1937. 18p. Mimeographed. 50c
> Addressed to Negro youth, this pamphlet discusses requirements, training, income, and opportunities for Negro youth. Bibliography.

* Architecture as a career. Institute for Research. 1939. 16p. 75c
> Qualifications, training, typical course of study, opportunities, requirements for registration, advantages, and disadvantages. List of thirty-two schools of architecture. Three illustrations.

Description of the profession of architecture. National Roster.
1945. 3p. Free
> See p. 34 for description of series.

See also Landscape architect

ARCHITECTURAL ENGINEER   0-16.01
Description of profession of architectural engineer. National
Roster. 1946. Free
> In preparation. See p. 34 for description of series.

See also Engineer

ARMY OFFICER. *See* Soldier

ARMY SERVICEMAN. *See* Soldier

ARTIST   0-04.
Art. Greenleaf, Walter J. U. S. Office of Education. Supt. of
Documents, Washington 25, D.C. 1932. 13p. 5c
> Guidance leaflet number 20. Qualifications, training, opportunities, and compensation. List of universities and colleges offering a major in fine arts. Bibliography.

ARTIST—*Continued*

**Art as a career. Revised edition. Institute for Research. 1945. 20p. 75c

> Describes types of work in sculpture, graphic arts, and painting and drawing. Includes training, typical courses of study, qualifications, salaries, related positions, attractive and unattractive features. Chart shows number of established artists in each state classified according to muralists, painters, portrait painters, sculptors, and miniature and water color artists. Four illustrations.

Art opportunities today. Related Arts Service, 511 Fifth Ave., New York 17, N.Y. 1944. 4p. Free

> Seven well-known artists present brief opinions of the opportunities in their specific fields such as industrial design, advertising, home decoration, and teaching.

Arts and crafts—careers. Revised edition. Institute for Research. 1945. 24p. 75c

> Information concerning the potter, weaver, basketry and cane worker, woodworker, metalworker, bookbinder, leather worker, maker of jewelry, and maker of novelties. Five illustrations.

* Book illustration. Revised edition. Occupational Index. 1944. 6p. 25c

> Occupational abstract. Duties, qualifications, preparation, entrance, advancement, earnings, number of workers, advantages, and disadvantages. Annotated bibliography.

* Careers for women in advertising art. Institute for Research. 1944. 20p. 75c

> Describes work of the layout artist, illustrative artist, hand letterer, poster artist, and advertising photographer. Qualifications, training, opportunities, remuneration, attractive and unattractive features. Includes some information on work of fashion illustrator and fashion editor. Three illustrations.

* Commercial and industrial art as a career. Institute for Research. 1944. 16p. 75c

> Information concerning work of the advertising artist, costume designer, industrial designer, and art buyer. Qualifications, training, opportunities, salaries, attractive and unattractive features. Three illustrations.

* Commercial art. Shade, Chloris, ed. 2nd edition revised. Morgan-Dillon & Co. 1939. 24p. 32c

> Describes work of the commercial artist who illustrates the manufactured product attractively, letters the trade name, creates the trademark, designs the package in which the article is sold, and creates the posters, handbills, pamphlets, newspaper and magazine advertisements by means of which the product is kept in the mind of the public. Classified bibliography.

Commercial art and industrial design. Quarrie Corporation. 1938. 20p. Planographed. 10c

> Vocational monograph number 9.

* Fine and applied arts. Farnum, Royal B. Bellman Publishing Co. 1941. 24p. 50c

> Qualifications, requirements, opportunities, and earnings of the designer and artist. List of forty occupations that require a knowledge of art and design. Selected list of fifty-two schools of art and design. Bibliography.

* If you are considering applied art. Ulp, Clifford M. Rochester Institute of Technology. 1944. 16p. 10c
> Discussion of duties, qualifications, and working conditions in the fields of illustration and advertising art, design, and interior decoration.

The sign painter. Baltimore Department of Education. 1942. 7p. 10c
> Nature of work, qualifications, remuneration, and opportunities. Bibliography.

ASTRONOMER 0-39.47
Description of the profession of astronomy (including astrophysics). National Roster. 1945. 2p. Free
> See p. 34 for description of series.

AUTOMOBILE MANUFACTURING INDUSTRY WORKER
5, 7, 9-02.
Information for recent college graduates seeking employment. General Motors Corporation, Clearing Point Activity, 3044 W. Grand Blvd., Detroit 2, Mich. 1944. 6p. Multigraphed. Free
> Information concerning the types of work for which college students and graduates are employed in General Motors and the general procedure followed in their recruiting program.

Job descriptions for the automobile manufacturing industry. Division of Occupational Analysis. Supt. of Documents, Washington 25, D.C. 1935. 778p. Out of print, but available in many libraries and U. S. Employment Service offices.
> See p. 58 for comment on National Job Descriptions. Describes jobs found in the manufacture of automobiles and other motor vehicles. Illustrated.

AUTOMOBILE MECHANIC 5-81.010
Auto and garage service. Davis, Anne S., ed. Commonwealth Book Co. 1938. 20p. Mimeographed. 75c
> Information presented according to the NVGA outline. See p. 26 for for description of series. Covers repair and servicing fields in the general garage, storage garage, and filling station.

Auto mechanic. Baltimore Department of Education. 1942. 11p. 10c
> Description of the nineteen kinds of work, qualifications, remuneration, and training. Bibliography.

* Auto mechanics and garage management. Shade, Chloris, ed. 2nd edition revised. Morgan-Dillon & Co. 1939. 24p. 32c
> Types of mechanics and description of work, qualifications, preparation, and conditions of work. Description of work of auto mechanic and manager in repair garage, sales garage, storage garage, parking garage, and service garage or filling station. Classified bibliography.

Automotive mechanics (Diesel engine). Davis, Anne S., ed. Commonwealth Book Co. 1936 with 1939 supplement. 28p. Mimeographed. 75c
> Information presented according to the NVGA outline. See p. 26 for description of series. Includes operation, maintenance, and repair work.

AUTOMOBILE MECHANIC—*Continued*

**Employment outlook for automobile mechanics. Bureau of Labor
Statistics, U. S. Dept. of Labor. Supt. of Documents, Washington 25, D.C. 1945. 18p. 10c

> Occupational Outlook Division series. Nature of the occupation, edu-
> cation, training, earnings, hours, other working conditions, and status of
> occupation before and during the war. The employment prospects are dis-
> cussed under two headings: trend of motor-vehicle registrations and pros-
> pective labor demand and supply.

Establishing and operating an automobile repair shop. U. S. Dept.
of Commerce. Supt. of Documents, Washington 25, D.C. 1945

> Industrial series. Intended as a practical guide to experienced skilled
> repairmen who are considering opening their own shops. In preparation.

Garage mechanic—a job men like. Clarke, James M. Occupational
Index. 1936. 7p. 25c

> Discussion of duties, methods of entrance, and skills of specialists.

AUTOMOBILE-SERVICE-STATION ATTENDANT 7-60.500

Establishing and operating a service station. U. S. Dept. of Commerce. Supt. of Documents, Washington 25, D.C. 1945

> Industrial series. Intended as a practical guide to experienced persons
> considering starting their own businesses. In preparation.

* Gasoline filling stations. Revised edition. Occupational Index.
1944. 6p. 25c

> Occupational abstract. Duties, earnings, preparation, advantages, dis-
> advantages, and number employed. Annotated bibliography.

AUTOMOTIVE ENGINEER   0-19.01

Automotive engineer. Prepared for the War Department by the
National Roster. Supt. of Documents, Washington 25, D.C.
1945. 12p. 5c

> Occupational brief containing summary, earnings, outlook, qualifications,
> and training.

  See also Engineer

AVIATION MECHANIC. *See* Airplane mechanic

AVIATOR. *See* Airplane Pilot

BACTERIOLOGIST   0-39.36

Bacteriologist. Prepared for the War Department by the National
Roster. Supt. of Documents, Washington 25, D.C. 1945. 5c

> Occupational brief containing summary, earnings, outlook, qualifications,
> and training.

Description of profession of bacteriology. National Roster. 1945.
4p. Free

> See p. 34 for description of series.

* Handbook of descriptions of specialized fields in bacteriology. National Roster. Supt. of Documents, Washington 25, D.C. 1945.
8p. 5c

BAKER   4-01.100

* An appraisal and abstract of available literature on the occupation of the baker. Spiegler, Samuel. Occupational Index. 1938. 12p. 25c

    Duties, qualifications, training, compensation, number and geographic distribution, advantages, and disadvantages. Annotated bibliography of eleven references.

* Baking. Davis, Anne S., ed. Commonwealth Book Co. 1938. 20p. Mimeographed. 75c

    Information presented according to the NVGA outline. See p. 26 for description of series. Includes duties during apprenticeship.

Establishing and operating a retail bakery. U. S. Dept. of Commerce. Supt. of Documents, Washington 25, D.C. 1945

    Industrial series. Intended as a practical guide to experienced skilled persons who are considering their own shops. In preparation.

Job descriptions for the bakery products industry. Division of Occupational Analysis. Supt. of Documents, Washington 25, D.C. 1939. 322p. $1.00

    See p. 58 for comment on National Job Descriptions. Describes occupations concerned with the production of all bakery products except ice cream cones. Eighty-six illustrations.

BANK WORKER   0-98.00 through 0-98.19 and 1-06.

Banking. Griffin, Albert. Bellman Publishing Co. 1945. 28p. $1.00

    History and development of banking, brief description of work of principal departments, requirements, remuneration, and trends. Bibliography.

* Banking. Revised edition. Occupational Index. 1945. 6p. 25c

    Occupational abstract. Types of work, abilities, training, entrance and advancement, number and distribution of workers, earnings, advantages, disadvantages, and postwar prospects. Annotated bibliography.

Banking—a career and an opportunity. Science Research Associates. 1942. 2p. 15c

    Occupational reprint number 118. One illustration.

Banking and investments. Revised edition. Quarrie Corporation. 1944. 11p. Planographed. 10c

    Vocational monograph number 6.

Banking as a career. Institute for Research. 1940. 20p. 75c

    Duties, qualifications, training, lines of promotion, advantages, and disadvantages. Includes description of work of the cashier, teller, bookkeeper, clearing house clerk, central clearing clerk, and file clerk. Four illustrations.

Banking as a vocation. American Bankers Association, 22 E. 40th St., New York 16, N.Y. 1945. 5p. Mimeographed. Free

    Preparation, qualifications, rewards, working conditions, and possibilities for advancement.

BANK WORKER—*Continued*

Current policies in personnel relations in banks. Industrial Relations Section, Princeton University. Princeton, N.J. 1940. 50p. $1

> Gives a picture of conditions of work in a bank and the nature of work in personnel relations. Discussion of employment policies, promotional plans, employee rating, educational plans, financial security, health services, and group relations work. Bibliography.

* A job in banking. Schroeder, Joseph. Science Research Associates. 1941. 50p. 60c

> What beginning work in a bank might be, what it requires by way of preparation, and what are the possibilities for the future. The beginner is also shown the place of a bank in the community and the contribution a well-run bank can make to the financial health of that community. Sixteen illustrations. Annotated bibliography.

Preparing for an occupation in banking. American Institute of Banking, 22 E. 40th St., New York 16, N.Y. 1945. 2p. Mimeographed. Free

> Nature of work, qualifications, and training.

The role of women in banking. Science Research Associates. 1944. 2p. 15c

> Occupational reprint number 182.

Titles and descriptions of banking occupations. American Bankers Association, 22 E. 40th St., New York 16, N.Y. 1944. 40p. 50c

> List of 340 bank job titles and 255 job descriptions.

Women in banking. Association of Bank Women, Research Committee (Miss Catherine Pepper, Chairman), 55 Wall St., New York 15, N.Y. 1942 with 1944 supplement. 28p. 3c

> Includes a survey of women in twenty-two kinds of work in banks in each of the states.

BANKER   0-98.00

Investment banking as a career. Revised edition. Institute for Research. 1946. 20p. 75c

> In press.

Toward careers in finance. Investment Bankers Association of America, 33 South Clark St., Chicago 3, Ill. 1945. 24p. Free

> Description of work, qualifications, outlook, and training.

BARBER   2-32.01

An appraisal and abstract of available literature on the occupation of the barber. Schoettler, A. E. Occupational Index. 1937. 8p. 25c

> Duties, preparation, union requirements, rewards, number of workers, advantages, and disadvantages. Annotated bibliography.

* Barbering. Davis, Anne E., ed. Revised edition. Commonwealth Book Co. 1938. 20p. Mimeographed. 75c

> Information presented according to the NVGA outline. See p. 26 for description of series. Includes list of twenty-six schools certified by the Associated Master Barbers of America.

Barbers and beauticians. Science Research Associates. 1943. 4p.
Planographed. 15c
Occupational brief number 96. Two illustrations. Annotated bibliography.

BEAUTICIAN. *See* Beauty Operator

BEAUTY OPERATOR   2-32.15
Barbers and beauticians. Science Research Associates. 1943. 4p.
Planographed. 15c
Occupational brief number 96. Two illustrations. Annotated bibliography.

Beauty culture. Bander, Irving L. Bellman Publishing Co. 1940.
64p. Vari-typed. 50c
Description of types of positions in the beauty shop, the cosmetic field, education, editorial, and miscellaneous work. Requirements for license in each of the states. List of schools of beauty culture meeting requirements of their respective state laws. Bibliography.

* Beauty culture. Davis, Anne S., ed. Revised edition. Commonwealth Book Co. 1937. 29p. Mimeographed. 75c
Information presented according to the NVGA outline. See p. 26 for description of series. Includes summary of state laws for certification in each state.

* Beauty culture. Shade, Chloris, ed. 2nd edition revised. Morgan-Dillon & Co. 1939. 24p. 32c
Nature of work, opportunities, qualifications, training, earnings, and related occupations. Outline of legal requirements in each state. Bibliography.

Beauty-shop management as a career. Institute for Research. 1935.
16p. 75c
Temporarily out of print.

The cosmetologist. Baltimore Department of Education. 1941. 7p.
10c
Qualifications, training, income, advantages, and disadvantages. Bibliography.

Establishing and operating a beauty shop. U. S. Dept. of Commerce. Supt. of Documents, Washington 25, D.C. 1945
Industrial series. Intended as a practical guide to experienced skilled beauticians who are considering opening their own shops. In preparation.

Jobs in barber shops and beauty shops. Science Research Associates. 1939. 2p. Planographed. 15c
Occupational reprint number 81.

BEEKEEPER   3-07.70
* Beekeeping. Baldwin, Leo. Revised edition. Occupational Index.
1945. 6p. 25c
Occupational abstract. Duties, abilities, preparation, number of beekeepers, advantages, and disadvantages. Annotated bibliography.

BEEKEEPING—*Continued*

Bee keeping. Davis, Anne S., ed. Commonwealth Book Co. 1936 with 1939 supplement. 26p. Mimeographed. 75c

Information presented according to the NVGA outline. See p. 26 for description of series. Describes work of honey production, package-bee raising, and queen-bee breeding.

BELLBOY   2-22.11

The efficient bellman and elevator operator. Dahl, J. O. The Dahls, Haviland Road, Stamford, Conn. 1933. 36p. 35c

Written as a manual of instructions to beginners, it includes description of duties, responsibilities, and qualifications of the bellboy in hotels and restaurants.

BIOLOGIST   0-39.31

Agricultural and biological scientist (general survey). Prepared for the War Department by the National Roster. Supt. of Documents, Washington 25, D.C. 1945. 5c

Occupational brief containing summary, earnings, outlook, qualifications, and training.

**Biological work. Shade, Chloris, ed. 2nd edition revised. Morgan-Dillon and Co. 1940. 24p. 32c

Qualifications, training, conditions of work, advantages, and disadvantages. Description of work in public health, bacteriology, scientific agriculture, seed analysis, entomology, plant pathology, museum work, and conservation. List of eighty-two occupations offering employment in biological work. List of thirty-four Federal departments and bureaus employing biologists. Classified bibliography.

Biological work as a career. Revised edition. Institute for Research. 1946. 16p. 75c

In press.

Biology as a career. Lehigh University, Bethlehem, Pa. No date. 6p. Free

Opportunities, preparation, personal qualifications, and professional attractions of biology. Bibliography.

BLACKSMITH   4-86.

**An appraisal and abstract of available literature on the occupation of the blacksmith. Spiegler, Samuel. Occupational Index. 1938. 8p. 25c

Duties, abilities, compensation, number and geographic distribution, advantages and disadvantages. Annotated bibliography.

The smithy takes to the road. Horse and Mule Association of America, Inc., 407 So. Dearborn St., Chicago 5, Ill. No date. 15p. 5c

Advantages of conducting a traveling blacksmith shop.

BOILERMAKER   4-83.100

* Boilermaker. Revised edition. Occupational Index. 1945. 6p. 25c

Occupational abstract. Duties, abilities, preparation, entrance, advancement, number and distribution of workers, earnings, advantages, disadvantages, and postwar prospects. Annotated bibliography.

BOOK ILLUSTRATOR. *See* Artist

BOOKKEEPER   **1-01.; 1-02.**

Bookkeeping. Shade, Chloris, ed. 2nd edition revised. Morgan-Dillon & Co. 1939. 24p. 32c

> Qualifications, training, conditions of work, and trends. Bibliography.

* Bookkeeping. Spiegler, Samuel. Revised edition. Occupational Index. 1945. 6p. 25c

> Occupational abstract. Duties, qualifications, training, beginning jobs and possible advancement, number and geographic distribution, earnings, advantages, disadvantages, and postwar prospects. Annotated bibliography.

* Career as a bookkeeper. Institute for Research. 1941. 23p. 75c

> Duties, typical day's work, personal qualifications, and lines of promotion. Information concerning the bookkeeper, entry clerk, ledger clerk, statement clerk, payroll clerk, bookkeeping machine operator, calculating machine operator, and cashier. Six illustrations.

See also Accountant

BOTANIST   **0-39.35**

Botanist, plant pathologist and plant physiologist. Prepared for the War Department by the National Roster. Supt. of Documents, Washington 25, D.C. 1945. 5c

> Occupational brief containing summary, earnings, outlook, qualifications, and training.

Description of the profession of botany. National Roster. 1945. 3p. Free

> See p. 34 for description of series.

BRICKLAYER   **5-24.**

An appraisal and abstract of available literature on the occupation of the bricklayer. Spiegler, Samuel. Occupational Index. 1938. 8p. 25c

> Duties, preparation, compensation, advantages, disadvantages, number and distribution of workers. Annotated bibliography of twelve references.

* Bricklayer. Davis, Anne S., ed. Commonwealth Book Co. 1938. 23p. Mimeographed. 75c

> Information presented according to the NVGA outline. See p. 26 for description of series. Describes work of thirteen types of bricklayers such as terrazzo bricklayer, terra cotta bricklayer, and tile conduit bricklayer.

Bricklaying. McGarvey, George. U. S. Office of Education. Supt. of Documents, Washington 25, D.C. 1941. 238p. 40c

> An analysis of the trade of bricklaying together with suggestive courses of training for apprentices and journeymen workers. Although written for instructors of bricklaying apprentices, it contains information of interest to anyone considering the field of masonry construction.

See also Mason

BUILDING CONSTRUCTION ENGINEER 0-16.01; 0-99.21

* Building contractor. Spiegler, Samuel. Revised edition. Occupational Index. 1944. 6p. 25c

> Occupational abstract. Duties, abilities and preparation, entrance and advancement, compensation, advantages, disadvantages, and postwar prospects. Annotated bibliography.

Construction contracting as a career. Institute for Research. 1935. 20p. 75c

> Temporarily out of print.

Establishing and operating a building contracting business. U. S. Dept. of Commerce. Supt. of Documents, Washington 25, D.C. 1945

> Industrial series. Intended as a practical guide to experienced skilled persons who are considering starting their own business. In preparation.

BUILDING MANAGER. *See* Building superintendent

BUILDING SUPERINTENDENT 0-87.10

Wanted: building managers. Science Research Associates. No date. 2p. Planographed. 15c

> Occupational reprint number 16.

BUS DRIVER 5-36.010

* Bus and truck driver. Revised edition. Occupational Index. 1944. 6p. 25c

> Occupational abstract. Duties, qualifications, entrance, advancement, hours, earnings, number and distribution of workers, advantages, and disadvantages. Bibliography.

See also Motor transportation worker; Truck driver

BUSINESS WORKER 0-70. through 0-99.

Business administration. Cam, Gilbert. Bellman Publishing Co. 1940. 27p. Vari-typed. 50c

> Description of general types of positions, qualifications, requirements, and opportunities. Information about ninety-six schools of business administration and description of twenty-four subjects usually offered. Bibliography.

* Business as a career. New York University, Washington Square, New York 3, N.Y. 1945. 48p. Free

> Discussion of twenty-two careers in business. Useful chart of business opportunities, listing eighty-two typical positions in fourteen basic activities in business.

Establishing and operating your own business. Bureau of Foreign and Domestic Commerce, U. S. Dept. of Commerce. Supt. of Documents, Washington 25, D.C. 1945. 30p. 10c

> Discussion of opportunities, chances of success, and a check list of questions to be considered before investing in a business.

Executives. Science Research Associates. 1943. 4p. Planographed. 15c

> Occupational brief number 73. Two illustrations. Annotated bibliography.

* Jobs in Business. B'nai B'rith Vocational Service Bureau. 1746 M St., N.W., Washington 6, D.C. 1941. 44p. 10c
  A section devoted to the occupations named below with the last para-graph of each addressed to Jewish youth: accounting, advertising, banking, clerical work, credit, personnel, sales, and statistics. Bibliography at end of each unit. Illustrated.

Merchandising. Revised edition. Quarrie Corporation. 1943. 13p. Planographed. 10c
  Vocational monograph number 21.

* Merchandising as a career. Institute for Research. 1939. 21p. 75c
  Function of the merchant, description of work of wholesaler, broker, commission merchant, sales agent, importers and exporters, retailer, and auctioneer. Includes department store positions in merchandise, service, publicity, and finance. Three illustrations. Bibliography.

The Negro in business. Corcoran, J. P. Xavier University. 1938. 20p. Mimeographed. 50c
  Addressed to Negro youth, this pamphlet includes the number and kinds of retail establishments operated by Negroes. Bibliography.

—* Post high-school training for a business career. Association of Business Institutes of the State of New York, 225 Broadway, New York 7, N.Y. 1944. 8p. Free
  Discusses preparation in financial control and record keeping, administration, buying and selling. List of seven schools approved as business institutes in New York State.

Some selected business occupations. Corcoran, J. P. Xavier University. 1938. 16p. 50c
  Discussion of the retail business occupations of Negroes.

Starting your own business. Revised edition. Occupational Index. 1941. 6p. 25c
  Occupational abstract. Discussion of starting, succeeding, and growing in business. Also includes compensation, advantages, and disadvantages. Annotated bibliography.

  See also Clerical worker

BUTCHER. *See* Meat cutter

BUYER   0-74.11; 0-91.
  Background for purchasing. Science Research Associates. No date. 2p. Planographed. 15c
  Occupational reprint number 36. One illustration.

The buyer. Science Research Associates. No date. 2p. Planographed. 15c
  Occupational reprint number 73. Two illustrations. Annotated bibliography.

* Career as a merchandise buyer. Institute for Research. 1937. 23p. 75c
  Duties, typical day's work, personal qualifications, training, attractive and unattractive features. Kind of work, line of promotion, and salary range of the store buyer, assistant buyer, stock clerk, and merchandise manager. Additional information concerning the chain store buyer and mail order buyer. Bibliography.

BUYER—*Continued*
* Career as a purchasing agent. Institute for Research. 1940. 22p. 75c

> Includes a description of the work of the industrial, public utility, Government, school, and institutional purchasing agent. Two illustrations.

Description of profession of purchasing agent. National Roster. 1946. Free

> In preparation. See p. 34 for description of series.

Purchasing agent and buyers. Science Research Associates. 1943. 4p. Planographed. 15c

> Occupational brief number 76. Two illustrations. Annotated bibliography.

CABINETMAKER   4-32.100
* Cabinet making. Shade, Chloris, ed. 2nd edition revised. Morgan-Dillon & Co. 1940. 23p. 32c

> Description of work, qualifications, opportunities, and conditions of work. Bibliography.

* Cabinetmaker. Spiegler, Samuel. Revised edition. Occupational Index. 1944. 6p. 25c

> Occupational abstract. Duties, abilities, preparation, entrance and advancement, compensation, number and distribution of workers, advantages, disadvantages, and postwar prospects. Annotated bibliography.

CABLE ENGINEER   0-17.02
Description of the profession of electrical engineering including radio and communications engineering. National Roster. 1945. 5p. Free

> See p. 34 for description of series.

See also Engineer

CANNING AND PRESERVING WORKER   6, 8-04.
Cannery workers. Science Research Associates. 1945. 4p. 15c

> Occupational brief number 118. Description of work in canning factories, wages and hours, advantages, disadvantages, and the future of the canning industry. Two illustrations. Annotated bibliography.

CARPENTER   5-25
An appraisal and abstract of available literature on the occupation of the carpenter. Spiegler, Samuel. Occupational Index. 1938. 8p. 25c

> Duties, abilities, compensation, number and distribution of workers, advantages, and disadvantages. Annotated bibliography of twenty-two references.

Carpenters. Science Research Associates. 1943. 4p. Planographed. 15c

> Occupational brief number 56. Two illustrations. Annotated bibliography.

* Carpentry. Shade, Chloris, ed. 2nd edition revised. Morgan-Dillon & Co. 1940. 24p. 32c
  Description of carpentry in rough work, frame work, stair building, finish and trim work, and general carpentry work. Chart shows related occupations and lines of promotion. Bibliography.

National standards for carpentry apprenticeship. Federal Committee on Apprenticeship. Supt. of Documents, Washington 25, D.C. 1942. 7p. 10c
  Basic requirements for journeymanship and an example of a standard apprenticeship agreement.

CARRIER TRAFFIC MANAGER. *See* Traffic manager

CARTOGRAPHER   **0-48.15**
Cartography (map making). Bauer, Hubert A. Bellman Publishing Co. 1945. 32p. 75c
  Qualifications, training, and opportunities.

CARTOONIST   **0-04.41**
The cartoonist. Science Research Associates. No date. 2p. Planographed. 15c
  Occupational reprint number 55. One illustration.

* Motion picture cartooning. Western Personnel Service. 1941. 15p. 25c
  Description of production of cartoon films, the work of the animator, caricaturist, and layout artist, and information concerning specific cartoon employers. Includes discussion of training and apprenticeship, chances for promotion, salaries, and outlook. Suggested reading pertains to production methods and development.

CERAMIC ENGINEER   **0-15.11**
Ceramic engineer. Selina, Ruth. Occupational Index. 1946. 6p. 25c
  Nature of the work, qualifications, preparation, earnings, number and distribution of workers, and postwar prospects. Annotated bibliography.

* Ceramic engineering as a career. Institute for Research. 1937. 23p. 75c
  Historical background, personal qualifications, requirements, and typical day's work. List of twelve schools offering instruction in ceramic engineering. Various types of work done in mining, plant control, plant development work, engineering, and plant supervisory duties. Six illustrations.

Ceramics—what it is, what it offers as a career. Illinois Ceramic Institute, Urbana, Ill. 1944. 24p. Free
  Addressed to youth who are going to attend college, for the occupations that are peculiar to the ceramics industry require advanced training in chemistry and physics. Positions generally involve research (in clay, enamel, glass, cement), management and supervision. One page is addressed to parents. Illustrated.

Clay working as a career. Institute for Research. 1946. Revised edition. 16p. 75c
  In press.

CERAMIC ENGINEER—*Continued*
Description of the profession of ceramic engineering. National
Roster. 1945. 3p. Free
> See p. 34 for description of series.

**Handbook of descriptions of specialized fields in ceramic technology
and engineering. National Roster. Supt. of Documents, Washington 25, D.C. 1944. 9p. 5c
> Occupational summary, related fields, functional activities, fields of
> specialization, and related occupations.

See also Engineer

CHAIN STORE MANAGER. *See* Retail manager

CHEESE MANUFACTURE WORKER
                                        4, 6-06.400 through 4, 6-06.499
The romance of cheese. Kraft Cheese Company, 500 Peshtigo
Court, Chicago 90, Ill. 1944. 52p. Free
> This description of the process of cheese making contains many pictures
> of workers but no other occupational information.

CHEMICAL ENGINEER   0-15.01
Chemical engineer. Prepared for the War Department by the National Roster. Supt. of Documents, Washington 25, D.C. 1945. 5c
> Occupational brief containing summary, earnings, outlook, qualifications,
> and training.

* Chemical engineering. Reed, Charles. Bellman Publishing Co.
1944. 23p. 75c
> Qualifications, training, and opportunities. Includes description of
> types of positions available in chemical engineering and a list of industries
> in which chemical engineers are employed.

* Chemistry and chemical engineering as careers. Institute for Research. 1939. 24p. 75c
> Training, typical course of study, salaries, attractive and unattractive
> sides. Discussion of opportunities in numerous industries such as textiles,
> metals, agriculture, glass, explosives, rubber, and synthetic resin compounds.
> Four illustrations.

Description of the profession of chemical engineering. National
Roster. 1945. 4p. Free
> See p. 34 for description of series.

**Handbook of descriptions of specialized fields in chemistry and
chemical engineering. National Roster. Supt. of Documents,
Washington 25, D.C. 1944. 103p. 30c
> Occupational summary, related fields, functional activities, fields of spe-
> cialization, and related occupations.

See also Chemist; Engineer

CHEMICAL PRODUCTS INDUSTRY WORKER   4, 6, 8-53.
— Chemicals. Labor market information for USES counseling—Industry Series. U. S. Dept. of Labor. Washington 25, D.C. 1945. 8p. Mimeographed. Free
> Statement including a description of the nature and location of the industry; nature of unskilled, skilled, and professional jobs; training, requirements, working conditions, wages, hours, union affiliation and employment prospects. Charts show wage rates by occupation and employment in major branches. Bibliography.

CHEMIST   0-07.
    Chemical editing. Scientific Research Associates. 1944. 2p. 15c
> Occupational reprint number 163. Two illustrations.

    Chemist. Prepared for the War Department by the National Roster. Supt. of Documents, Washington 25, D.C. 1945. 5c
> Occupational brief containing summary, earnings, outlook, qualifications, and training.

    Chemistry. Corcoran, J. P. Xavier University. 1938. 18p. 50c
> Description of various uses of chemistry, qualifications, training, and opportunities for Negro chemists. Bibliography.

    Chemistry. Revised edition. Quarrie Corporation. 1944. 9p. Planographed. 10c
> Vocational monograph number 7.

    Chemistry and chemical engineering. Greenleaf, Walter J. U. S. Office of Education. Supt. of Documents, Washington 25, D.C. 1932. 14p. 5c
> Guidance leaflet number 19. Number of wage earners in each of thirty chemical industries. Also includes training, opportunities, and salaries. Bibliography.

**Chemistry in industry. Shade, Chloris, ed. 2nd edition revised. Morgan-Dillon & Co. 1939. 24p. 32c
> Describes work performed by chemist, technician, research chemist, chemical engineer, consultant, and chemical salesman. Qualifications, training, remuneration, and working conditions. Outline of twenty-seven divisions of industrial chemistry. Classified bibliography.

    Chemists. Science Research Associates. 1943. 4p. Planographed. 15c
> Occupational brief number 29. Two illustrations. Annotated bibliography.

    Description of profession of chemistry. National Roster. 1945. 6p. Free
> See p. 34 for description of series.

    Farm chemurgy. Building America, 2 W. 45th St., New York 19, N.Y. 1945. 30p. 30c
> A description of work in chemurgy, industrial and governmental research, how it will affect agriculture and industry, and future outlook. Illustrated. Bibliography.

CHEMIST—*Continued*

Here comes tomorrow—the chemurgic way of life. Schoffelmayer, Victor. Row, Peterson and Co. 1942. 64p. 96c

> The use of the processes of chemistry, physics, and other sciences in such ways that farm crops, farm and industrial wastes, and animal products become basic raw materials for use by industry. See p. 41 for description of series. Forty illustrations.

* If you are considering industrial chemistry. Van Peursem, Ralph L. Rochester Institute of Technology. 1944. 19p. 10c

> Gives physical and personal characteristics which are important for success as a control chemist, production operator, production supervisor, and research chemist. Bibliography.

* Industrial chemist. Spiegler, Samuel. Revised edition. Occupational Index. 1941. 6p. 25c

> Occupational abstracts. Describes work of the control chemist, research chemist, chief chemist, technician, and chemical engineer. Abilities essential to success, preparation necessary, entrance, advancement, earnings, number and distribution of workers, advantages, and disadvantages. Annotated bibliography.

List of institutions the Committee deems to be qualified to offer professional training for chemists and chemical engineering. American Chemical Society, 1155 16th St., N.W., Washington 6, D.C. 1945. 1p. Free

> List of 137 colleges for training of chemists and list of 51 colleges for chemical engineers.

Opportunities for chemists in literature service work. Science Research Associates. 1944. 4p. 15c

> Occupational reprint number 174. One illustration.

Patent work as a field for chemists. Science Research Associates. 1944. 2p. 15c

> Occupational reprint number 170. One illustration.

Selling fine chemicals. Science Research Associates. 1944. 4p. 15c

> Occupational reprint number 171. One illustration.

**Vocational guidance in chemistry and chemical engineering. American Chemical Society, 1155 16th St., N.W., Washington 6, D.C. 1944. 19p. 10c

> Types of work, qualifications, training, professional development, opportunities, and list of twenty-six industrial fields open to chemists and chemical engineers. Five illustrations. Bibliography.

*Your future in chemistry. Kimball, V. F., and Bhagwat, M. R. Science Research Associates. 1943. 50p. 60c

> Description of work in the numerous types of chemical jobs. Also discussion of occupations which combine chemistry with other subjects. Twenty-three illustrations. Bibliography.

> *See also* Chemical engineer

CHIROPODIST   0-52.01

Chiropody. Davis, Anne S., ed. Revised edition. Commonwealth
Book Co. 1938. 19p. Mimeographed. 75c
Information presented according to the NVGA outline. See p. 26 for
description of series. List of six schools accredited by the National Association of Chiropodists. Number of registered chiropodists in each of the states.

* Chiropody (podiatry). Lelyveld, Joseph. Bellman Publishing Co.
1941. 24p. 50c
Description of work, training, qualifications, opportunities, and license
requirements. Data concerning the six schools approved by the National
Association of Chiropodists.

**Chiropody. National Association of Chiropodists, 3500 14th St.,
N.W., Washington 10, D.C. 1945. 4p. Free
Qualifications, educational requirements, income, and list of the six
colleges approved by the National Association of Chiropodists.

Chiropody as a career. Belleau, W. E. Park Publishing House,
4141 W. Vliet St., Wilwaukee, Wis. 1945. 32p. 50c
Nature of work, qualifications, training, and summary of state laws
regulating chiropody. Includes number of registered chiropodists in each
state. Bibliography.

CHIROPRACTOR   0-42.10

Chiropractic—a career. Nugent, J. J. National Chiropractic Association, 92 Norton St., New Haven, Conn. 1945. 24p. Free
Scope of practice, qualifications, compensation, training, and license requirements. An insert folder presents the educational requirements for
licensure in each of the states as of November 1, 1945, and a list of the
five accredited schools in the United States and Canada.

CITY AND COUNTY MANAGER   0-94.

An appraisal and abstract of available literature on city and county
management as an occupation. Pence, Edith. Occupational Index.
1937. 8p. 25c
Duties, abilities, preparation, number and geographic distribution of
workers, advantages, and disadvantages. Annotated bibliography of thirty-
seven references.

* City and county management. Shade, Chloris, ed. Morgan-Dillon
& Co. 1940. 24p. 32c
History and growth of occupation, number and distribution of workers,
duties, typical day's work, qualifications, training, trends, and code of
ethics. Bibliography.

Public Administration. Science Research Associates. 1943. 4p.
Planographed. 15c
Occupational brief number 52. Two illustrations. Annotated bibliog-
raphy.

CITY PLANNING ENGINEER   0-16.01

Description of profession of planners. National Roster. 1946. Free
In preparation. See p. 34 for description of series.

CITY PLANNING ENGINEER—*Continued*

* Planning jobs and jobs in planning. Ehrlich, Otto H. Bellman Publishing Co. 1945. 40p. $1

Discussion of local, state, and regional planning and of land, water, and energy planning. Information about jobs in social planning, industrial planning, national and international planning, such as industry analyst, marketing specialist, transportation economist, and state planning engineer. Bibliography.

See also Engineer

CIVIL ENGINEER 0-16.01

* Civil engineer. Prepared for the War Department by the National Roster. Supt. of Documents, Washington 25, D.C. 1945. 5c

Occupational brief containing summary, earnings, outlook, qualifications, and training.

Civil engineering. Greenleaf, Walter J. U. S. Office of Education. Supt. of Documents, Washington 25, D.C. 1932. 9p. 5c

Guidance leaflet number 11. Description of various branches of civil engineering, what preliminary education is required, where professional training is offered, length of training, and salaries. Bibliography.

Civil Engineering. Revised edition. Quarrie Corporation. 1944. 12p. Planographed. 10c

Vocational monograph number 8.

* Civil engineering as a career. Institute for Research. 1941. 16p. 75c

Nature of work, qualifications, training, opportunities, earnings, attractive and unattractive features. Describes the various branches of civil engineering and the requirements for registration. Three illustrations. Bibliography.

Civil engineers. Science Research Associates. 1943. 4p. Planographed. 15c

Occupational brief number 26. Two illustrations. Annotated bibliography.

Description of profession of civil engineering. National Roster. 1945. 6p. Free

See p. 34 for description of series.

* Handbook of description of specialized fields in civil engineering National Roster. Supt. of Documents, Washington 25, D.C. 1945. 27p. 10c

Rolling stones—the way of life of a civil engineer. Bennitt, Ralph. Row, Peterson and Co. 1942. 64p. 96c

Story of a civil engineer's struggles and experiences. See p. 41 for description of series. Thirty-one illustrations.

See also Engineer

CIVIL SERVICE WORKER 0-00. through 9-99.

Careers in New York state government. State of New York. Dept. of Civil Service, Albany, N.Y. 1944. 48p. Free

Salary range, kinds of work performed, and the minimum qualifications required for beginners in typical non-professional positions: dairy and food inspector, game protector, elevator operator, custodian, steam fireman, clerk, telephone operator, hospital attendant, X-ray technician, employment interviewer, factory inspector, fireman, guard, motor vehicle license examiner, and patrolman. The scope of the examination and sample questions are included in the description of each position.

Civil service. Corcoran, J. P. Xavier University. 1938. 18p. Mimeographed. 50c
> Description of Civil Service examinations, factors governing appointment, list of positions, requirements, and opportunities for Negro youth.

**Civil service. Shade, Chloris, ed. 2nd edition revised. Morgan-Dillon & Co. 1940. 24p. 32c
> Number and classification of government employees under Civil Service. Duties in several types of work, qualifications, training, salaries, advantages, and disadvantages. Bibliography.

* Clerical careers in government service. Institute for Research. 1942. 24p. 75c
> Duties, opportunities, salary, promotional possibilities, attractive and unattractive features. Description of the merit system and positions in clerical, administrative, and accounting work. One illustration. Bibliography.

Getting a job with Uncle Sam. Science Research Associates. No date. 4p. Planographed. 15c
> Occupational reprint number 41. Two illustrations.

* The government service. Doyle, George C. Bellman Publishing Co. 1941. 15p. 50c
> Opportunities for employment and advancement in Civil Service, requirements for becoming a government employee, and qualifications for a successful career. Also disadvantages, advantages, remuneration, and benefits of Civil Service. Bibliography.

—How to get a U. S. government job. Franklin Institute, Rochester, N.Y. 1942. 32p. Free
> A recruiting bulletin giving information about Civil Service positions. Qualifications, salaries, subjects of examination, and manner of appointment for railway postal clerk, city mail carrier, post office clerk, rural mail carrier, clerk, accountant, nurse, and guard.

* Jobs in the Civil Service. Raebeck, Helen. B'nai B'rith Vocational Service Bureau, 1746 M St., N.W., Washington, D.C. 1942. 33p. 10c
> Discussion of positions for professional, semi-professional, clerical, and manual workers in Federal and municipal employment. Bibliography. Illustrated.

Working for the Federal Government. Supt. of Documents, Washington 25, D.C. 1945. 64p. 15c
> Information concerning Civil Service positions. Nature of work, salary, and requirements are summarized for typical jobs in the postal service, trades and manual occupations, photography and graphic arts, clerical work, scientific fields, medicine and nursing, engineering and drafting, home economics, accounting, law, library, and teaching. Illustrated.

> *See also* Government service worker

CLEANING AND DYEING INDUSTRY WORKER. *See* Laundry industry worker

CLERGYMAN 0-08.10

Catholic clergyman. Prepared for the War Department by the National Roster. Supt. of Documents, Washington 25, D.C. 1945. 5c

Occupational brief containing summary, earnings, outlook, qualifications, and training.

Clergymen and religious workers. Science Research Associates. 1943. 4p. Planographed. 15c

Occupational brief number 91. Two illustrations. Annotated bibliography.

Nine questions about entering the ministry. Board of Christian Education, Presbyterian Church in the U.S.A., 808 Witherspoon Bldg., Philadelphia 7, Pa. 1944. 8p. Free

Points out the need for religious leaders, the compensation, and training.

Protestant clergyman. Prepared for the War Department by the National Roster. Supt. of Documents, Washington 25, D.C. 1945. 5c

Occupational brief containing summary, earnings, outlook, qualifications, and training.

Rabbi. Prepared for the War Department by the National Roster. Supt. of Documents, Washington 25, D.C. 1945. 5c

Occupational brief containing summary, earnings, outlook, qualifications, and training.

To be a priest. Rumble, Leslie. Radio Replies Press, 500 Robert St., St. Paul 1, Minn. 1944. 46p. 10c

Discusses work of the priest. Includes list of sixty-nine religious orders of men.

See also Religious Worker

CLERICAL WORKER 1-01. through 1-49.

Beginning jobs in business. Science Research Associates. 1941. 4p. Planographed. 15c

Occupational reprint number 71. Three illustrations.

* Careers for women in office work. Institute for Research. 1944. 30p. 75c

Duties performed, training, personal qualifications, opportunities, lines of promotion, and salaries. Discussed under thirty-two occupations: four in the stenographic group, ten in the accounting group, seven machine operators, and eleven clerical positions. Five illustrations.

* Clerical careers in government service. Institute for Research. 1942. 24p. 75c

Description of the merit system and positions in clerical, administrative, and accounting work. Duties, opportunities, salary, promotional possibilities, attractive and unattractive features. Includes description of work of stenographer, typist, junior clerk, senior clerk, statistical clerk, editorial clerk, accounting and auditing clerk, fingerprint classifier, executive positions, and operators of thirteen types of office machines. One illustration. Bibliography.

Clerical occupations. Schloerb, Lester and Medsker, Leland. Revised edition. Science Research Associates. 1945. 50p. 60c
Description of work, salaries, and outlook. Includes a table showing comparison of salaries for eighteen types of clerical positions in 1938 and in 1942. Twelve illustrations. Annotated bibliography.

Filing as a vocation. Weeks, Bertha. National Vocational Guidance Association, 82 Beaver St., New York 5, N.Y. 1945. 5p. 10c
Reprint describing duties, qualifications, and compensation.

**Job descriptions for office occupations. Division of Occupational Analysis. Supt. of Documents. Washington 25, D.C. 1945. 204p. $1.25
See p. 58 for comment on National Job Descriptions. Includes history, developments and present status of office occupations. Describes office occupations under these headings: accountants and auditors; bookkeepers and cashiers; buyers and purchasing agents; checkers; credit, collection, and adjustment jobs; general clerks; managers and officials; material-handling jobs; office boys and messengers; office machine operators; personnel jobs; stenographers and typists; and telephone operators. Bibliography.

Office, clerical and secretarial work. Revised edition. Quarrie Corporation. 1943. 11p. Planographed. 10c
Vocational monograph number 24.

Office clerks. Science Research Associates. 1943. 4p. Planographed. 15c
Occupational brief number 11. Two illustrations. Annotated bibliography.

Office workers. Keliher, Alice, ed. Hinds, Hayden and Eldredge, Inc. 1940. 56p. 80c
See p. 28 for description of Picture Fact Books.

White collar jobs. Science Research Associates. 1943. 2p. 15c
Occupational reprint number 132.

See also Business worker

CLINICAL LABORATORY TECHNICIAN. *See* Laboratory technician

CLOTH DESIGNER   0-46.91

Textile design. Federated Council on Art Education and Institute of Women's Professional Relations, Connecticut College, New London, Conn. 1939. 48p. 15c
Skills required, personal qualifications, opportunities, earnings, and methods of securing beginning work. List of art schools and colleges offering instruction in textile design. Bibliography.

* Textile designing as a career. Institute for Research. 1944. 20p. 75c
Information concerning the designer in the apparel fabric field and the decorative fabric field. Includes a list of thirty-three art schools which

CLOTH DESIGNER—*Continued*

give instruction in textile design, four specialized textile schools, and six institutions which offer a degree course in textile engineering with an option in textile design. Six illustrations.

CLOTHES DESIGNER   0-46.01

* Costume design. Neelsen, Marion. Bellman Publishing Co. 1942. 24p. 50c

Training, qualifications, possibilities for employment, opportunities for advancement, and remuneration in thirteen types of positions. Description of basic courses usually offered in costume design schools which give instruction in draping, drafting, dress construction, sketching, textiles, fashion analysis, and history of costume. Bibliography.

* Costume design. Shade, Chloris, ed. 2nd edition revised. Morgan-Dillon & Co. 1939. 24p. 32c

Description of work in designing for custom-made trade and for wholesale trade. Some information about related occupations such as fashion editor, stage costume designer, and plastics designer. Qualifications, training, and conditions of work. Bibliography.

Fashion Institute of Technology and Design. Ritter, Mortimer C. The Institute, 225 W. 24th St., New York 11, N.Y. 1945. 3p. Free

Discusses qualities necessary to become a successful designer or scientific manager in the apparel industry. Bibliography.

Picking up pins. Mademoiselle, 122 E. 42nd St., New York 17, N.Y. 1945. 4p. 10c

Description of dress designing, qualifications, training, and earnings.

Vocations for women—designing. National Federation of Business and Professional Women's Clubs. 1940. 4p. 10c

Includes biographical sketches of several successful costume designers. Bibliography.

CLOTHING INDUSTRY WORKER   4, 6, 8-21. through 8-27.

Clothing manufacturing workers. Science Research Associates. 1943. 4p. Planographed. 15c

Occupational brief number 83. Two illustrations. Annotated bibliography.

COAL INDUSTRY WORKER   5, 7-21.; 6, 8-56.

Black land—the way of life in the coal fields. Korson, George. Row, Peterson and Co. 1941. 72p. 96c

See p. 41 for description of series. Forty illustrations.

COAST GUARDSMAN   2-68.40

A career in the United States Coast Guard. Institute for Research. 1943. 27p. 75c

Description of the functions of the Coast Guard and its branches of service. Qualifications, attractive and unattractive features, and salaries of enlisted men and officers and retirement pay. Seven illustrations. Bibliography.

COMMERCIAL ARTIST. *See* Artist

COMMUNICATION AND UTILITY WORKER. *See* Telephone and telegraph industry worker

CONFECTIONER 4, 6, 8-05.

The confectioner. Davis, Anne S., ed. Commonwealth Book Co. 1936. 19p. Mimeographed. 75c

> Information presented according to the NVGA outline. See p. 26 for description of series. Describes work of making and marketing candy.

Job descriptions for the confectionery industry. Division of Occupational Analysis. Supt. of Documents, Washington 25, D.C. 1939. 218p. $1.25

> See p. 58 for comment on National Job Descriptions. Describes jobs concerned with the manufacture of hard candies, soft or cream candies, and popcorn confections. Does not include jobs in the manufacture of confections made exclusively of chocolate, or the blanching and roasting of nuts. Illustrated.

CONSTRUCTION INDUSTRY WORKER

5, 7-23. through 5, 7-33.

Construction. Labor market information for USES counseling—Industry Series. U. S. Dept. of Labor, Washington 25, D.C. 1945. 4p. Mimeographed. Free

> Statement including a description and location of the industry, training, working conditions, and employment prospects. Chart shows the proportion of the various types of workers. Bibliography.

Job descriptions for the construction industry. Division of Occupational Analysis. Supt. of Documents, Washington 25, D.C. 1936. 5 volumes, $5.75

> See p. 58 for comment on National Job Descriptions. Describes occupations in the construction of highways, buildings, bridges, viaducts, sewers, tunnels, waterworks, and river and harbor work. Illustrated.

New career opportunities in the building industry for high school graduates planning to enter college. Wood, Arthur A. Johns-Manville Corporation, 22 E. 40th St., New York 16, N.Y. 1945. 23p. Free

> Includes fifteen reasons why the building industry offers opportunities in the postwar world, a suggested formula for analyzing a contemplated career, and a list of colleges offering training to students who seek a building industry career.

Probable volume of postwar construction. U. S. Bureau of Labor Statistics. Supt. of Documents, Washington 25, D.C. 1945. 58p. 10c

> Estimation of employment in the first five postwar years for each major occupation in the construction industry.

Sandhog—the way of life of the tunnel builders. Chase, Borden. Row, Peterson and Co. 1941. 64p. 96c

> See p. 41 for description of series. Thirty-one illustrations.

CONSTRUCTION INDUSTRY WORKER—*Continued*

Skilled artisans. Corcoran, J. P. Xavier University. 1938. 18p. 50c

Description of work and opportunities for Negro youth in the building trades and mechanics.

Stabilizing the construction industry. Colean, Miles L. National Planning Association, 800 21st St., N.W., Washington 6, D.C. 1945. 39p. 25c

Background information for the counselor concerning instruments of stabilization and the development and operation of a stabilization program.

CONSUMER COOPERATIVE WORKER   1-80.

Consumer cooperative workers. Science Research Associates. 1945. 4p. 15c

Occupational brief number 107. Two illustrations. Annotated bibliography.

— Co-ops and their workers. Cooperative League of the USA, 343 So. Dearborn St., Chicago 4, Ill. 1944. 4p. Free

Includes a list of vocational opportunities in cooperatives in ten fields such as store, office, service station, production, trucking, and wholesale operations.

COOK   2-26.

* Cooking. Bradley, Alice. Bellman Publishing Co. 1940. 20p. Varityped. 50c

Types of positions, training, qualifications, and compensation. List of training schools of cookery and description of typical courses. Bibliography.

COPY WRITER   0-06.94

* Careers for women as advertising copy writers. Institute for Research. 1944. 24p. 75c

Describes work through the medium of newspapers, radio, magazines, and billboard posters.

CORSETIER   1-75.01; 4-27.981

Corsetier. Davis, Anne S., ed. Commonwealth Book Co. 1938. 22p. Mimeographed. 75c

Information presented according to the NVGA outline. See p. 26 for description of series. Work described includes both the manufacture and sale of foundation garments.

COSMETICIAN. *See* Beauty Operator

COSTUME DESIGNER. *See* Clothes designer

COTTON INDUSTRY WORKER   3-47.

White gold—the way of life in the cotton kingdom. Schoffelmayer, Victor. Row, Peterson and Co. 1941. 64p. 96c

See p. 41 for description of series. Forty-four illustrations.

COUNTY AGRICULTURAL AGENT. *See* Agricultural agent, County

CREDIT CLERK 0-85.10; 1-12.02

Agents and credit workers. Science Research Associates. 1943. 4p. Planographed. 15c

> Occupational brief number 72. Two illustrations. Annotated bibliography.

Career as a credit manager. Institute for Research. 1946. Revised edition. 32p. 75c

> In press.

CRIMINOLOGY EXPERT 0-66.30 through 0-66.39

* Criminological work as a career. Institute for Research. 1941. 23p. 75c

> Qualifications, requirements, and rewards for police work, penal institution work, probation and parole work, psychological work, preventive work, and crime detection including work with the Federal Bureau of Investigation. Police service includes patrolman, traffic officer, license worker, record worker, and jail worker. Three illustrations. Bibliography.

DAIRY FARMER 3-04.10

Dairy farmer. Science Research Associates. 1943. 4p. Planographed. 15c

> Occupational brief number 32. Two illustrations. Annotated bibliography.

* Dairy farming as a career. Revised edition. Institute for Research. 1945. 24p. 75c

> Attractive and unattractive sides, personal qualifications, training, opportunities, and salaries. Example of a curriculum for a four-year course in dairy husbandry. Three illustrations.

Dairying. Davis, Anne S., ed. Commonwealth Book Co. 1936 with 1939 supplement. 32p. Mimeographed. 75c

> Information presented according to the NVGA outline. See p. 26 for description of series. Describes work in the production and sale of milk, butter, and cheese.

* Dairying. Shade, Chloris, ed. 2nd edition revised. Morgan-Dillon & Co. 1940. 24p. 32c

> Development of the dairy industry, nature of work, qualifications, advantages, disadvantages, and rewards. Bibliography.

DAIRY HUSBANDMAN 0-68.03

Animal, dairy and poultry scientist. Prepared for the War Department by the National Roster. Supt. of Documents, Washington 25, D.C. 1945. 5c

> Occupational brief containing summary, earnings, outlook, qualifications, and training.

Description of the professional fields in the animal, dairy and poultry sciences. National Roster. 1945. 4p. Free

> See p. 34 for description of series.

DAIRY FARMER—*Continued*

* Handbook of descriptions of specialized fields in animal, dairy, and poultry husbandry and dairy products technology. National Roster. Supt. of Documents, Washington 25, D.C. 1945. 18p. 10c
  Occupational summary, related fields, functional activities, fields of specialization, and related occupations.

DAIRY PRODUCTS INDUSTRY WORKER   4, 6, 8-06.
Careers in the dairy products industry. Institute for Research. 1937. 31p. 75c
  Types of positions, qualifications, opportunities, salaries, attractive and unattractive features. Describes work in a creamery plant, ice cream plant, cheese manufacturing plant, large dairy corporation, and a control laboratory of a milk plant and general dairy products plant. Typical day's work of a creamery plant superintendent and control laboratory worker. Four illustrations.

Milk from farm to family. National Dairy Council, 111 No. Canal St., Chicago 6, Ill. No date. 23p. Free
  Includes pictures and description of the pasteurization and bottling processes.

DENTAL HYGIENIST   0-50.07
An appraisal and abstract of available literature on dental hygiene as an occupation. Woodhouse, Chase Going. Occupational Index. 1936. 12p. 25c
  Duties, preparation, license requirements, rewards, advantages, and disadvantages. Chart shows the number of registered dental hygienists in each state and the number employed in each type of practice—schools, private dentists' offices, hospitals, or clinics. Annotated bibliography of eighteen references.

* Career as a dental hygienist. Institute for Research. 1938. 22p. 75c
  Typical day's work of dental hygienist in the industrial clinic, school, dentist's office, state or county board of health, and on school staff for student health. Summary of state laws licensing dental hygienists. Number of licensed dental hygienists in each of the states licensing dental hyigenists classified according to places of employment. One illustration. Bibliography.

Curriculum in dental hygiene. University of Michigan, Ann Arbor, Mich. 1944. 20p. Free
  A recruiting bulletin giving nature of the work and requirements for admission to the curriculum in dental hygiene.

The dental hygienist. The Chronicle. No date. 6p. 5c
  Guide post to occupational information number 6. Bibliography.

Dental hygienist. Science Research Associates. No date. 2p. Planographed. 15c
  Occupational reprint number 24. One illustration.

**Dental hygienist. Women's Bureau, U. S. Dept. of Labor. Supt. of Documents, Washington 25, D.C. 1945. 17p. 10c
  Number 10 of series "The outlook for women in occupations in the medical and other health services." Definition, opportunities, hours, and

advancement. Prewar number and distribution of dental hygienists, wartime changes, and postwar outlook. Minimum requirements for entrance to a school for training dental hygienists, for licensure, for membership in the American Dental Hygienists' Association, and for beginning Civil Service positions. List of sixteen schools offering training. Two illustrations. Bibliography.

— **Dental hygienist—a career for women. American Dental Hygienists' Association, 1704 No. Troy St., Arlington, Va. 1944. 8p. Free.
Description of work, duties, and requirements. Length of course, fee, and dates when the sixteen recognized schools for dental hygienists were organized. Statutory requirements for license are abstracted from laws of thirty-five states.

Description of the sub-profession of dental hygienists. National Roster. 1945. 2p. Free
See p. 34 for description of series.

DENTAL TECHNICIAN 0-50.06

An appraisal and abstract of available literature on the occupation of the dental mechanic. Spiegler, Samuel. Occupational Index. 1938. 8p. 25c
Duties, preparation, earnings, number and distribution of workers, advantages, and disadvantages. Annotated bibliography of ten references.

Mechanical dentistry. Davis, Anne S., ed. Revised edition. Commonwealth Book Co. 1939. 17p. Mimeographed. 75c
Information presented according to the NVGA outline. See p. 26 for description of series. Describes work of making artificial restorations for the mouth from impressions taken by dentists. Does not cover the work of the dental assistant.

DENTIST 0-13.10

* An appraisal and abstract of available literature on the occupation of the dentist. Pavan, Ann. Occupational Index. 1939. 12p. 25c
Duties, preparation, qualifications, earnings, number and geographic distribution of dentists, advantages, and disadvantages. Annotated bibliography of fifteen references.

Dental education—a statement for individuals in the Armed Forces. American Dental Association, 222 E. Superior St., Chicago 11, Ill. 1945. 9p. Free
Admission requirements for dental study. List of forty approved dental schools and sixteen schools of dental hygiene.

Dentist. Prepared for the War Department by the National Roster. Supt. of Documents, Washington 25, D.C. 1945. 5c
Occupational brief containing summary, earnings, outlook, qualifications, and training.

Dentistry. Corcoran, J. P. Xavier University. 1938. 17p. Mimeographed. 50c
Addressed to Negro youth, this pamphlet discusses qualifications, training, earnings, and opportunities for Negro dentists. Bibliography.

DENTIST—*Continued*

Dentistry. Greenleaf, Walter J. U. S. Office of Education. Supt. of Documents, Washington 25, D.C. 1932. 10p. 5c
Guidance leaflet number 7. Requirements, training, and compensation. Bibliography.

Dentistry. Miner, Leroy. Bellman Publishing Co. 1940. 23p. Vari-typed. 50c
Qualifications, opportunities, earnings, and license requirements. Includes description of special dental services such as oral surgery, orthodontia, and exodontia. Presents points to be considered in the selection of a dental school and list of approved schools. Bibliography.

Dentistry. Revised edition\ Quarrie Corporation. 1943. 9p. Planographed. 10c
Vocational monograph number 10.

* Dentistry. Shade, Chloris, ed. 2nd edition revised. Morgan-Dillon & Co. 1940. 24p. 32c
Qualifications, training, and state requirements for license. Some information about the work of specialists. List of thirty-nine approved schools of dentistry and sixteen schools of dental hygiene. Bibliography.

⌐Dentistry. University of Michigan, Ann Arbor, Mich. 1940. 17p. Free
Nature of practice, qualifications, educational requirements, opportunities afforded, advantages and disadvantages.

Dentistry as a career. Institute for Research. 1939. 16p. 75c
Qualifications, opportunities, training, typical course of study, duties, license requirements, trends, advantages, and disadvantages. List of thirty-nine dental schools. Some information about the dental technician, dental hygienist, and dental assistant. One illustration. Bibliography.

**Dentistry as a professional career. American Dental Association, 222 E. Superior St., Chicago 44, Ill. 1941. 72p. 10c
Historical background, educational requirements, state licensing requirements, and list of the thirty-nine approved dental schools of the United States. Discussion of auxiliary fields of service: dental hygienist, dental assistant, and dental technician. Bibliography. (Out of print; revised edition is in preparation.)

Dentists. Science Research Associates. 1945. 4p. Planographed. 15c
Occupational brief number 112. Two illustrations. Annotated bibliography.

Description of profession of dentist. National Roster. 1946. Free
In preparation. See p. 34 for description of series.

Graduate, postgraduate and refresher courses in the dental schools of the United States. American Dental Association, 222 E. Superior St., Chicago 44, Ill. 1945. 27p. Mimeographed. Free
Compiled for information of dentists in the armed forces who are interested upon their return to civilian life to pursue graduate and refresher courses in the dental schools.

**Women dentists. Women's Bureau, U. S. Dept. of Labor. Supt. of Documents, Washington 25, D.C. 1945. 21p. 10c
Number 9 of the series "The outlook for women in occupations in the medical and other health services." Prewar number and distribution of

dentists, wartime changes, and postwar outlook. Minimum requirements for entrance to and graduation from a dental school, for a state license, for Civil Service positions, and for the U. S. Naval Reserve women dentists. Three illustrations. Bibliography.

DENTIST'S ASSISTANT   1-32.10

The dental assistant. The Chronicle. No date. 6p. 5c
> Guidepost to occupational information number 7. Bibliography.

**Physician's and dentists' assistants. Women's Bureau, U. S. Dept. of Labor. Supt. of Documents, Washington 25, D.C. 1945. 10c
> Number 11 of the series "The outlook for women in occupations in the medical and other health services." Duties, number and distribution of workers, qualifications, and postwar outlook. Bibliography.

DEPARTMENT STORE WORKER   0-72.99

Department store work. Shade, Chloris, ed. 2nd edition revised. Morgan-Dillon & Co. 1940. 24p. 32c
> Description of work in the divisions of merchandising, publicity or sales promotion, finance and control, store operation and personnel, and management. Training, working conditions, and opportunities. Classified bibliography.

Shoppers' special—the way of life in a department store. Bedell, Clyde. Row, Peterson and Co. 1941. 64p. 96c
> In describing the management of a special sale of Swedish glass, the duties of various workers are presented. See p. 41 for description of series. Thirty-six illustrations.

Vocations for women—department store work. National Federation of Business and Professional Women's Clubs. 1941. 4p. 10c
> Includes description of many non-selling jobs. One illustration. Bibliography.

DETECTIVE   2-66.

* Careers in the F. B. I. Institute for Research. 1942. 18p. 75c
> Describes work of the investigative staff. Information about careers in the FBI Technical Laboratory such as identification specialist and fingerprint classifier. Five illustrations. Bibliography.

* Detective. Revised edition. Occupational Index. 1944. 6p. 25c
> Occupational abstract. Duties, preparation, entrance, advancement, abilities, compensation, number and distribution of workers, advantages, disadvantages, and future trend of employment. Annotated bibliography.

The Federal Bureau of Investigation. The Bureau, U. S. Dept. of Justice, Washington 25, D.C. 1944. 46p. Free
> Describes the background, jurisdiction, and activities of the FBI. Duties, qualifications, and salaries are given for clerical, laboratory, and identification work.

DIESEL-ENGINE OPERATOR   5-72.210

The diesel engine—careers. Institute for Research. 1935. 12p. 75c
> Temporarily out of print.

DIESEL-ENGINE OPERATOR—*Continued*

Diesel engineering. Shade, Chloris, ed. 2nd edition revised. Morgan-Dillon & Co. 1939. 24p. 42c

> Description of work in production, distribution, and operation. Preparation needed, wages, and conditions of work. Bibliography.

* Diesel engines. Revised edition. Occupational Index. 1945. 6p. 25c

> Occupational abstract. Duties, abilities, preparation, entrance and advancement, earnings, number and distribution of workers, advantages, disadvantages, and postwar prospects. Annotated bibliography.

A survey of the diesel engine industry. Advisory Board on Industrial Education, Board of Education, 110 Livingston St., Brooklyn 2, N.Y. 1936. 44p. Mimeographed. 25c

> A report of the recommendation for training in the public schools. Suggests course of study, prerequisites for entrance to classes, and instructions to counselors.

What are the opportunities for college men in the Diesel engine industry? Diesel Engine Manufacturers Association, 1 North LaSalle St., Chicago 2, Ill. 1945. 4p. Free

> Brief statement concerning training and opportunities.

DIESEL MECHANIC   5-83.931

* Employment opportunities for diesel-engine mechanics. Bureau of Labor Statistics, U. S. Dept. of Labor. Supt. of Documents, Washington 25, D.C. 1945. 10p. 5c

> Occupational Outlook Division series. Nature and importance of the occupation, characteristics of the Diesel engine, prospects for expansion in use of Diesel engines, opportunities for Diesel mechanics, training for Diesel maintenance, and summary.

DIETICIAN   0-39.93

* An appraisal and abstract of available literature on dietetics as an occupation. Murtland, Cleo. Occupational Index. 1938. 10p. 25c

> Duties, abilities, preparation, number employed, salaries, advantages, and disadvantages. Annotated bibliography of fifty-three references.

Courses for student dietitians, approved by the Executive Board. The American Dietetic Association, 620 N. Michigan Ave., Chicago 11, Ill. 1945. 5p. 15c

> List of institutions offering administrative and hospital courses approved by the American Dietetic Association. Tabulated information includes name of dietitian, tuition fees, enrollment, and length of course.

Description of the profession of dieticians. National Roster. 1945. 2p. Free

> See p. 34 for description of series.

The dietician. Davis, Anne S., ed. Commonwealth Book Co. 1936 with 1939 supplement. Mimeographed. 75c

> Information presented according to the NVGA outline. See p. 26 for description of series. Includes duties of hospital, hotel, and restaurant dietitian, the consultant dietitian, and organizer of dietary departments.

Dietitian. Prepared for the War Department by the National Roster. Supt. of Documents, Washington 25, D.C. 1945. 13p. 5c
Occupational brief containing summary, earnings, outlook, qualifications, and training.

List of institutions offering training courses approved by the American Dietetic Association. The Association, 620 No. Michigan Ave., Chicago 11, Ill. 1945. 4p. 15c
Institutions approved as of October 1945.

> Dietitians are urgently needed. American Dietetic Association, 620 No. Michigan Ave., Chicago 11, Ill. 1944. 8p. Free
Illustrated leaflet showing dietitians at work in Army, hospital, food administration, and community nutrition.

**Dietetics as a profession. Amercian Dietetic Association, 620 No. Michigan Ave., Chicago 11, Ill. 1944. 35p. 25c
Employment opportunities in eighteen fields of activity, conditions of work, salaries, personal qualifications, and methods of securing positions. Illustrated. Bibliography.

* Hospital dietetics as a career. Institute for Research. 1939. 24p. 75c
Duties, typical day's work, educational requirements, personal qualifications, opportunities, salaries, attractive and unattractive features, and qualifications for dietetic internship. Also list of hospitals offering courses approved by the American Dietetic Association. Three illustrations. Bibliography.

DIETITIAN. *See* Dietician

DIPLOMATIC SERVICE WORKER 0-94.
* The diplomatic service as a career. Institute for Research. 1939. 16p. 75c
Discussion of work in the Foreign Service of the United States. Includes duties, qualifications, training, salaries, advantages, disadvantages, examination requirements, and methods of making appointments. Four illustrations.

Diplomatic service workers. Science Research Associates. 1943. 4p. Planographed. 15c
Occupational brief number 92. Two illustrations. Annotated bibliography.

DOCTOR OF MEDICINE. *See* Physician

DOMESTIC SERVICE WORKER 2-00. to 2-09.
Duties and responsibilities of the general household employee. White, Marie. U. S. Office of Education. Supt. of Documents, Washington 25, D.C. 1938. 32p. 10c
Prepared for the purpose of providing bases for determining content for vocational courses in household employment. Information is summarized on abilities desired by homemakers, qualities considered essential, training, and wages.

DOMESTIC SERVICE WORKER—*Continued*

* Household workers. Brown, Jean C. Science Research Associates. 1940. 50p. 60c

> Description of household work, training for domestic service, working conditions, typical earnings for each type of household work, and the outlook for domestic service. Ten illustrations. Annotated bibliography.

Household workers. Keliher, Alice, ed. Hinds, Hayden **and** Eldredge, Inc. 1941. 56p. 80c

> Includes a discussion of the advantages in household employment. See p. 28 for description of Picture Fact Books.

Household workers. Science Research Associates. 1943. 4p. Planographed. 15c

> Occupational brief number 95. Two illustrations. Annotated bibliography.

Job descriptions for domestic service and personal service occupations. Division of Occupational Analysis. Supt. of Documents, Washington 25, D.C. 1939 261p. $1

> See p. 58 for comment on National Job Descriptions. Includes description of occupations concerned with personal services to individuals in and about their homes.

DRAFTSMAN   0-48.

Architectural drafting and design. Shade, Chloris, ed. 2nd edition revised. Morgan-Dillon & Co. 1939. 24p. 32c

> Duties, nature of work, qualifications, training, and rewards. Bibliography.

* Drafting and designing. Davis, Anne S., ed. Commonwealth Book Co. 1936 with 1939 supplement. 23p. Mimeographed. 75c

> Information presented according to the NVGA outline. See p. 26 for description of series. Information about draftsmen and designers in the machine and metal trades.

Draftsmen. Science Research Associates. 1943. 4p. Planographed. 15c

> Occupational brief number 40. Two illustrations. Annotated bibliography.

* Mechanical drafting and design. Shade, Chloris, ed. 2nd edition revised. Morgan-Dillon & Co. 1940. 24p. 32c

> Duties and nature of the work, qualifications, training, and rewards. Bibliography.

DRAMA CRITIC. *See* Actor and actress

DRESSMAKER   4.25.030

* Dressmaker. Revised edition. Occupational Index. 1945. 6p. 25c

> Occupational abstract. What the dressmaker does, abilities, preparation, entrance, advancement, number of workers, earnings, advantages, disadvantages, and postwar prospects. Annotated bibliography.

* Dressmaking and alterations. Davis, Anne S., ed. Commonwealth Book Co. 1936. 25p. Mimeographed. 75c
    Information presented according to the NVGA outline. See p. 26 for description of series. Includes work in the wholesale garment factory, department store, small custom shop, and home economics extension. Bibliography.

Dressmaking and costume design. Revised edition. Quarrie Corporation. 1942. 15p. Planographed. 10c
    Vocational monograph number 11.

DRUG AND COSMETIC INDUSTRY WORKER
4, 6, 8-53.000 through 8-53.149

* The drug and cosmetic industry. Ewing, Clare O. Bellman Publishing Co. 1944. 24p. 50c
    Describes work involved in the manufacture of drug, perfume, and cosmetic products and in supplying the raw materials. Qualifications, opportunities, compensation, and training. Bibliography.

Postwar market, sales and industrial progress survey of the drug, chemical, cosmetic and allied lines. National Paper Box Manufacturers Association, Liberty Trust Bldg., Philadelphia 7, Pa. 1945. 24p. $2.50; $1 to schools and libraries.
    One of a series of postwar industrial surveys, discussing employment, demand for products, and packaging problems.

DRUG STORE MANAGER. *See* Manager, Retail Drug

DRUGGIST. *See* Pharmacist

ECONOMIST
0-39.14

Description of the profession of economists. National Roster. 1945. 4p. Free
    See p. 34 for description of series.

Economist. Prepared for the War Department by the National Roster. Supt. of Documents, Washington 25, D.C. 1945. 5c
    Occupational brief containing summary, earnings, outlook, qualifications, and training.

Handbook of descriptions of specialized fields in economics. National Roster. 1946
    In preparation.

EDITOR
0-06.

* Editorial work as a career. Institute for Research. 1941. 22p. 75c
    Describes work of editorial staff in a book publishing house, encyclopedia staff, government position and on newspaper or magazine staff. Qualifications, opportunities, salaries, advantages and disadvantages. Bibliography.

Editors and reporters. Science Research Associates. 1943. 4p. Planographed. 15c
    Occupational brief number 89. Two illustrations. Annotated bibliography.

EDITOR—*Continued*

* Motion picture editing. Western Personnel Service. 1941. 9p.
25c
> Specific information about number of film editors, their work, earnings,
> and promotional steps. The suggested reading pertains to technical proc-
> esses and methods of film editing.

Reporter and editor. Prepared for the War Department by the
National Roster. Supt. of Documents, Washington 25, D.C. 1945.
5c
> Occupational brief containing summary, earnings, outlook, qualifications,
> and training.

ELECTRICAL ENGINEER   0-17.01

Description of the profession of electrical engineering including
radio and communications engineering. National Roster. 1945.
5p. Free
> See p. 34 for description of series.

Electrical engineer. Prepared for the War Department by the National Roster. Supt. of Documents, Washington 25, D.C. 1945.
13p. 5c
> Occupational brief containing summary, earnings, outlook, qualifications,
> and training.

* The electrical engineer—some facts concerning electrical engineering
as a career. American Institute of Electrical Engineers, 33 W.
39th St., New York 18, N.Y. No date. 21p. 10c
> Information concerning the work done by electrical engineers, the op-
> portunities available, the types of persons most likely to succeed, the edu-
> cation required, and other facts of interest. "This information should
> encourage students having the necessary abilities and preferences to decide
> upon electrical engineering and to secure a suitable type of education, and
> it should warn those not having suitable qualifications to seek other careers."
> Bibliography.

Electrical engineering. Greenleaf, Walter J. U. S. Office of Education. Supt. of Documents, Washington 25, D.C. 1932. 11p.
5c
> Guidance leaflet number 12. Duties, qualifications, salary, and training.

Electrical engineering. Revised edition. Quarrie Corporation. 1942.
13p. Planographed. 10c
> Vocational monograph number 12.

Electrical engineering as a career. Institute for Research. 1936.
16p. 75c
> Training, qualifications, compensation, opportunities, advantages, disad-
> vantages, and a typical day's work. Describes work of the operating engi-
> neer, designing engineer, and the research engineer and gives the policy of
> several electrical corporations in selecting and training employees. Three
> illustrations.

Electrical engineers. Science Research Associates. 1943. 4p.
Planographed. 15c
> Occupational brief number 27. Two illustrations. Annotated bibliog-
> raphy.

Handbook of descriptions of specialized fields in electrical engineering. National Roster. 1946
> In preparation.

* If you are considering a career in the electrical field. Morecock, Earle M. Rochester Institute of Technology. 1944. 18p. 10c
> Describes nature of work, opportunities for beginners, requirements for the better positions, and the probable promotion sequence.

> *See also* Engineer

ELECTRICAL EQUIPMENT MANUFACTURER   5, 7, 9-00.
Electrical manufacturing. Stephenson, Howard and Williams, R. E. Bellman Publishing Co. 1941. 32p. 75c
> Qualifications, training, opportunities, and list of positions in electrical manufacturing. Includes list of seventeen technical institutes and one hundred and eight colleges offering courses in electrical engineering. Description of seventeen subjects included in college courses in engineering. Good bibliography.

ELECTRICIAN   4-97.
* An appraisal and abstract of available literature on the occupation of the electric lineman. Spiegler, Samuel. Occupational Index. 1939. 12p. 25c
> Duties, abilities, preparation, compensation, number and distribution of workers, advantages, disadvantages, union organization, and trends. Annotated bibliography of fourteen references.

Careers in electrical wiring and electrical contracting. Institute for Research. 1941. 30p. 75c
> Qualifications, training, attractive and unattractive features, opportunities, and related jobs. Four illustrations.

Careers resulting from rural electrification. Institute for Research. 1941. 22p. 75c
> Information concerning the promotion superintendent, manager of project, electrification adviser, chief engineer, wiring contractor, lineman, and bookkeeper. Discussion of opportunities developed as a result of rural electrification such as irrigation and cold storage locker plants. Four illustrations.

* Electrical installation. Shade, Chloris, ed. 2nd edition revised. Morgan-Dillon & Co. 1940. 24p. 32c
> Nature of the work, qualifications, training, and opportunities. Information about related occupations such as refrigerator service and radio repair. Classified bibliography.

The electrician. Baltimore Department of Education. 1941. 7p. 10c
> Description of various types of work, qualifications, remuneration, advantages, and disadvantages. Bibliography.

Electrician. Davis, Anne S., ed. Commonwealth Book Co. 1938. 25p. Mimeographed. 75c
> Information presented according to the NVGA outline. See p. 26 for description of series. Information pertains to the electrician in the trade and industrial fields.

ELECTRICIAN—*Continued*

Electricians and electrical workers. Science Research Associates. 1943. 4p. Planographed. 15c

> Occupational brief number 25. Two illustrations. Annotated bibliography.

Establishing and operating an electrical appliance and radio shop. U. S. Dept. of Commerce. Supt. of Documents, Washington 25, D.C. 1945

> Industrial series. Intended as a practical guide to experienced skilled electricians who are considering starting their own business. In preparation.

National apprenticeship and training standards for the electrical industry. Apprentice-Training Service, U. S. Dept. of Labor, Washington 25, D.C. 1945. 34p. Free

> Includes an example of an apprenticeship agreement, standards, discussion of basic related instruction, content of training for electrical construction, and list of state apprenticeship agencies.

ELECTRONICS INDUSTRY WORKER
4, 6, 8-98.000 through 5, 7, 9-00.999

* Electronics. Revised edition. Occupational Index. 1944. 6p. 25c

> Occupational abstract. Describes the following jobs in electronics: research, development and design, manufacturing, operating, and sales engineering. Abilities, training, entrance, advancement, earnings, advantages, and disadvantages. Annotated bibliography.

Electronics. Science Research Associates. 1943. 4p. Planographed. 15c

> Occupational brief number 51. Two illustrations. Annotated bibliography.

ELEVATOR OPERATOR. *See* Bellboy

EMPLOYMENT INTERVIEWER   0-68.71

Employee counseling: a selected list of references. U. S. Civil Service Commission, Washington 25, D.C. 1944. 22p. Free

> Annotated bibliography followed by a supplementary list published eight months later.

Employee counseling—a survey of a new development in personnel relations. Industrial Relations Section, Princeton University, Princeton, N.J. 1944. 64p. $1

> Discussion of the growth and aims of counseling programs in industry and government, the duties of employee counselors, qualifications, training, and probable future trends. Annotated bibliography.

EMPLOYMENT MANAGER   0-39.82

Description of the profession of personnel administration. National Roster. 1945. 4p. Free

> See p. 34 for description of series.

EMPLOYMENT SERVICE WORKER 0-68.70 to 0-68.79

* Careers in the U. S. Employment Service. Institute for Research. 1945. 29p. 75c

Qualifications, requirements, salaries, and attractive and unattractive features. Description of work of director of employment service, employment office manager, senior interviewer, technical personnel assistant, employer relations representative, statistical clerk, informational representative, supervisor of research and statistics, supervisor of procedures, and employment counselor. One illustration.

ENGINEER 0-15. through 0-20.

**Annual report. Engineers' Council for Professional Development, 29 W. 39th St., New York 18, N.Y. 1945. 56p. 25c

Contains reports of committees on guidance and selection of engineering students, on engineering schools, on professional training, and on professional recognition. Contains list of one hundred and thirty-five accredited undergraduate engineering schools, arranged by states, and indicating special curricula. A second list names the fifteen schools offering accredited undergraduate curricula in aeronautical engineering, three in agricultural engineering, fourteen in architectural, ten in ceramic, fifty in chemical, one hundred and eighteen in civil engineering, one hundred and eighteen in electrical, one in fuel technology, eight in general engineering, nineteen in industrial, one hundred and twelve in mechanical, thirty in metallurgical, twenty-nine in mining engineering, three in naval architecture and marine engineering, thirteen in petroleum engineering, and four in sanitary engineering.

The list of accredited curricula is available December 15 each year, at 25c per copy, 6 copies for $1.

* A career in engineering. Stewart, Lowell O. Science Research Associates. 1942. 50p. 60c

Information is given in the form of an interview between an experienced engineer and a boy considering a career in engineering. Twenty-three illustrations. Bibliography.

**Career in engineering—requirements, opportunities. Stewart, Lowell O. Iowa State College Press, Ames, Iowa. 1941. 87p. 75c

The work of the engineer is discussed under three headings: (1) the degree-granting departments such as agricultural, architectural, ceramic, chemical, civil, electrical, general, and mechanical engineering; (2) functional specialization such as design, development and experiment, construction and manufacturing, sales, commercial, application, service, and operations; (3) opportunities in specific industries such as automotive, radio, refrigeration and air conditioning, telephone, and aviation. Good discussions are included on who should study engineering and the factors determining success. Illustrated. Bibliography.

Engineer Foundry. War Department Technical Manual. Supt. of Documents, Washington 25, D.C. 1944. 65p. 15c

Description of work of pattern making, preparing mold, and making metal castings. Definitions, lists of foundry equipment, and five courses of study for specialist training. Forty-eight illustrations.

ENGINEER—*Continued*

Engineering. Smith, Richard H. Bellman Publishing Co. 1940. 59p. Vari-typed. 75c

> Qualifications, earnings, and opportunities. Includes discussion of who should not enter engineering. Criteria of fitness for engineering includes social responsibility, originality, curiosity, and capacity to analyze. Bibliography.

**Engineering as a career—a message to young men, teachers, parents. Engineers' Council for Professional Development, 29 W. 39th St., New York 18, N.Y. 1942. 36p. 10c

> Discussion of kind of work, functions, qualifications, preparation, opportunities, earnings, and requirements of registration. Branches of engineering covered are: civil, mining, metallurgical, ceramic, mechanical, electrical, chemical, and related fields. Annotated bibliography.

Engineers (general survey). Prepared for the War Department by the National Roster. Supt. of Documents, Washington 25, D.C. 1945. 14p. 5c

> Occupational brief containing summary, earnings, outlook, qualifications, and training.

Where do we go from here? Allis-Chalmers Manufacturing Company, Milwaukee 1, Wis. No date. 16p. Free

> Includes pictures of many activities of engineers.

See also

Aeronautical engineer	Landscape engineer
Agricultural engineer	Marine engineer
Air conditioning engineer	Mechanical engineer
Automotive engineer	Metallurgical engineer
Cable engineer	Mining engineer
Ceramic engineer	Naval architect
Chemical engineer	Petroleum engineer
Civil engineer	Planning engineer
Diesel-engine engineer	Refrigerating engineer
Electrical engineer	Safety engineer
Fire protection engineer	Sound engineer
Industrial engineer	Traffic engineer

ENTOMOLOGIST　　　　　　　　　　　　　　　0-39.65

Description of the profession of entomology. National Roster. 1945. 3p. Free

> See p. 34 for description of series.

* Handbook of descriptions of specialized fields in entomology. National Roster. Supt. of Documents, Washington 25, D.C. 1945. 14p. 10c

> Occupational summary, functions of the various major branches of entomology, fields of specialization, and related activities.

Zoologist, entomologist, and parasitologist. Prepared for the War Department by the National Roster. Supt. of Documents, Washington 25, D.C. 1945. 5c

> Occupational brief containing summary, earnings, outlook, qualifications, **and training.**

ETHNOLOGIST 0-39.13
Description of the profession of anthropology. National Roster.
1945. 3p. Free
See p. 34 for description of series.

ETYMOLOGIST 0-39.16
Description of the professional occupations in foreign languages.
National Roster. 1945. 2p. Free
See p. 34 for description of series.

EXPLORER 0-39.79
* Exploring as a career. Institute for Research. 1937. 24p. 75c
Qualifications, training, opportunities, attractive and unattractive sides.
Includes list of twenty-eight types of scientific work in exploratory work
and seven positions of a non-scientific nature. List of American museums
and types of expeditions. Three illustrations.

FACTORY WORKER 4, 6, 8-00. to 5, 7, 9-18.
* Careers for women in factory work. Institute for Research. 1942.
19p. 75c
Information concerning machine tending, assembly work, packaging,
inspecting, and testing. Description of work in individual factories such
as book binding, candy making, and aircraft assembly. Six illustrations.
Bibliography.

FARM HAND 3-11. through 3-19.
Farm laborers. Science Research Associates. 1943. 4p. Planographed. 15c
Occupational brief number 35. Two illustrations. Annotated bibliography.

FARM MANAGER 3-37.
Farm management as a career. Institute for Research. 1946.
Revised edition. 20p. 75c
In press.

FARMER 3-04. through 3-09.
Agriculture. Jones, Maurice. Bellman Publishing Co. 1940. 43p.
Vari-typed. 50c
Discussion of thirteen kinds of work in farming, fourteen in the industrial field, eight in educational fields of agriculture, three in research, four
in regulatory and farm management services. Includes list of sixty-six
schools of agriculture and description of courses of study in agricultural
economics, agronomy, agricultural engineering, animal husbandry, bacteriology, biochemistry, biology, and dairy technology. Bibliography.

Agriculture. Quarrie Corporation. 1938. 9p. Planographed. 10c
Vocational monograph number 3.

Agriculture. Union of American Hebrew Congregations, Cincinnati, Ohio. 1937. 30p. Mimeographed. 25c
Discussion of requirements, advantages, disadvantages, opportunities, and
trends. Last half of booklet is addressed to Jewish youth. Bibliography.

FARMER—*Continued*

Farm workers. Keliher, Alice, ed. Hinds, Hayden and Eldredge, Inc. 1940. 56p. 80c

See p. 28 for description of Picture Fact Books.

Farming. Tyler, H. S. Revised edition. Occupational Index. 1941. 6p. 25c

Occupational abstract. The farmer's jobs, abilities needed for success, income, number of workers, advantages, and disadvantages. Annotated bibliography.

General agriculture as a career. Institute for Research. 1930. 20p. 75c

Description of the life of the farmer, qualifications, opportunities, salary, advantages and disadvantages. Also information concerning the teaching of agriculture. Two illustrations.

General farmers. Science Research Associates. 1943. 4p. Planographed. 15c

Occupational brief number 30. Two illustrations. Annotated bibliography.

**General farming. Shade, Chloris, ed. 2nd edition revised. Morgan-Dillon & Co. 1940. 24p. 32c

Nature of work, qualifications, advantages, disadvantages, and future outlook. List of one hundred and seven occupations in and related to agriculture other than productive farming. Classified bibliography.

A letter to G.I. Joe. Science Research Associates. 1944. 4p. 15c

Occupational reprint number 168. One illustration.

Matching men and farms. Zeran, Franklin R. U. S. Office of Education. Supt. of Documents, Washington 25, D.C. 1944. 38p. 10c

Suggestions for helping young men analyze the opportunities in farming. Describes work of a farm operator, conditions of work, methods of determining farming opportunities, and factors in determining the aptness of an individual as a farm operator.

**Opportunities in agriculture. Dept. of Vocational Education, Virginia Polytechnic Institute, Blacksburg, Va. 1941. 137p. 20c

Written as a guide to the youth of Virginia in the selection of occupations for those who are considering agriculture as the field of their life work. For each of eighteen fields, information is presented on importance of work, classification, duties, working conditions, compensation, opportunities, qualities desired, educational requirements, advantages, and disadvantages. Bibliography at end of each section.

* Opportunities in farming. Chapman, Paul. Science Research Associates. 1941. 50p. 60c

Information concerning the twelve types of farms recognized by the Bureau of the Census. Requirements, incomes, favorable and unfavorable factors. Fourteen illustrations. Annotated bibliography.

Shall I be a farmer? U. S. Dept. of Agriculture. Supt. of Documents, Washington 25, D.C. 1944. 34p. 5c

Addressed to discharged servicemen. Advantages and disadvantages of farming, and brief information about various kinds of farming such as truck farming, poultry farming, fruit growing, and dairying. Other information such as capital investment needed for equipment and for stocking the various kinds of farms.

Why I want my boy to be a farmer. Science Research Associates.
No date. 4p. Planographed. 15c
   Occupational reprint number 35. Two illustrations.
   See also Animal farmer; Animal husbandman; Dairy husband-
man; Poultry husbandman

FASHION DESIGNER   0-46.
* Careers in fashion designing. Institute for Research. 1940. 24p.
75c
   Description of work, training recommended, personal qualifications,
   duties, typical day's work, opportunities, salaries, advantages, and disadvantages. Information about related occupations of fashion illustrator,
   sketcher or copyist, costume stylist, fashion editor, and designer of accessories. Three illustrations. Bibliography.

Fashion designing. Science Research Associates. No date. 4p.
Planographed. 15c
   Occupational reprint number 96. Two illustrations.
   See also Clothes designer

FILE CLERK   1-17.
Filing as a vocation. Weeks, Bertha. National Vocational Guidance Association, 82 Beaver St., New York 5, N.Y. 1945. 5p.
10c
   Reprint describing duties, qualifications, working conditions, advantages,
   disadvantages, compensation, and advancement.

FILLING-STATION ATTENDANT. *See* Automobile-service-
station attendant

FIRE PROTECTION ENGINEER   0-16
Description of the profession of fire protection engineering. Na-
tional Roster. 1945. 4p. Free
   See p. 34 for description of series.
   See also Engineer

FIREMAN   2-63.10
* City fireman. Revised edition. Occupational Index. 1945. 6p. 25c
   Occupational abstract. Duties, qualifications, training, entrance, advancement, earnings, number and distribution of workers, advantages, and
   disadvantages. Bibliography.

Police and fire protection. Shade, Chloris, ed. Morgan-Dillon &
Co. 1939. 24p. 32c
   The second part of the booklet gives information about the work of
   the fireman. Chart shows the organization of the fire department in a
   large city. Bibliography.
   See also Police officer

FISHERMAN   3-87.
Fishermen and oystermen. Science Research Associates. No date.
4p. 15c
   Requirements, wages, and trends. Annotated bibliography.

FLORIST. *See* Manager, Retail Floral

FOOD MANAGER. *See* Manager, Catering

FOOD STORE WORKER. *See* Sales clerk

FOREIGN SERVICE WORKER   0-39.99
* Consular and foreign trade services of the United States as careers.
Institute for Research. 1936. 16p. 75c
>   Describes positions in the American Foreign Service and in the Bureau
>   of Foreign and Domestic Commerce. Requirements, promotion, salaries,
>   advantages and disadvantages. One illustration.

* Foreign service. Shade, Chloris, ed. 2nd edition revised. Morgan-
Dillon & Co. 1940. 23p. 32c
>   Brief history of the Foreign Service of the United States. Qualifica-
>   tions, duties, salaries, and advancement of officers and employees of the
>   Foreign Service. Bibliography.

Postwar demands for women in foreign service. Science Research
Associates. 1944. 2p. 15c
>   Occupational reprint number 176.

— The problem of foreign trade education. Foreign trade education
committee of the National Foreign Trade Council Inc., 26 Beaver
St., New York 4, N.Y. 1942. 35p. Free
>   One section discusses foreign service as a career, listing personal quali-
>   fications and recommending academic courses of study.

The U. S. foreign service. Science Research Associates. No date.
2p. Planographed. 15c
>   Occupational reprint number 28. One illustration.

See also Diplomatic service worker

FOREMAN   5-91. through 5.99.
Foremen. Science Research Associates. 1943. 4p. Planographed.
15c
>   Occupational brief number 21. Two illustrations. Annotated bibliog-
>   raphy.

FOREST RANGER   0-38.03
Description of the profession of forestry including range management. National Roster. 1945. 3p. Free
>   See p. 34 for description of series.

FORESTER   0-38.01
* Careers in forestry. Elliott, Charles N. Revised edition. Science
Research Associates. 1945. 50p. 60c
>   Description of work, qualifications, training, and future outlook. Sug-
>   gestions for a local survey of forestry jobs. List of schools of forestry
>   recognized by the Society of American Foresters with the number of de-
>   grees conferred by each in 1940. Twenty-one illustrations. Bibliography.

Description of the profession of forestry including range management. National Roster. 1945. 3p. Free
>   See p. 34 for description of series.

Forest practice handbook. Revised edition. Pacific Northwest Loggers Association. Joint Committee on Forest Conservation, 364 Stuart Bldg., Seattle 1, Wash. 1937. 31p. 10c
Presents the rules of forest practice for the Douglas fir region. This is not designed for occupational information, but in the description of methods a clear picture of the duties involved in forest conservation may be obtained. Includes topics such as fire protection, hazard reduction, providing a seed supply, conservation of young growth, and partial logging.

Forester. Prepared for the War Department by the National Roster. Supt. of Documents, Washington 25, D.C. 1945. 5c
Occupational brief containing summary, earnings, outlook, qualifications, and training.

Foresters. Science Research Associates. 1943. 4p. Planographed. 15c
Occupational brief number 61. Two illustrations. Annotated bibliography.

Forestry. Davis, Anne S., ed. Commonwealth Book Co. 1938. 23p. Mimeographed. 75c
Information presented according to the NVGA outline. See p. 26 for description of series. Emphasis given to opportunities in the U. S. Forest Service. Bibliography.

Forestry. Greenleaf, Walter J. U. S. Office of Education. Supt. of Documents, Washington 25, D.C. 1932. 11p. 5c
Guidance leaflet number 16. Training, opportunities for employment, and compensation. Bibliography.

Forestry. Science Research Associates. No date. 4p. Planographed. 15c
Occupational reprint number 53. Two illustrations.

* Forestry. Shade, Chloris, ed. 2nd edition revised. Morgan-Dillon & Co. 1940. 24p. 32c
Classification of eleven activities of foresters with examples of typical work performed. Qualifications, preparation, compensation, and list of twenty schools accredited by the Society of American Foresters. Chart shows organization of the U. S. Forest Service. Classified bibliography.

Forestry. Swain, Lewis. Bellman Publishing Co. 1940. 26p. Vari-typed. 50c
Training, qualifications, and opportunities for employment in the United States government, states, cities, industrial organizations, and private enterprise. Information about twenty-four professional schools of forestry. Bibliography.

* Forestry as a career. Institute for Research. 1940. 24p. 75c
Positions in forestry, typical week's work, personal qualifications, training, opportunities, promotional steps, attractive and unattractive features. Table showing the kinds of positions held by the graduates from twenty schools of forestry from 1936 to 1939. Four illustrations. Bibliography.

Green kingdom—the way of life of a forest ranger. Du Puy, William A. Row, Peterson and Co. 1940. 64p. 96c
Training; finding a job; various assignments; work involved in fighting forest fires, erosion, and insects; and future opportunities. See p. 41 for description of series. Forty-five illustrations.

FORESTER—*Continued*

Handbook of descriptions of specialized fields in forestry. National Roster. Supt. of Documents, Washington 25, D.C. 1945. 11p. 5c

Occupational summary, functional activities, related occupations, and fields of specialization.

**Handbook of information on entering positions in forestry. Allen, Shirley W. Society of American Foresters, 825 Mills Bldg., Washington 6, D.C. 1945. 56p. 25c

Duties, working conditions, requirements, training, and salary for each of forty positions such as range examiner, wood technologist, junior planter, junior arborist, dispatcher, pest control worker, towerman, and skilled woods worker. List of nineteen schools of forestry which meet standards set up by the Society of American Foresters.

Recommended college preparation for students planning to enter the National Park Service through the park ranger Civil Service examination. National Park Service, U. S. Dept. of the Interior, Chicago 54, Ill. 1944. 10p. Mimeographed. Free

Qualifications for entrance in park ranger examinations. Description of each of the recommended college subjects.

FOUNDRY WORKER
4, 6, 8-82.

**Employment opportunities in foundry occupations. Bureau of Labor Statistics, U. S. Dept. of Labor. Supt. of Documents, Washington 25, D.C. 1945. 10c

Occupational Outlook Division series. Presents employment prospects, training, and working conditions.

Foundrymen. Science Research Associates. 1943. 4p. Planographed. 15c

Occupational brief number 41. Two illustrations. Annotated bibliography.

Job descriptions for job foundries. Division of Occupational Analysis. Supt. of Documents, Washington 25, D.C. 1938. 336p. $1.25

One of the series of National Job Descriptions. Describes occupations in job foundries fitted to undertake any type of work assigned to them. Does not include occupations existing in foundries operating on a production basis. Illustrated.

**Jobs in the foundry. Bowman, Ernest L. Science Research Associates. 1944. 50p. 60c

Description of work of the pattern maker, core maker, molder, and apprentice. Qualifications, wages and hours, lines of promotion, and future outlook. Includes comparison of wages of ten types of foundry workers in 1937 and 1942. Twelve illustrations. Annotated bibliography.

FUEL TECHNOLOGIST. *See* Metallurgist

FUNERAL DIRECTOR. *See* Undertaker

FURNITURE MANUFACTURING INDUSTRY WORKER
4, 6, 8-36.

Furniture workers. Science Research Associates. 1943. 4p. Planographed. 15c
> Occupational brief number 82. Two illustrations. Annotated bibliog-
> raphy.

Trends in the furniture manufacturing industry. Leffler, George L.
and Brown, Mary Virginia. Bureau of Business Research, Pennsylvania State College, State College, Pa. 1944. 45p. Mimeographed. Free
> Trends in geographic shifts in the industry, labor costs, and production.

GARAGE MANAGER. *See* Manager, Retail Automotive Service

GARDENER. *See* Truck farmer

GARMENT INDUSTRY WORKER   4, 6, 8-14. through 8-27.
The garment worker. Science Research Associates. 1939. 4p.
Planographed. 15c
> Occupational reprint number 89. Two illustrations.

Job descriptions for the garment manufacturing industry. Division
of Occupational Analysis. Supt. of Documents, Washington 25,
D.C. 1939. 237p. $1
> See p. 58 for comment on National Job Descriptions. Describes jobs
> concerned with the manufacture of apparel from woven and knitted fab-
> rics. Illustrated.

GENETICIST   0-39.99
Description of the profession of genetics. National Roster. 1945.
2p. Free
> See p. 34 for description of series.

GEOGRAPHER   0-39.79
Description of the professional occupation of geography. National
Roster. 1945. 3p. Free
> See p. 34 for description of series.

Jobs in geography. Science Research Associates. 1944. 2p. 15c
> Occupational reprint number 175. One illustration.

GEOLOGIST   0-39.45
* Careers in geology. Institute for Research. 1939. 23p. 75c
> Discussion of historical geology, such as astronomic geology; general
> geology, such as physiography and stratigraphy; and structural geology,
> such as geophysics and geochemistry. Description of duties, typical day's
> work, training, typical course of study, advantages, and disadvantages.
> Three illustrations.

Description of the profession of geology. National Roster. 1945.
3p. Free
> See p. 34 for description of series.

GEOLOGIST—*Continued*

Geologist. Prepared for the War Department by the National Roster. Supt. of Documents, Washington 25, D.C. 1945. 5c
>Occupational brief containing summary, earnings, outlook, qualifications, and training.

* Geology as a career. Lehigh University, Bethlehem, Pa. No date. 6p. Free
>Opportunities, preparation, personal qualifications, and professional attractions of geology. Bibliography.

**Handbook of descriptions of specialized fields in geology. National Roster. Supt. of Documents, Washington 25, D.C. 1945. 16p. 10c
>Occupational summary, related fields, functional activities, fields of specialization, and related occupations.

GEOPHYSICIST   0-39.45

Geophysicist. Prepared for the War Department by the National Roster. Supt. of Documents, Washington 25, D.C. 1945. 13p. 5c
>Occupational brief containing summary, earnings, outlook, qualifications, and training.

Handbook of descriptions of specialized fields in geophysics. National Roster. 1946
>In preparation.

GIRL SCOUT PROFESSIONAL WORKER   0-27.99

**Girl scouting as a profession. Adams, Margaret. Bellman Publishing Co. 1945. 23p. 75c
>Qualifications, opportunities, remunerations, and description of national staff positions and local professional positions such as executive secretary, field, district, and functional secretaries. Bibliography.

Girls—you can prepare for tomorrow's job today. Girl Scouts, 155 E. 44th St., New York 17, N.Y. 1945. 4p. Free
>Brief description of professional work with the Girl Scouts, qualifications, training, and working conditions.

**Professional opportunities in girl scouting. Girl Scouts, 155 E. 44th St., New York 17, N.Y. 1945. 24p. Free
>Description of national staff positions and local professional positions such as executive secretary and field secretary. Qualifications, standards of work, and preparation.

Trail of the trefoil—the way of life of a girl scout. Price, Edith B. Row, Peterson and Co. 1941. 64p. 96c
>In the description of girl scout activities, glimpses of the work of the leader are given. See p. 41 for description of series. Forty-three illustrations.

GLASS INDUSTRY WORKER   4, 6, 8-65.

Glass. Labor market information for USES counseling—Industry Series. U. S. Dept. of Labor, Washington 25, D.C. 1945. 6p. Free
>Statement including nature and location of industry, requirements, conditions of work, union affiliations, wages, and employment prospects. Chart shows employment by states. Bibliography.

GOVERNMENT SERVICE WORKER   0-39.99
Careers in government service. Institute for Research. 1935. 24p.
75c
> Temporarily out of print.

The first federal in-service internship program. The National Institute of Public Affairs, 400 Investment Bldg., Washington 5, D.C.
1944. 13p. 10c
> Report of in-service internship program in public service training includes summary of qualifications of candidates, methods of selection, training program to increase work efficiency, and the specific work assignments.

Government service. Revised edition. Quarrie Corporation. 1942.
13p. Planographed. 10c
> Vocational monograph number 13.

The internship program. National Institute of Public Affairs, 400
Investment Bldg., Washington 5, D.C. 1945. 6p. Free
> Announcement of the eleventh internship program in the Federal Government. General information and requirements for eligibility.

Jobs in government. Science Research Associates. 1943. 4p.
Planographed. 15c
> Occupational brief number 10. Two illustrations. Annotated bibliography.

Training for government service. Indiana University, Bloomington,
Ind. 1940. 16p. Free
> By government positions is meant not only positions in Federal but also in state and municipal corporations. Positions are not described but a general undergraduate curriculum is set forth which should equip one for positions of junior grade.

> *See also* Civil Service worker

GROCERY STORE WORKER. *See* Sales clerk

GUIDANCE AND PERSONNEL WORKER. *See* Personnel
manager

HEALTH EDUCATOR   0-27.20
Educational qualifications of health educators. American Public
Health Association. 1943. 5p. Free

HERPETOLOGIST   0-39.68
Description of the profession of zoology including fish and wildlife
management. National Roster. 1945. 3p. Free
> See p. 34 for description of series.

HIGHWAY MAINTENANCE MAN   0-16.01; 7-61.010
* Highway jobs. Royall, R. E. Science Research Associates. 1944.
50p. 60c
> A study of employment in highway construction and maintenance. Includes a table presenting information about highway engineering positions under the U. S. Civil Service. Twelve illustrations.

HISTORIAN   0-06.91
Description of the professional occupation of historian. National
Roster. 1945. 2p. Free
See p. 34 for description of series.

HOME DEMONSTRATION AGENT   0-12.30
Vocations for women—home demonstration work. National Federation of Business and Professional Women's Clubs. 1941. 4p.
10c
Describes work of the county home demonstration agent with farm
women. Five illustrations.

HOME ECONOMICS EXPERT   0-11.50; 0-31.01; 0-32.96
Business home economics, expanding field. Goeppinger, Katherine.
American Home Economics Association, 620 Mills Bldg., Wash-
ington 6, D.C. 1944. 3p. 10c
Summary of fifty-eight questionnaires answered by home economics
businesswomen concerning trends.

Career as a home economist in the food field. Revised edition. Institute for Research. 1945. 20p. 75c
Describes duties, qualifications, and opportunities of nutritionist, food
service director, journalist, and specialist in foods engaged in advertising
or sales promotion work. Three illustrations. Bibliography.

Careers for the home economist. Science Research Associates. No
date. Planographed. 2p. 15c
Occupational reprint number 66.

Cooking with words. Mademoiselle, 122 E. 42nd St., New York 17,
N.Y. 1945. 5p. 10c
Describes the opportunities for the home economist in journalism, ad-
vertising and sales promotion, and public service.

Description of profession of home economist. National Roster.
1946. Free
In preparation. See p. 34 for description of series.

Handbook of descriptions of specialized fields in home economics.
National Roster. 1946
In preparation.

Employment opportunities for women with limited home economics
training. Brown, Clara M. and Arnesen, Ruth. Burgess Publishing Company, 426 So. 6th St., Minneapolis 15, Minn. 1944.
44p. Mimeographed. $1.25
Types of business offering employment, qualifications and remuneration
for various jobs, and additional information about each of the fourteen
types of jobs for which a limited amount of home economics training
would be an asset.

Home economics. Corcoran, J. P. Xavier University. 1938. 19p.
50c
Description of work in various branches of home economics, with information concerning the occupational opportunities for Negro youth. Bibliography.

Home economics. Greenleaf, Walter J. U. S. Office of Education. Supt. of Documents, Washington 25, D.C. 1932. 14p. 5c
Guidance leaflet number 21. Discussion of opportunities in various branches of home economics, salaries, and training.

Home economics. Milwaukee-Downer College, Milwaukee, Wis. 1944. 21p. Free
College bulletin giving information about preparation for foods and nutrition, including dietetics and institutional management; textiles and clothing; and home economics education. Illustrated.

Home economics. Revised edition. Quarrie Corporation. 1944. 14p. Planographed. 10c
Vocational monograph number 14.

Home economics. University of Wisconsin, Madison, Wis. No date. 8p. Free
Recruiting leaflet containing thirteen illustrations useful for bulletin board.

* Home economics as a career. Institute for Research. 1940. 20p. 75c
Qualifications, training, opportunities, salaries, advantages and disadvantages. Discussion of work in home making, teaching, extension work, food and nutrition, business, institutional management, research, social service, journalism, textile, clothing, and merchandising. Three photographs.

The home economics horoscope. American Home Economics Association, 620 Mills Bldg., Washington 6, D.C. 1944. 4p. 10c
Twelve women, representing twelve different types of careers in home economics, tell about their work.

* Home economics in business. Shade, Chloris, ed. 2nd edition revised. Morgan-Dillon & Co. 1939. 24p. 32c
Discussion of work in merchandising, research and testing, budgetary service, technical journalism, institutional management, commercial service, and commercial design. Qualifications, number of workers, training, and typical courses. Bibliography.

Home economics teaching as a career. American Home Economics Association, 620 Mills Bldg., Washington 6, D.C. 1945. 9p. 10c
Description of the work, qualifications, opportunities, and advantages. Illustrated.

The home economist—her day. Science Research Associates. 1944. 2p. 15c
Occupational reprint number 159. Four illustrations.

Home economists. Science Research Associates. 1943. 4p. Planographed. 15c
Occupational brief number 64. Two illustrations. Annotated bibliography.

**Preparation for the business field of home economics. American Home Economics Association, 620 Mills Bldg., Washington 6, D.C. 1942. 24p. 25c
Description of sixteen types of work in business home economics followed by general discussion of salaries, preparation, personal qualifications, and methods of securing employment.

HOME ECONOMICS EXPERT—*Continued*

Your career in home economics. American Home Economics Association, 620 Mills Bldg., Washington 6, D.C. No date. 4p. Single copies 10c; ten or more, 3c each

> Illustrated folder containing brief descriptions of ten types of work in home economics.

HORTICULTURIST   0-39.62

Description of the profession of horticulture. National Roster. 1945. 3p. Free

> See p. 34 for description of series.

**Handbook of descriptions of specialized fields in horticulture. National Roster. Supt. of Documents, Washington 25, D.C. 1945. 6p. 5c

> Occupational summary, related fields, functional activities, fields of specialization, educational qualifications, and related nonprofessional occupations.

Horticulture as a career. Revised edition. Institute for Research. 1946. 20p. 75c

> In press.

Horticulturist, agronomist and soil scientist. Prepared for the War Department by the National Roster. Supt. of Documents, Washington 25, D.C. 1945. 5c

> Occupational brief containing summary, earnings, outlook, qualifications, and training.

* Jobs in horticulture. Wernicke, Gilbert. Science Research Associates. 1944. 50p. 60c

> Includes an estimate of future openings in each of thirteen horticultural occupations, such as fruit grower, truck farmer, florist, nurseryman, landscape gardener, and research horticulturist. Twelve illustrations. Annotated bibliography.

HOSIERY INDUSTRY WORKER   4, 6, 8-27.

Postwar employment prospects for women in the hosiery industry. Bureau of Labor Statistics, U. S. Dept. of Labor. Supt. of Documents, Washington 25, D.C. 1945. 12p. 5c

> Occupational Outlook Division series. Presents employment prospects, working conditions, and requirements.

HOSPITAL LIBRARIAN. *See* Librarian

HOSPITAL MANAGER. *See* Manager, Institution

HOSTESS   2-25.30 through 2-25.39

* The hostess. Davis, Anne S., ed. Commonwealth Book Co. 1936 with 1939 supplement. 24p. Mimeographed. 75c

> Information presented according to the NVGA outline. See p. 26 for description of series. Discussion of work of the air, train, dining room, recreation car, hotel, and steamship hostess. Bibliography.

HOTEL AND RESTAURANT INDUSTRY WORKER
2-24. through 2-29.

At your service—the way of life in a hotel. Bemelmans, Ludwig.
Row, Peterson and Co. 1941. 64p. 96c
> Information about work is given as on a conducted tour. See p. 41
> for description of series. Forty-six illustrations. Bibliography.

Dining room management for the head hostess. Sinclair, Winifred
V. Revised edition. The Dahls, Haviland Road, Stamford, Conn.
1944. 64p. 35c
> A manual of instructions for beginners. Includes description of duties,
> qualifications, and responsibilities. Other manuals in this series are: Cafe-
> teria supervision, Business methods for executive housekeepers, Storeroom
> management and control for quantity cookery profits, The beverage service
> manual, Efficient maid in hotels and clubs, and Dishwashing standards and
> practices for quantity cookery kitchens.

* Hotel business. Huntington, Richard. Bellman Publishing Co.
1940. 24p. 50c
> Qualifications, duties, and brief description of sixty-six jobs. Chart
> shows salaries in thirteen positions in hotels of various sizes. List of in-
> stitutions offering instruction in hotel work. Bibliography.

The hotel industry. Davis, Anne S., ed. Commonwealth Book Co.
1936 with 1939 supplement. 30p. Mimeographed. 75c
> Information presented according to the NVGA outline. See p. 26
> for description of series. Includes names of schools offering four-year
> courses in hotel administration.

Hotel workers. Science Research Associates. 1945. 4p. Planographed. 15c
> Occupational brief number 111. Two illustrations. Annotated bibliog-
> raphy.

Job descriptions for hotels and restaurants. Division of Occupational Analysis. Supt. of Documents, Washington 25, D.C. 1938.
479p. 2 vols. $1 each
> See p. 58 for comment on National Job Descriptions. Describes occupa-
> tions in the hotel and restaurant industry, including jobs in formal dining
> rooms and cafes, cafeterias, office shops, tea rooms, dairy lunches, and auto-
> mats. Illustrated.

— * Jobs for G. I. Joe in America's hotels. American Hotel Association,
221 W. 57th St., New York 19, N.Y. 1944. 25p. Free
> Job descriptions, including physical activities, working conditions, and
> personal requirements, for twelve typical jobs in hotels: room clerk, assistant
> steward, second cook, engineer and assistant, meat butcher, pastry cook,
> wine steward, maintenance man, electrician, plumber, cashier, and assistant
> housekeeper. Illustrated.

HOTEL AND RESTAURANT MANAGER   0-71.
Hotel management as a career. Institute for Research. 1938. 16p.
75c
> Duties, qualifications, opportunities, advantages, disadvantages, and list
> of schools offering courses in hotel management. Describes work in hous-
> ing, accounting, food service, engineering and maintenance.

HOUSEHOLD WORKER. *See* Domestic service worker

HYGIENIST   0-26.19

— Educational qualifications of industrial hygienists. American Public Health Association. 1941. 3p. Free

  See also Dental hygienist

ICE CREAM INDUSTRY WORKER
4, 6, 8-06.00. through 8-06.299

Ice cream from farm to family. National Dairy Council, 111 No. Canal St., Chicago 6, Ill. 1943. 23p. Free

  Includes full-page pictures of workers in the receiving room, the laboratory, pasteurization, homogenization, freezing, flavoring, and packaging.

* Job opportunities for the veteran in the wholesale ice cream industry. International Association of Ice Cream Manufacturers, 1105 Barr Bldg., Washington 6, D.C. No date. 28p. Single copies free

  Contains a description of the various jobs in the ice cream industry.

ICHTHYOLOGIST   0-39.66

Description of the profession of zoology including fish and wildlife management. National Roster. 1945. 3p. Free

  See p. 34 for description of series.

INDUSTRIAL ARTIST. *See* Artist

INDUSTRIAL DESIGNER   0-46.88

* Industrial design. Shade, Chloris, ed. 2nd edition revised. Morgan-Dillon & Co. 1940. 24p. 32c

  Nature of work, qualifications, training, and conditions of work. Some information about related occupations such as city planning, store styling, and window display. Bibliography.

Industrial designing as a career. Institute for Research. 1940. 19p. 75c

  History and development of the work, duties, personal qualifications, training, opportunities, income, attractive and unattractive features. Also describes the work in a design studio. Illustrated.

Redesign for living. Mademoiselle, 122 E. 42nd St., New York 17, N.Y. 1945. 4p. 10c

  Reprint of article describing industrial design applied to home management. Bibliography.

INDUSTRIAL ENGINEER   0-18.01

Description of the profession of industrial engineering. National Roster. 1946. 3p. Free

  See p. 34 for description of series.

**Handbook of description of specialized fields in industrial engineering and business management. National Roster. 1945. 14p. 10c

Industrial design—a new career for you in postwar years. J. Gordon Lippincott and Company, 500 Fifth Ave., New York 18, N.Y. 1945. 4p. Free

  Qualifications, earnings, training, and opportunities. Four illustrations.

Industrial design as a profession. J. Gordon Lippincott and Company, 500 Fifth Ave., New York 18, N.Y. 1945. 4p. Free
> Description of the work, qualifications, and training. Three illustrations.

Industrial engineer. Prepared for the War Department by the National Roster. Supt. of Documents, Washington 25, D.C. 1945. 5c
> Occupational brief containing summary, earnings, outlook, qualifications, and training.

* Management engineering. Barnes, Nathaniel. Bellman Publishing Co. 1941. 12p. 50c
> Description of work, requirements, training, and opportunities. List of twenty-eight schools of engineering with accredited curricula in industrial engineering. Bibliography.

See also Engineer

INDUSTRIAL HYGIENIST. *See* Hygienist

INDUSTRIAL NURSE. *See* Nurse

INSTRUMENT MAKER   5, 7-08.; 5, 7-09.; 4-75.130
Aircraft instrument manufacture. The Chronicle. 1943. 6p. 5c
> Guidepost to occupational information number 44. Bibliography.

* Instrument makers. Schmid, Edward and Brand, Michael. Science Research Associates. 1943. 50p. 60c
> Divisions of the instrument industry, description of work, training, working conditions, wages, and future outlook. Twenty-six illustrations. Bibliography.

The manufacture of surgical and dental instruments and equipment. The Chronicle. 1943. 6p. 5c
> Guidepost to occupational information number 46. Bibliography.

Optical instrument and fire control instrument manufacture. The Chronicle. 1943. 6p. 5c
> Guidepost to occupational information number 45. Bibliography.

INSURANCE SALESMAN   1-57.10
About you women. Union Central Insurance Company, 3d and Vine St., Cincinnati 1, Ohio. No date. 13p. Free
> Calls attention to opportunities for women.

Career underwriting—a life work. Life Insurance Sales Research Bureau, 115 Broad St., Hartford 5, Conn. 1945. 63p. $1.50
> Discussion of the professional aspects of life underwriting, trends during period 1934-1944 of total number of agents compared to insurance in force, opportunities, financial possibilities, and advantages. Attractive two-color charts.

Careers in fire and casualty insurance. Institute for Research. 1941. 32p. 75c
> Duties, requirements for state license, opportunities, advantages and disadvantages. Describes work of general agent, survey agent, contract agent, insurance broker, underwriter, rate man, adjuster, and others in the large departmentalized agency.

INSURANCE SALESMAN—*Continued*

Careers in life insurance. Institute for Research. 1939. 29p. 75c

> Duties, responsibilities, requirements for state license, and lines of advancement for salesmen of ordinary, group, and industrial insurance. Description of home office work of actuary, secretary, underwriter, and advertising workers. Bibliography.

Connecticut Mutual career—a frank discussion of its advantages and disadvantages and the requirements for success. Connecticut Mutual Life Insurance Company, 140 Garden St., Hartford, Conn. 1934. 20p. Free

> Lists seven personal characteristics of the successful life insurance salesman. Although representing workers in only one company, the excellent table on earnings of salesmen over a ten-year period probably typifies the earnings of insurance salesmen in general.

Insurance. Revised edition. Quarrie Corporation. 1944. 9p. Planographed. 10c

> Vocational monograph number 15.

Insurance as a career. Hartford Accident and Indemnity Company, Hartford 15, Conn. 1945. 14p. Free

> Advantages of insurance selling.

* Insurance salesman. Revised edition. Occupational Index. 1945. 6p. 25c

> Occupational abstract. Nature of work, preparation, entrance, training, earnings, advancement, number and distribution of workers, advantages, disadvantages, and postwar prospects. Annotated bibliography.

Life insurance. Corcoran, J. P. Xavier University. 1938. 19p. Mimeographed. 50c

> Addressed to Negro youth, this pamphlet discusses qualifications, nature of work, salary, and opportunities for Negro life insurance workers.

Life insurance. Shade, Chloris, ed. 2nd edition revised. Morgan-Dillon & Co. 1940. 24p. 32c

> Duties of the life underwriter, training, qualifications, opportunities, and earnings. Classified bibliography.

The life insurance career. Union Central Life Insurance Company, 3d and Vine St., Cincinnati 1, Ohio. 1945. 22p. Free

> Discussion of advantages, earnings, and kind of work.

New careers coming—what chance has a man in the life insurance business? Howe, John. John Hancock Life Insurance Company, Boston, Mass. 1945. 8p. Free

Vocations for women—insurance. National Federation of Business and Professional Women's Clubs. 1941. 4p. 10c

> Includes photographs and brief biographical sketches of thirteen women insurance agents.

> *See also* Real estate salesman

INTERIOR DECORATOR   0-43.40

* If you are considering interior decoration. Stampe, Jean M. Rochester Institute of Technology. 1944. 22p. 10c

> In the form of an interview between an interior decorator and a high school student, information is presented about the field of work, qualifications, and opportunities. An interest inventory is included. Bibliography.

Interior decoration. Shade, Chloris, ed. 2nd edition revised. Morgan-Dillon & Co. 1939. 24p. 32c

> Duties, qualifications, training, and conditions of work. Some information about related occupations such as stage designer, industrial artist, and stylist. Bibliography.

* Interior decoration. Whiton, Sherrill. Bellman Publishing Co. 1941. 16p. 50c

> Qualifications, opportunities, and description of work of the interior designer, consultant decorator, corporation, civil service, department store, and retail furniture store decorators. List of forty-one schools offering courses in interior decoration.

Interior decoration and window display. Science Research Associates. 1943. 4p. Planographed. 15c

> Occupational brief number 59. Two illustrations. Annotated bibliography.

Interior decoration as a career. Institute for Research. 1936. 16p. 75c

> Temporarily out of print.

Interior decorator. Davis, Anne S., ed. Commonwealth Book Co. 1938. 23p. Mimeographed. 75c

> Information presented according to the NVGA outline. See p. 26 for description of series. Includes description of courses required in a two-year training course.

* Interior decorator. Revised edition. Occupational Index. 1944. 6p. 25c

> Occupational abstract. Duties, preparation, entrance, advancement, compensation, abilities essential to success, advantages, and disadvantages. Annotated bibliography.

IRON AND STEEL INDUSTRY WORKER
4, 6-81. through 4, 6, 8-94.

Iron and steel foundries. Labor market information for USES counseling—Industries Series. U. S. Dept. of Labor, Washington 25, D.C. 1945. 10p. Mimeographed. Free

> Statement of nature of work, requirements, working conditions, wages, and employment prospects. Includes patternmaking, molding, and coremaking. Chart shows distribution of workers by occupational groups. Bibliography.

* The iron and steel industry. Watson, Ralph H. Bellman Publishing Co. 1941. 28p. 75c

> Information about seventeen kinds of work and description of the subdivisions of the industry such as mining, quarrying, coke ovens, blast furnace, wrought iron processes, forges, and foundries. List of schools offering approved courses in metallurgy.

IRON AND STEEL INDUSTRY WORKER—*Continued*

Iron and steel workers. Science Research Associates. 1943. 4p. Planographed. 15c

> Occupational brief number 14. Two illustrations. Annotated bibliography.

The Loop course for college and university graduates. Bethlehem Steel Company, Bethlehem, Pa. 1941. 24p. Free

> Addressed to college undergraduates who are considering careers in the steel industry. Gives information about the entrance requirements for the Loop Course which gives to college graduates who have decided to make the steel industry their life work a sound basic knowledge of steel-making. Illustrated.

JEWELER DESIGNER   0-46.94

Jewelry designing and engraving. Davis, Anne S., ed. Commonwealth Book Co. 1936. 25p. Mimeographed. 75c

> Information presented according to the NVGA outline. See p. 26 for description of series. Includes work on hand-wrought and machine-made jewelry.

JOURNALIST   0-06.

Job opportunities in journalism. Science Research Associates. No date. 2p. Planographed. 15c

> Occupational reprint number 64. One illustration.

* Jobs in rural journalism. Watson, Elmo S. Science Research Associates. 1945. 50p. 60c

> Discussion of opportunities and rewards of "small town newspaper work." Includes table presenting average earnings of newspaper employees in nine types of work according to size of city. Nine illustrations. Annotated bibliography.

Journalism. Corcoran, J. P. Xavier University. 1937. 17p. Mimeographed. 50c

> Addressed to Negro youth, this pamphlet discusses qualifications, training, income, and the outlook for Negroes in journalism. Bibliography.

Journalism. Greenleaf, Walter J. U. S. Office of Education. Supt. of Documents, Washington 25, D.C. 1932. 6p. 5c

> Guidance leaflet number 8. Discussion of journalism, requirements, and training.

Journalism. Lake, Carroll. Bellman Publishing Co. 1940. 60p. Vari-typed. 75c

> Qualifications, opportunities, advantages, disadvantages, and description of fourteen types of positions in journalism. List of schools of journalism and description of professional courses. Bibliography.

* Journalism. Shade, Chloris, ed. 2nd edition revised. Morgan-Dillon and Co. 1939. 24p. 32c

> Information about workers engaged in managing, editing, and writing. Qualifications, training, and conditions of work. List of Class A and Class B schools of journalism. Classified bibliography.

* Journalism. Spiegler, Samuel. Revised edition. Occupational Index. 1945. 6p. 25c
> Occupational abstract. Duties, abilities, training, entrance, advancement, compensation, number and distribution of workers, advantages, and disadvantages. Annotated bibliography.

**Journalism as a career. Revised edition. Institute for Research. 1944. 23p. 75c
> Describes work of publisher, editorial staff, business department, and mechanical department. Includes information concerning rewrite man, copyreader, special writer, critic, correspondent, and columnist. Discusses qualifications, training, opportunities, salaries, attractive and unattractive features. Three illustrations. Bibliography.

— Journalism as a career. Lehigh University, Bethlehem, Pa. No date. 6p. Free
> Opportunities, preparation, personal qualifications, and professional attractions of journalism. Bibliography.

Journalism—writing for print. Revised edition. Quarrie Corporation. 1944. 14p. Planographed. 10c
> Vocational monograph number 16.

News workers. Keliher, Alice, ed. Hinds, Hayden and Eldredge, Inc. 1939. 56p. 80c
> See p. 28 for description of Picture Fact Books.

Nose for news—the way of life of a reporter. Arnold, Elliott. Row, Peterson and Co. 1941. 64p. 96c
> See p. 41 for description of series. Twenty-five illustrations.

Schools and departments of journalism offering majors in journalism. American Association of Schools and Departments of Journalism, Ohio State University, Columbus 10, Ohio. 1945. 4p. Mimeographed. Free
> List of thirty-four institutions of higher learning holding membership in the American Association of Schools and Departments of Journalism. A second list of thirty-three additional institutions giving journalism courses in sufficient numbers to permit a major in journalism.

See also Editor; Writer

KINDERGARTEN TEACHER   0-30.02
**Kindergarten work as a career. Institute for Research. 1940. 16p. 75c
> Development and present status of the kindergarten, a typical day's work, personal qualifications, preparation, opportunities, salaries, attractive and unattractive features. Brief information on nursery school work. Two illustrations.

LABOR RELATIONS WORKER. *See* Personnel manager

LABOR TRAINING MANAGER   0-39.87
Description of the profession of personnel administration. National Roster. 1945. 4p. Free
> See p. 34 for description of series.

LABORATORY TECHNICIAN 0-50.

Laboratory technicians. Science Research Associates. 1943. 4p. Planographed. 15c

Occupational brief number 63. Two illustrations. Annotated bibliography.

Motion picture laboratory technicians. Western Personnel Service. 1944. 11p. 25c

Describes the laboratory in production, the experience and background of laboratory technicians, earnings, and outlook. The suggested reading consists of technical manuals and methods of operation.

See also Medical technician

LABORATORY TECHNOLOGIST. *See* Laboratory technician

LABORER 8. or 9.

Unskilled laborers. Science Research Associates. 1943. 4p. Planographed. 15c

Occupational brief number 18. Two illustrations. Annotated bibliography.

LANDSCAPE ARCHITECT 0-03.20

Description of the profession of landscape architect. National Roster. 1945. 3p. Free

See p. 34 for description of series.

* Landscape architect. Revised edition. Occupational Index. 1944. 6p. 25c

Occupational abstract. Duties, abilities, preparation, compensation, number employed, advantages, disadvantages, and postwar prospects. Annotated bibliography.

Landscape architecture as a career. Institute for Research. 1938. 16p. 75c

Temporarily out of print.

See also Architect

LANDSCAPE ENGINEER 0-16.21

Description of profession of civil engineering. National Roster. 1945. 6p. Free

See p. 34 for description of series.

See also Engineer

LANDSCAPE GARDENER 3-40.06

* Landscape gardening. Shade, Chloris, ed. 2nd edition revised. Morgan-Dillon & Co. 1940. 24p. 32c

Duties, opportunities, qualifications, training, and conditions of work. Some information about related occupations such as tree surgery, horticulture, and city planning. List of twenty-seven schools offering instruction in landscape architecture, nine of which meet the requirements of the American Society of Landscape Architects. Bibliography.

Landscape gardening and tree surgery. Davis, Anne S., ed. Commonwealth Book Co. 1936 with 1939 supplement. 31p. Mimeographed. 75c

>Information presented according to the NVGA outline. See p. 26 for description of series. Includes list of universities offering courses for the degree of landscape architecture.

Landscapers, nurserymen. Science Research Associates. 1943. 4p. Planographed. 15c

>Occupational brief number 60. Two illustrations. Annotated bibliography.

LARYNGOLOGIST (THROAT SPECIALIST). *See* Physician

LAUNDRY INDUSTRY WORKER   5, 7, 9-57.

Cleaning and dyeing. Davis, Anne S., ed. Commonwealth Book Co. 1936. 17p. Mimeographed. 75c

>Information presented according to the NVGA outline. See p. 26 for description of series. Includes work of dyer, spotter, cleaner, tailor, and seamstress.

Cleaning and dyeing. Shade, Chloris, ed. 2nd edition revised. Morgan-Dillon & Co. 1940. 24p. 32c

>Nature of work, duties of worker such as the sorter and marker, inspector, spotter, the drycleaner, and presser. Number of workers, qualifications, and conditions of work. Bibliography.

Cleaning and dyeing workers. Science Research Associates. 1943. 4p. Planographed. 15c

>Occupational brief number 94. Two illustrations. Annotated bibliography.

Cleaning and pressing jobs. Science Research Associates. No date. 4p. Planographed. 15c

>Occupational reprint number 77.

The dry cleaning industry—careers. Institute for Research. 1936. 23p. 75c

>Description of jobs in the industry, qualifications, salaries, typical day's work, advantages, and disadvantages. Six illustrations.

Establishing and operating a dry cleaning business. U. S. Dept. of Commerce. Supt. of Documents, Washington 25, D.C. 1945

>Industrial series. Intended as a practical guide to experienced skilled persons who are considering starting their own business. In preparation.

Establishing and operating a laundry. U. S. Dept. of Commerce. Supt. of Documents, Washington 25, D.C. 1945

>Industrial series. Intended as a practical guide to experienced persons who are considering opening their own businesses. In preparation.

Job descriptions for the cleaning, dyeing, and pressing industry. Division of Occupational Analysis. Supt. of Documents, Washington 25, D.C. 1938. 374p. $1

>One of the series of National Job Descriptions. Describes occupations in establishments that clean, dye, and press garments, hats, and wearing apparel. Illustrated.

LAUNDRY INDUSTRY WORKER—*Continued*

Job descriptions for the laundry industry. Division of Occupational Analysis. Supt. of Documents, Washington 25, D.C. 1937. 291p. $1.25
One of the series of National Job Descriptions. Describes occupations in commercial laundries such as finished-work laundries, wet-wash laundries, and those existing in hotels and institutions. Illustrated.

* The laundry business. Davis, Anne S., ed. Revised edition. Commonwealth Book Co. 1938. 32p. Mimeographed. 75c
Information presented according to the NVGA outline. See p. 26 for description of series. Describes work of manager and production workers.

* Laundry industry. Shade, Chloris, ed. 2nd edition revised. Morgan-Dillon & Co. 1940. 24p. 32c
Classes of workers and their general qualifications, duties, training, and working conditions. Statistics about power laundries. Bibliography.

Laundry workers. Science Research Associates. 1943. 4p. Planographed. 15c
Occupational brief number 93. Two illustrations. Annotated bibliography.

Occupational possibilities in the power laundry industry. American Institute of Laundering, Joliet, Ill. 1944. 10p. Mimeographed. Free
Nature of the work, opportunities for men and women, qualifications and recommended preparation for each of eighteen job titles.

Vocations for women—laundries. Gove, Gladys F. National Federation of Business and Professional Women's Clubs. 1945. 4p. 15c
Discussion of work of director, personnel manager, sales manager, and public relations worker in laundries.

LAWYER   0-22.10

Description of profession of lawyer. National Roster. 1946. Free
In preparation. See p. 34 for description of series.

**Law. Gifford, James P. Bellman Publishing Co. 1945. 24p. 50c
Types of legal work, qualifications for the profession, training, and earnings. List of ninety schools of law. Bibliography.

Law. Greenleaf, Walter J. U. S. Office of Education. Supt. of Documents, Washington 25, D.C. 1932. 13p. 5c
Guidance leaflet number 5. Discussion of law as a career, requirements, and training.

Law. Quarrie Corporation. 1942. 11p. Planographed. 10c
Vocational monograph number 17.

* Law. Shade, Chloris, ed. Morgan-Dillon & Co. 1940. 24p. 32c
Duties of the general lawyer, the specialists, and the salaried lawyer. Some information about the judge, law teacher, and insurance adjuster. Qualifications, training, number and distribution of lawyers. Suggestions for the interested student. Classified bibliography.

Law. Union of American Hebrew Congregations, Cincinnati, Ohio. 1937. 43p. 25c
> Discussion of requirements, qualifications, and opportunities. The last half of the booklet is addressed to Jewish youth. Bibliography.

* Law as a career. Revised edition. Institute for Research. 1944. 16p. 75c
> Discussion of training, opportunities, income, advantages, disadvantages, and legal ethics. Includes description of specialized work of the trial, criminal, tax, real estate, and collection lawyer. One illustration.

Law schools and bar admission requirements in the United States; 1944 review of legal education. American Bar Association, 1140 No. Dearborn St., Chicago 10, Ill. 1945. 27p. Single copies free.
> Enrollment, tuition, and requirements of each of the hundred and ten law schools on the approved list of the American Bar Association; also information on the fifty law schools not on the approved list. Minimum educational and residence requirements for admission to legal practice are given for each of the states.

Lawyer. Prepared for the War Department by the National Roster. Supt. of Documents, Washington 25, D.C. 1945. 5c
> Occupational brief containing summary, earnings, outlook, qualifications, and training.

* Lawyer. Selina, Ruth. Revised edition. Occupational Index. 1945. 6p. 25c
> Occupational abstract. Nature of work, qualifications, preparation, entrance, advancement, earnings, number and distribution, advantages, and disadvantages. Annotated bibliography.

**Lawyers and the promotion of justice. Brown, Esther. Russell Sage Foundation, 130 E. 22nd St., New York 10, N.Y. 1938. 302p. $1
> Detailed discussion of law as a profession; education; examinations for admission to the bar; number of lawyers, compared with population, 1850 to 1930; income; and trends.

Look before you leap; finding your place in the legal profession. American Bar Association, 1140 No. Dearborn St., Chicago 10, Ill. 1945. 13p. Single copies free; 5c in quantity
> Description of specialized practices such as legal aid, law office management, judicial administration, and legal staff work in business.

* Patent law as a profession. Fenning, Karl. Bellman Publishing Co. 1945. 24p. 75c
> Duties, qualifications, preliminary education, training, and a description of work in the Government, in independent practice, in corporations, and in litigation.

— A report on pre-legal education. Vanderbilt, Arthur T. American Bar Association, 1140 No. Dearborn St., Chicago 10, Ill. 1945. 54p. Single copies free; 5c in quantity
> Analysis of the work of the lawyer and resume of methods of studying law form the introduction to the summary of recommendations of a hundred and eighteen leaders of the profession to the prospective law student. Advice is given concerning subjects that should be studied in college, the faculties that should be trained, and the interests that should be developed in preparation for the life of a lawyer.

LEATHER INDUSTRY WORKER   4, 6, 8-59. through 8-62.

Leather workers. Science Research Associates. 1943. 4p. Planographed. 15c
> Occupational brief number 84. Two illustrations. Annotated bibliog-
> raphy.

Postwar market, sales and industrial progress survey of the leather
industries. National Paper Box Manufacturers Association, Liberty Trust Bldg., Philadelphia 7, Pa. 1945. 24p. $2.50; $1 to
schools and libraries.
> One of a series of postwar industrial surveys, discussing employment,
> demand for products, and packaging problems.

The story of leather. Ohio Leather Company, 1052 No. State St.,
Girard, Ohio. 1935. 80p. Free
> A trip through a modern leather plant, thirty-three of the photographs
> showing various workers engaged in the production of leather.

LIBRARIAN   0-23.

A B C's for hospital librarians. Pomeroy, Elizabeth. American library Association, 520 No. Michigan Ave., Chicago 11, Ill. 1943.
19p. 25c
> Suggestions for conducting a hospital library as a therapeutic technique.
> Includes a description of the work and qualifications.

**Books and people; a career in library service. American Library
Association, 520 No. Michigan Ave., Chicago 11, Ill. 1945. 8p.
Single copies free; 25 copies 75c
> Brief statement of what library service offers, kinds of positions, salaries,
> and training. List of the thirty-four accredited library schools. Illustrated.

* Children's librarian. Beard, Sarah A. Revised edition. Occupational Index. 1943. 6p. 25c
> Occupational abstract. Entrance, advancement, earnings, preparation,
> advantages, disadvantages, and distribution of workers. Annotated bibliog-
> raphy.

Description of the profession of library science. National Roster.
1945. 2p. Free
> See p. 34 for description of series.

Librarian. Prepared for the War Department by the National
Roster. Supt. of Documents, Washington 25, D.C. 1945. 5c
> Occupational brief containing summary, earnings, outlook, qualifications,
> and training.

Librarians. Science Research Associates. 1945. 4p. Planographed.
15c
> Occupational brief number 115. Two illustrations. Annotated bibliog-
> raphy.

Librarianship. Corcoran, J. P. Xavier University. 1938. 16p. 50c
> Description of work, training, and opportunities for Negro librarians.
> Bibliography.

Librarianship. Greenleaf, Walter J. U. S. Office of Education.
Supt. of Documents, Washington 25, D.C. 1932. 9p. 5c
> Guidance leaflet number 9. Training, opportunities, and compensation.
> Bibliography.

Librarianship. Revised edition. Quarrie Corporation. 1944. 9p. Planographed. 10c
Vocational monograph number 18.

Librarianship as a career. Institute for Research. 1941. 19p. 75c
Qualifications, opportunities, compensation, advantages, and disadvantages. Describes work of the chief librarian, order librarian, cataloger, reference, circulation, children's, county or regional, school, and special librarian. Five illustrations. Bibliography.

**Library work. Leonard, Ruth and Hazen, Margaret. Bellman Publishing Company. 1945. 24p. 50c
Qualifications, training, salaries, advantages, and disadvantages. Includes a list of accredited library schools and a description of basic courses. Bibliography.

Library workers. Keliher, Alice, ed. Hinds, Hayden and Eldredge, Inc. 1940. 56p. 80c
Contents: Libraries past and present, the public library and the community, the librarian at work, special libraries and library services, a house of treasures, behind the scenes in a large library, and becoming a librarian. See p. 28 for description of Picture Fact Books.

Passing the book. Science Research Associates. 1943. 4p. 15c
Occupational reprint number 149. One illustration.

Something special. Special Libraries Association, 31 E. Tenth St., New York 3, N.Y. 1945. 4p. Free
A leaflet intended to recruit special librarians into the profession. Describes duties and advantages. Gives a list of organizations that maintain special libraries and a list of firms that have installed special libraries within the past year.

Special librarianship as a career. Savord, Ruth. Institute of Women's Professional Relations, Connecticut College, New London, Conn. 1945. 16p. 15c
Qualifications, requirements, rewards, advantages, and disadvantages. Gives names of the twelve library schools offering courses in Special Library Service. Sponsored by the Special Libraries Association. Bibliography.

This might be you. Special Libraries Association, 31 E. Tenth St., New York 3, N.Y. 1945. 4p. Free
Describes the work of the librarian in the fields of aviation, chemistry, radio, and finance.

Training for hospital librarianship. Walter, Frank K. University of Minnesota Library, Minneapolis 14, Minn. 1938. 5p. 10c
A reprint from *The Library Journal* describing the first organized training course for hospital librarians.

**Training for library work—a statement for prospective librarians. Board of Education for Librarianship, American Library Association, 520 No. Michigan Ave., Chicago 11, Ill. 1945. 5p. Mimeographed. Single copies free
Brief discussion of opportunities in library service, necessary education, and special fields of library service.

LIBRARIAN—*Continued*

Treasure shelves—the way of life in a library. Fargo, Lucile F. Row, Peterson and Co. 1941. 64p. 96c
> See p. 41 for description of series. Follows the members of the library staff as they go about their work. Thirty-eight illustrations.

Why not look into library work? New York Library Association, Public Library, Brooklyn, N.Y. No date. 6p. Free
> Description of work, advantages, and need for trained librarians. List of six library schools in New York State. Bibliography.

See also Medical record librarian

LINGUIST   0-68.39

Description of the professional occupations in foreign languages. National Roster. 1945. 2p. Free
> See p. 34 for description of series.

Foreign language specialist. Prepared for the War Department by the National Roster. Supt. of Documents, Washington 25, D.C. 1945. 5c
> Occupational brief containing summary, earnings, outlook, qualifications, and training.

Globalingo—jobs in foreign service, intelligence, communications, rehabilitation, offer new incentives for mastery of languages. Mademoiselle, 122 E. 42nd St., New York 17, N.Y. 1944. 5p. 10c
> Includes some sample questions from an old Civil Service examination for the United States Foreign Service.

Occupational opportunities for students majoring in Spanish or Portuguese. Pan American Union, Washington, D.C. 1944. 2p. Free
> Brief mimeographed statement of positions for which mastery of a foreign language is a prime requisite (foreign language teaching, translating, and interpreting) and those in which such knowledge is useful as an auxiliary tool.

**Vocational opportunities for foreign language students. The Modern Language Journal, 284 Hoyt St., Buffalo 13, N.Y. 1941. 34p. 25c
> Discussion of the six occupations in which a knowledge of foreign language is a primary requirement, the twelve occupations in which it is a distinct advantage, and the forty-two kinds of work in which foreign languages are an asset in achieving success.

LINOTYPE OPERATOR   4-44.110

Linotype operator. Revised edition. Occupational Index. 1944. 6p. 25c
> Occupational abstract. Duties, abilities, preparation, entrance and advancement, earnings, number and distribution of workers, advantages, disadvantages, and postwar prospects. Annotated bibliography.

LITHOGRAPHER   4-46.

**Lithographer. Davis, Anne S., ed. Commonwealth Book Co. 1938. 31p. Mimeographed. 75c
> Information presented according to the NVGA outline. See p. 26 for description of series. Includes description of work of the artist, stone engraver, proofer, grainer, plate maker, pressman, and binder.

LOCOMOTIVE MAINTENANCE MAN. *See* Railroad mechanic

LONGSHOREMAN   9-47.10

Longshoremen and stevedores. Science Research Associates. 1943.
4p. Planographed. 15c
> Occupational brief number 23. Two illustrations. Annotated bibliography.

LUMBER INDUSTRY WORKER   4, 6, 8-29. through 8-39.

Establishing and operating a small sawmill business. U. S. Dept. of
Commerce. Supt. of Documents, Washington 25, D.C. 1945
> Industrial series. Intended as a practical guide to experienced skilled persons who are considering starting their own business. In preparation.

Job descriptions for the lumber and lumber products industries.
Division of Occupational Analysis. Supt. of Documents, Washington 25, D.C. 1939. 347p. $1.25
> One of a series of National Job Descriptions. Describes general wood working occupations common to a number of industries, including the sawmill, planing mill, and excelsior industries. Illustrated.

Lumbermen. Science Research Associates. 1943. 4p. Planographed.
15c
> Occupational brief number 47. Two illustrations. Annotated bibliography.

Timber!—the way of life in the lumber camps. Stevens, James.
Row, Peterson and Co. 1942. 72p. 96c
> See p. 41 for description of series. Forty illustrations.

MACHINIST   4-75.

Job descriptions for job machine shops. Division of Occupational
Analysis. Supt. of Documents,Washington 25, D.C. 1938. 196p
75c
> One of a series of National Job Descriptions. Describes occupations in job machine shops fitted to undertake any job assigned to them. Does not include occupations found in machine shops operating on a production basis. Ninety-six illustrations.

Jobs in machine shops. Science Research Associates. 1938. 2p.
Planographed. 15c
> Occupational reprint number 79.

* Jobs in the machine shop. Bowman, Ernest. Revised edition. Science Research Associates. 1945. 50p. 60c
> Description of jobs, wages and hours, requirements, and opportunities. Information concerning training of apprentices. Thirty-one illustrations. Annotated bibliography.

* The machinist. Baltimore Department of Education. 1942. 7p.
Free
> Description of the various branches of work, qualifications, opportunities, and remuneration. Bibliography.

Machinist—a basic trade. Science Research Associates. No date.
2p. Planographed. 15c
> Occupational reprint number 10.

MACHINIST—*Continued*

Machinist apprenticeship standards. Apprentice-Training Service, U. S. Dept. of Labor, Washington 25, D.C. 1943. 18p. Free
> Standards adopted by representative employers and International Association of Machinists. Includes an illustration of the various work processes and an example of an apprenticeship agreement.

Machinists. Science Research Associates. 1943. 4p. Planographed. 15c
> Occupational brief number 40. Two illustrations. Annotated bibliography.

Machinists at work. Keliher, Alice, ed. Hinds, Hayden and Eldredge, Inc. 56p. 80c
> See p. 28 for description of Picture Fact Books.

Operatives. Science Research Associates. 1943. 4p. Planographed. 15c
> Occupational brief number 19. Two illustrations. Annotated bibliography.

There's work to be done. Allis-Chalmers Manufacturing Co., Milwaukee 1, Wis. 1941. 22p. Free
> Describes the apprentice training program of twelve trades. The four-year apprentice courses are offered for blacksmith, brass molder, electrical mechanic, iron molder, machinist, pattern maker, plate worker, sheet metal worker, toolmaker, and woodworker. Three-year courses are offered for mechanical drafting and welding. Twenty illustrations.

Training courses at Caterpillar Tractor Company. The Company, Peoria 8, Ill. 1945. 28p. Free
> The description of work, eligibility, terms of agreement, trial period, shop and classroom schedules are given for apprentice courses for machinist, pattern-maker, and foundryman. Profusely illustrated.

See also Airplane mechanic; Automobile mechanic

MAIL CARRIER   1-28.

An appraisal and abstract of available literature on the occupation of the letter carrier. Corre, Mary. Occupational Index. 1936. 8p. 25c
> Qualifications of city carrier, rural carrier, and substitute carrier. Number employed, rewards, advantages, and disadvantages. Annotated bibliography of twenty-four references.

Sky mail clerk. Science Research Associates. 1941. 2p. 15c
> Occupational Reprints number 121. Two illustrations.

MAIL CLERK. *See* Civil Service worker

MAINTENANCE ENGINEER. *See* Building superintendent

MAINTENANCE MAN   5-83.611

Building maintenance workers. Science Research Associates. 1943. 4p. Planographed. 15c
> Occupational brief number 57. Two illustrations. Annotated bibliography.

Job descriptions for industrial service and maintenance occupations. Division of Occupational Analysis. Supt. of Documents, Washington 25, D.C. 1939. 265p. $1.50
    One of a series of National Job Descriptions. Describes occupations concerned with the operation of equipment such as elevators, cranes, and heating and ventilating equipment, and occupations concerned with lubricating, cleaning, adjusting, and minor repair of the premises and mechanical equipment of industrial plants.

MANAGEMENT ENGINEER. *See* Industrial engineer

MANAGER, CATERING   **0-71.15**
If you are considering food administration. Hoke, Georgie C. Rochester Institute of Technology. 1944. 23p. 10c
    Discussion of the various duties of the food manager and the hospital dietitian. Qualifications, training, advantages, and difficulties of the food administrator.

MANAGER, INSTITUTION   **0-99.84**
Hospital management as a career. Institute for Research. 1940. 20p. 75c
    Duties, typical day's work, qualifications, training, opportunities, and salaries. Kinds and number of workers, and their salaries are given for small and large hospitals in general administration, nursing department, dietary, housekeeping, and mechanical departments, and accessory professional services.

Hospitiology. Hospital for Joint Diseases, 1919 Madison Ave., New York 35, N.Y. 1937. 7p. Free
    Describes the work of hospital service, hospital administration, and hospital planning.

MANAGER, RECREATION ESTABLISHMENT   **0-98.54**
Motion picture theatre operation as a career. Institute for Research. 1939. 24p. 75c
    Duties, qualifications, training, earnings, lines of promotion, advantages, and disadvantages. Duties of members of a motion picture theatre's staff such as projectionist, electrician, and cashier. Three illustrations.
Theatre. Davis, Anne S., ed. Commonwealth Book Co. 1938. 26p. Mimeographed. 75c
    Information presented according to the NVGA outline. See p. 26 for description of series. Discussion of vocations in legitimate stage theatres and moving picture theatres. Limited to occupations in the exhibiting field and does not describe positions of actor, producer, or distributor.

MANAGER, RETAIL APPAREL   **0-72.01**
Establishing and operating an apparel store. U. S. Dept. of Commerce. Supt. of Documents, Washington 25, D.C. 1945
    Industrial series. Intended as a practical guide to experienced persons considering opening their own shops. In preparation.

MANAGER, RETAIL AUTOMOTIVE SERVICE   **0-72.12**
Auto sales and service workers. Science Research Associates. 1943. 4p. Planographed. 15c
    Occupational brief number 67. Two illustrations. Annotated bibliography.

MANAGER, RETAIL AUTOMOBILE SERVICE—*Continued*

Garage management as a career. Institute for Research. 1935. 19p. 75c

> Information concerning work in a sales garage, repair garage, storage garage, service garage, and parking garage. Discussion of private garage and community garage management. Three illustrations.

MANAGER, RETAIL DRUG STORE   0-72.31

Are you going to be a druggist? Science Research Associates. No date. 2p. Planographed. 15c

> Occupational reprint number 62. Two illustrations.

* Drug store operation as a career. Institute for Research. 1940. 16p. 75c

> Description of work, a typical day, personal qualifications, opportunities, attractive and unattractive features. In addition to information concerning owning and operating a drug store, data are given about the work of the pharmacist and fountain manager. Bibliography.

MANAGER, RETAIL FLORAL   0-72.41

Careers in the floral industry. Institute for Research. 1935. 24p. 75c

> Temporarily out of print.

* The florist industry. Shade, Chloris, ed. 2nd edition revised. Morgan-Dillon & Co. 1939. 23p. 32c

> Description of work in production, wholesale and retail distribution. Qualifications, preparation, and conditions of work. Some information about related occupations such as floral artist, plant pathologist, and entomologist. Bibliography.

Nursery and flower growing. Davis, Anne S., ed. Commonwealth Book Co. 1936 with 1939 supplement. 26p. Mimeographed. 75c

> Information presented according to the NVGA outline. See p. 26 for description of series. Describes the work of retail growing and selling.

MANAGER, RETAIL FOOD   0-72.21

Establishing and operating a grocery store. U. S. Dept. of Commerce. Supt. of Documents, Washington 25, D.C. 1945

> Industrial series. Intended as a practical guide to experienced persons who are considering starting their own businesses. In preparation.

MANAGER, RETAIL GENERAL MERCHANDISE   0-72.51

Establishing and operating a variety and general merchandise store. U. S. Dept. of Commerce. Supt. of Documents, Washington 25, D.C. 1945

> Industrial series. Intended as a practical guide to experienced persons who are considering starting their own businesses. In preparation.

MANAGER, RETAIL HARDWARE   0-72.71

Establishing and operating a hardware store. U. S. Dept. of Commerce. Supt. of Documents, Washington 25, D.C. 1945

> Industrial series. Intended as a practical guide to experienced persons who are considering starting their own businesses. In preparation.

MANUFACTURER   **4, 6, 8-01. through 9-18.**
* Manufacturing as a career. Institute for Research. 1941. 24p. 75c
  Historical background, opportunities, salaries, attractive and unattractive features. Discussion of twenty-four department workers such as planning manager, foreman, shop manager, purchasing agent, and shipping
  manager. Four illustrations.

Opportunities for employment. Proctor & Gamble Co., Cincinnati 1,
Ohio. 1945. 30p. Free
  Describes the fields of work in the major departments and the types
  of positions which the new employee may anticipate. Organization charts
  show the relationships between the various groups in these departments:
  manufacturing (factory, chemical, engineering, and industrial relations),
  sales, advertising and promotion, finance, and buying. Twenty-nine illustrations.

MARINE   **2-68.30**
A career in the United States Marine Corps. Institute for Research. 1943. 21p. 75c
  History of the Marine Corps, qualifications, training, and description
  of service schools. Salaries and retirement pay of officers and enlisted
  men. Eight illustrations. Bibliography.

Jobs in the Marines and Coast Guard. Science Research Associates.
1943. 4p. 15c
  Occupational brief number 5. Three illustrations. Annotated bibliography.

MARINE ARCHITECT   **0-03.30**
Description of the profession of naval architect. National Roster.
1945. 3p. Free
  See p. 34 for description of series.

The marine engineer and the naval architect. Science Research Associates. No date. 2p. Planographed. 15c
  Occupational reprint number 67.

MARINE ENGINEER   **0-19.01**
Description of the profession of marine engineering. National Ros-
ter. 1945. 2p. Free
  See p. 34 for description of series.
  See also Engineer

MARKET GARDENER. *See* Truck farmer

MASON   **5, 7-24.**
Brick and stone masons. Science Research Associates. 1943. 4p.
Planographed. 15c
  Occupational brief number 55. Two illustrations. Annotated bibliog-
  raphy.
  See also Bricklayer

MATHEMATICIAN   **0-39.79**
Description of the profession of mathematics. National Roster.
1945. 2p. Free
  See p. 34 for description of series.

MATHEMATICIAN—*Continued*

Mathmagicians. Science Research Associates. 1943. 4p. 15c
Occupational reprint number 136. Two illustrations.

**Mathematics as a career. Lehigh University, Bethlehem, Pa. No date. 6p. Free
Opportunities, preparation, personal qualifications, and professional attractions of mathematics.

MEAT CUTTER 5-58.

Butcher. Spiegler, Samuel. Revised edition. Occupational Index. 1944. 6p. 25c
Occupational abstract. Duties, abilities, preparation, entrance and advancement, compensation, advantages, disadvantages, and postwar prospects. Annotated bibliography.

MEAT PACKING INDUSTRY WORKER 4, 6, 8-09.

Home-study courses in the meat packing business. Institute of Meat Packing, University of Chicago, Chicago 37, Ill. 1944. 9p. Free
The description of courses and topics covered give an idea of kinds of work. Some courses are entitled: meat packing science, by-products of the meat packing industry, beef operations, pork operations, and production and marketing of livestock.

The meat packing industry. Heckler, Edwin L. Bellman Publishing Co. 1944. 23p. 50c
Includes description of individual jobs and range of income.

Meat packing workers. Science Research Associates. 1945. 4p. 15c
Occupational brief number 119. Description of variety of jobs, wages and hours, advantages, disadvantages and future prospects. Two illustrations. Annotated bibliography.

MECHANIC AND REPAIRMAN 5, 7-79. through 9-83.

General and auto mechanics. Science Research Associates. 1943. 4p. Planographed. 15c
Occupational brief number 48. Two illustrations. Annotated bibliography.

Machine shop mechanics. Davis, Anne S., ed. Commonwealth Book Co. 1936 with 1939 supplement. 24p. Mimeographed. 75c
Information presented according to the NVGA outline. See p. 26 for description of series. Includes procedures in apprentice training.

* Machine shop mechanics. Shade, Chloris, ed. 2nd edition revised. Morgan-Dillon & Co. 1939. 24p. 32c
Description of work of machinist, tool maker, and die maker. Qualifications, training, apprenticeship requirements, and conditions of work. Bibliography.

See also Airplane mechanic; Automobile mechanic; Machinist; Railroad mechanic

MECHANICAL ENGINEER   0-19.01

Description of the profession of mechanical engineering. National
Roster. 1945. 7p. Free
See p. 34 for description of series.

Handbook of descriptions of specialized fields in mechanical engineering. National Roster. 1946
In preparation.

* If you are considering a career in the mechanical field. Martin,
Herman. Rochester Institute of Technology. 1944. 16p. 10c
Names major divisions of mechanical industries. Job charts are presented for machine designer, technical supervisor, instrument maker, power
plant supervisor, and production supervisor.

Mechanical engineer. Prepared for the War Department by the
National Roster. Supt. of Documents, Washington 25, D.C.
1945. 14p. 5c
Occupational brief containing summary, earnings, outlook, qualifications,
and training.

* Mechanical engineering. Cowdrey, I. H. Bellman Publishing Co.
1941. 20p. 50c
Qualifications, training, opportunities, and rewards. Distribution of
mechanical engineers in industry. Information about seventy-five schools
of mechanical engineering. Bibliography.

Mechanical engineering. Greenleaf, Walter J. U. S. Office of Education. Supt. of Documents, Washington 25, D.C. 1934. 11p. 5c
Guidance leaflet number 13. Branches of mechanical engineering, training, opportunities, and salaries. Bibliography.

Mechanical engineering. Quarrie Corporation. 1942. 11p. Planographed. 10c
Vocational monograph number 19.

Mechanical engineering as a career. Institute for Research. 1939.
20p. 75c
Temporarily out of print.

Mechanical engineers. Science Research Associates. 1943. 4p.
Planographed. 15c
Occupational brief number 28. Two illustrations. Annotated bibliog-
raphy.

The power engineer. Science Research Associates. No date. 2p.
Planographed. 15c
Occupational reprint number 38. One illustration.

See also Engineer

MEDICAL LABORATORY TECHNICIAN. *See* Medical tech-
nician

MEDICAL PATHOLOGIST. *See* Pathologist

MEDICAL RECORD LIBRARIAN 0-23.25

* A career as a medical records librarian. Institute for Research. 1943. 22p. 75c

> Duties, typical day's work, qualifications, number of workers, salaries, attractive and unattractive features. List of the ten schools approved by the American Association of Medical Record Librarians. Four illustrations.

Essentials of an acceptable school for medical record librarians and list of approved schools. Council on Medical Education and Hospitals of the American Medical Association, 535 No. Dearborn St., Chicago 10, Ill. 1945. 2p. Free

> Includes list of ten approved schools.

Hospital administration and medical record library science. Northwestern University, Lake Shore Drive, Chicago, Ill. 1945. 20p. Free

> College bulletin containing description of work and training of the medical records librarian who is responsible for the proper custody of the medical records of patients.

Medical record librarians. Westmoreland, M. G. American Association of Medical Record Librarians, 18 E. Division St., Chicago 10, Ill. 1944. 3p. Free

> Reprint from *Hygeia* presenting nature of work and requirements. Two illustrations.

**Medical record librarians. Women's Bureau. 1945. 9p. 10c

> Number 6 of the series "The outlook for women in occupations in the medical services." Duties, earnings, hours, and advancement. Prewar number and distribution of medical record librarians, wartime changes, and postwar outlook. List of the ten approved schools and requirements for entrance to an approved school for training and for registration by the Registry of the American Association of Medical Record Librarians. Two illustrations. Bibliography.

> *See also* Librarian

MEDICAL TECHNICIAN 0-50.01

Approved schools for clinical laboratory technicians. Council on Medical Education and Hospitals of the American Medical Association, 535 No. Dearborn St., Chicago 10, Ill. 1944. 4p. Free

> For each of the two hundred forty-seven approved schools there is given the following information: college affiliation, minimum prerequisite college training, length of training in months, maximum enrollment, tuition, and whether certificate, diploma, or degree may be earned.

Approved schools for clinical laboratory technicians. Registry of Medical Technologists, Ball Memorial Hospital, Muncie, Ind. 1945. 4p. Free

> Information about the schools approved for clinical laboratory technicians by the Council on Medical Education and Hospitals of the American Medical Association, arranged by states; also a statement of essentials of an acceptable school.

* Career as a laboratory technician. Institute for Research. 1939. 14p. 75c

> Importance of the laboratory to the physician, steps necessary to become a technician, typical day's work, qualifications, training, salaries, ad-

vantages and disadvantages. Minimum standards for training schools and minimum standards to secure a certificate of registration from the Board of Registry of the American Society of Clinical Pathologists. Bibliography.

The clinical laboratory technician. The Chronicle. No date. 6p. 5c
Guidepost to occupational information number 5. Bibliography.

Description of the occupation of medical laboratory technicians. National Roster. 1945. 3p. Free
See p. 34 for description of series.

— Educational and experience qualifications of public health laboratory workers. American Public Health Association, 1790 Broadway, New York 19, N.Y. 1943. 5p. Free
Includes qualifications for various kinds of laboratory workers: director, pathologist, bacteriologist, chemist, and parasitologist.

Laboratory technician. Davis, Anne S., ed. Revised edition. Commonwealth Book Co. 1938. 26p. Mimeographed. 75c
Information presented according to the NVGA outline. See p. 26 for description of series. List of schools for clinical laboratory technicians conforming to the standards adopted by the American Medical Association.

Medical laboratory technician. Prepared for the War Department by the National Roster. Supt. of Documents, Washington 25, D.C. 1945. 5c
Occupational brief containing summary, earnings, outlook, qualifications, and training.

**Medical laboratory technicians. Women's Bureau, U. S. Dept. of Labor. Supt. of Documents, Washington, D.C. 1944. 10p. 10c
Number four of series "The outlook for women in occupations in the medical services." Definitions, number and distribution of medical laboratory technicians, wartime changes, earnings, hours, advancement, opportunities, and postwar outlook. Minimum requirements for entrance and completion of training in a school for clinical laboratory technicians approved by the American Medical Association. Requirements for registration as a medical technologist and for beginning Federal Civil Service positions. Bibliography.

* Medical laboratory technologist. Boeshore, Elizabeth. Revised edition. Occupational Index. 1945. 6p. 25c
Occupational abstract. Duties, preparation, entrance, advancement, earnings, number and distribution of workers, advantages, and disadvantages. Also a list of desirable characteristics prepared by directors of twenty-five training schools for technicians. Bibliography.

Medical technology. Shade, Chloris, ed. 2nd edition revised. Morgan-Dillon & Co. 1940. 24p. 32c
Duties, qualifications, preparation necessary, earnings, and conditions of work. List of schools offering four-year courses. Information about related occupations and hints to prospective students. Bibliography.

— Medical technology, a profession for women. Registry of Medical Technologists of the American Society of Clinical Pathologists, Muncie, Ind. 1945. 8p. Free
Well-illustrated folder, suitable for bulletin board, describing work, qualifications, opportunities, and training.

MEDICAL TECHNICIAN—*Continued*

The registry of medical technologists of the American Society of Clinical Pathologists. The Registry, Muncie, Ind. 1945. 21p. Free

> Information about eligibility for registration, technical training requirements, examination of applicants, and brief suggestions for prospective students.

You're needed in a laboratory. Cunningham, R. M. Registry of Medical Technologists, Muncie, Ind. 1944. 4p. Free

> Reprint from *Coronet* presenting nature of work and requirements.

MERCHANT MARINE   0-88. and 5, 7, 9-48.

Careers in the United States merchant marine. Institute for Research. 1942. 20p. 75c

> History of the American merchant marine. Description of work of the ship's personnel such as chief steward, deck yeoman, and engine cadet. Types of training available and a discussion of attractive and unattractive sides. Seven illustrations. Bibliography.

How to get a job on a ship. Tyarks, Fredric E. Revised edition. Harian Publications, 270 Lafayette St., New York 12, N.Y. 1939. 62p. 50c

> Describes the types of work, requirements, training, and opportunities of work in the Merchant Marine, Coast Guard, Navy, Marines, and tour conducting. List of steamship lines.

Jobs in the Merchant Marine. Science Research Associates. 1943. 4p. 15c

> Occupational brief number 4. Two illustrations. Bibliography.

United States maritime service. U. S. Maritime Commission, Educational Section, Commerce Bldg., Washington 25, D.C. 1944. 65p. Free

> Includes discussion of training courses established by the U. S. Maritime Service, basic qualifications, digest of regulations prescribing qualifications for training courses and for appointment of officers. One hundred twenty-four illustrations.

METAL INDUSTRY WORKER   4-80. through 4, 6-95.

An appraisal and abstract of available literature on the occupation of the sheet metal worker. Spiegler, Samuel. Occupational Index. 1938. 8p. 25c

> Duties, apprenticeship requirements, compensation, advantages, and disadvantages. Annotated bibliography of twelve references.

Establishing and operating a metal working shop. U. S. Dept. of Commerce. Supt. of Documents, Washington 25, D.C. 1945. 202p. 35c

> Industrial series number 16. Intended as a practical guide for the experienced skilled worker who is considering opening his own shop. Includes information concerning requirements, qualifications, equipment, and safety considerations.

Nonferrous metal workers. Science Research Associates. 1943. 4p. Planographed. 15c

> Occupational brief number 87. Two illustrations. Annotated bibliography.

Sheet metal worker. Science Research Associates. 1943. 4p.
Planographed. 15c
    Occupational brief number 43. Two illustrations. Annotated bibliography.

METALLURGICAL ENGINEER. *See* Metallurgist

METALLURGIST   0-07.32; 0-20.01
* Careers and mineral industries. School of Mineral Industries,
Pennsylvania State College, State College, Pa. 1944. 25p. **Free**
    Development of the mineral industries, employment, and compensation.
Discussion of geology, mineralogy, geophysics, meteorology, geography,
mineral economics, mining, mineral preparation, fuel technology, metallurgy, and ceramics. Only one page devoted to specific school. Cover
page is a mineral geography map. Twenty-two photographs show people
at work in mineral industries.

Description of the professions of metallurgy and metallurgical engineering. National Roster. 1945. 5p. Free
    See p. 34 for description of series.

Fuel technology as a career (coal). Institute for Research. 1938.
20p. 75c
    Development of fuel technology. Qualifications, training, opportunities, salaries, attractive and unattractive sides. Typical day's work in a
control laboratory, research laboratory, and by-product coke plant. Three
illustrations.

Handbook of descriptions of specialized fields in metallurgy and
mining engineering. National Roster. 1946
    In preparation.

Metallurgical engineer. Prepared for the War Department by the
National Roster. Supt. of Documents, Washington, D.C. 1945.
5c
    Occupational brief containing summary, earnings, outlook, qualifications,
and training.

Metallurgical engineering as a career. Institute for Research. 1937.
21p. 75c
    Duties, requirements, training, opportunities, lines of promotion, and
salaries. A typical day in metallurgical operation in a routine laboratory
and in a research laboratory. Three illustrations.

** Metallurgy. Williams, Robert. Bellman Publishing Co. 1941. 12p.
50c
    Qualifications, training, opportunities, and duties of the physical metallurgist and the production or process metallurgist. List of schools offering
courses in metallurgy. Example of typical course of study. Bibliography.

Wanted, coal-mining engineers — qualifications and selection of
young men for the coal industry. Mitchell, David R. and Moore,
B. V. American Institute of Mining and Metallurgical Engineers,
29 W. 39th St., New York 18, N.Y. 1942. 22p. 25c. Single
copies free to vocational schools
    The announcement of scholarships offered by four coal-mining companies. Qualifications, personal characteristics and abilities desired in
selection of successful candidates.

    See also Engineer

METEOROLOGIST 0-39.51

Description of the profession of meteorology. National Roster. 1945. 3p. Free
> See p. 34 for description of series.

Handbook of descriptions of specialized fields in meteorology. National Roster. 1946
> In preparation.

Meteorologist. Prepared for the War Department by the National Roster. Supt. of Documents, Washington 25, D.C. 1945. 5c
> Occupational brief containing summary, earnings, outlook, qualifications, and training.

**Meteorology as a career. Institute for Research. 1938. 24p. 75c
> Positions and salaries in the weather bureau. Describes qualifications, training, opportunities, typical day's work, attractive and unattractive features. Also describes work of airways observer, clerk, airline meteorologist, and research-teaching meteorologist. Three illustrations.

Post-war opportunities in meteorology and allied fields. American Meteorological Society, 5727 University Ave., Chicago 37, Ill. 1945. 6p. Free
> Describes work and opportunities in air line and industrial meteorology and in the U. S. Weather Bureau. Brief discussion of instrument research, geophysical technology, hydrometeorology, and earth science teaching.

MILLINER 4-23.100

Millinery. Davis, Anne S., ed. Commonwealth Book Co. 1938. 28p. Mimeographed. 75c
> Information presented according to the NVGA outline. See p. 26 for description of series. Includes work of designers, cutters, blockers, operators of power-driven machines, and trimmers.

MINERAL INDUSTRY WORKER 5, 7, 9-20. through 9-22.

**Careers in the mineral industries. Read, Thomas T. American Institute of Mining and Metallurgical Engineers, 29 W. 39th St., New York 18, N.Y. 1941. 31p. 25c. Single copies free to vocational schools
> In question and answer form, information is given about various kinds of work, cost and nature of training, employment opportunities and rewards expected. Suggested reading list and a directory of the fifty-four mineral technology schools in the United States.

Coal miners. Science Research Associates. 1943. 4p. Planographed. 15c
> Occupational brief number 15. Two illustrations. Annotated bibliography.

Mining (coal and iron). Davis, Anne S., ed. Commonwealth Book Co. 1936 with 1939 supplement. 26p. Mimeographed. 75c
> Information presented according to the NVGA outline. See p. 26 for description of series. Includes a list of thirty-four mineral technology schools.

Mining (petroleum and metal). Davis, Anne S., ed. Commonwealth Book Co. 1936 with 1939 supplement. 30p. Mimeographed. 75c
> Information presented according to the NVGA outline. See p. 26
> for description of series. Includes a list of sixteen schools offering courses
> in petroleum mining, refining, and metal mining.

Salt of the earth. Science Research Associates. No date. 2p. Planographed. 15c
> Occupational reprint number 42. One illustration.

MINING ENGINEER   0-20.01
Description of the profession of mining engineering. National Roster. 1945. 5p. Free
> See p. 34 for description of series.

Mining engineer. Prepared for the War Department by the National Roster. Supt. of Documents, Washington 25, D.C. 1945.
5c
> Occupational brief containing summary, earnings, outlook, qualifications,
> and training.

* Mining engineering. Locke, Charles E. Bellman Publishing Co.
1945. 23p. 50c
> Qualifications, requirements, training, and opportunities in twenty-three
> fields of work. List of schools. Bibliography.

* Mining engineering as a career. Institute for Research. 1939. 30p.
75c
> Types of positions in production work, investigation work, research,
> teaching, and consulting or executive work. Salaries, qualifications, typical
> day's work, working conditions, and opportunities. Includes list of twenty-
> eight schools of mining engineering accredited by the Engineers' Council
> for Professional Development and a list of twelve accredited schools
> offering courses in petroleum engineering. Six illustrations.
> *See also* Engineer

MODEL   2-43.40 through 2-43.49
Distinctive courses in the technique and psychology of the manne-
quin's art. Barbizon Studio of Fashion Modeling, 576 Fifth Ave.,
New York 19, N.Y. No date. 20p. Free
> A recruiting bulletin which includes a description of the scope of
> photographic and fashion modeling, general requirements, and the training
> program.

Getting into modeling. Barbizon Studio of Fashion Modeling, 576
Fifth Ave., New York 19, N.Y. No date. 6p. Free
> Personal requirements, training program, and opportunities.

* Modeling. Conover, Harry. Bellman Publishing Co. 1941. 12p.
50c
> Characteristics a model must have, preparations for becoming a model,
> and description of work in photographic and life modeling. Bibliography.

MORTICIAN. *See* Undertaker

MOTION PICTURE INDUSTRY WORKER　　5, 7, 9-56.

* The motion picture industry. Ramsaye, Terry. Bellman Publishing Co. 1945. 24p. 75c
  > Includes duties of many workers such as set director, sound editor, casting director, film editor, and production designer. Bibliography.

Motion picture workers. Science Research Associates. 1945. 4p. 15c
  > Occupational brief number 120. Description of various types of work, requirements, salaries, opportunities, related fields, and the future outlook. Two illustrations. Annotated bibliography.

Movie workers. Keliher, Alice, ed. Hinds, Hayden and Eldredge, Inc. 1939. 56p. 80c
  > See p. 28 for description of Picture Fact Books.

The outlook for motion pictures. Science Research Associates. 1944. 2p. 15c
  > Occupational reprint number 179. Two illustrations.

Talking shadows—the way of life in Hollywood. Jester, Ralph. Row, Peterson and Co. 1942. 64p. 96c
  > See p. 41 for description of series. Thirty illustrations.

MOTION PICTURE THEATRE MANAGER. *See* Manager, Recreation Establishment

MOTOR TRANSPORTATION WORKER　5, 7-36. through 7-39.

Bus and trucking service. Shade, Chloris, ed. 2nd edition revised. Morgan-Dillon & Co. 1939. 24p. 32c
  > The first half of booklet describes work in bus operation office, service, dispatching, instruction, and bus maintenance. The second part describes work in truck operation office, traffic, maintenance, and receiving and shipping. Bibliography.

  See also Bus driver; Truck driver

MUSEUM WORKER　　　　　　　　　　　0-39.99

Before your eyes—the way of life in a museum. Barton, Donald. Row, Peterson and Co. 1941. 64p. 96c
  > Includes duties of workers in various departments of a museum. See p. 41 for description of series. Forty-one illustrations.

**Careers in museum work. Institute for Research. 1939. 32p. 75c
  > Nature of work, qualifications, and opportunities for work on administrative, curatorial, educational, custodial, and technical staffs. Also description of work of museum scientists such as anthropologist, archeologist, ethnologist, geologist, ornithologist, paleontologist, taxidermist, and zoologist. Three illustrations. Bibliography.

MUSIC TEACHER　　　　　　　　　　　0-24.31

Musician and music teacher. Prepared for the War Department by the National Roster. Supt. of Documents, Washington 25, D.C. 1945. 5c
  > Occupational brief containing summary, earnings, outlook, qualifications, and training.

* School music as a career. Institute for Research. 1939. 24p. 75c
   Qualifications, preparation, salaries, and typical state requirements for certification. Includes description of a typical day's work as a small and large city school supervisor. Four illustrations.

Vocations for women—music teaching. National Federation of Business and Professional Women's Clubs. 1941. 4p. 10c
   Reprint of article entitled "Music teaching changes its tune."

MUSICIAN   0-24.

**Are you interested in music as a vocation? Music Educators National Conference, 80 E. Jackson Blvd., Chicago 4, Ill. 1945. 12p. 15c
   Describes fields of opportunity, remuneration, working conditions, and musical qualifications. Gives the course of study for a typical four-year music education course for instrumental or supervisory work. Also presents some typical state certification requirements in music education. Bibliography.

How to be an opera singer. Science Research Associates. 1941. 2p. Planographed. 15c
   Occupational reprint number 102.

Music. Greenleaf, Walter J. U. S. Office of Education. Supt. of Documents, Washington 25, D.C. 1934. 15p. 5c
   Guidance leaflet number 17. Requirements, training, and opportunities. Bibliography.

* Music. Helm, Everett. Bellman Publishing Co. 1940. 43p. Varityped. 50c
   Description of work in radio, cinema, and recording, and as concert artist, orchestra player, conductor, organist, composer, music critic, teacher, and music librarian. Requirements, opportunities, a list of schools of music, and description of courses usually offered. Bibliography.

* Music. Revised edition. Occupational Index. 1941. 6p. 25c
   Occupational abstract. Describes work of the singer, instrumentalist, conductor, composer, music critic, musicologist, and teacher of music. Abilities, training, entrance, advancement, earnings, number and distribution of workers, advantages, and disadvantages. Annotated bibliography.

Music. Revised edition. Quarrie Corporation. 1944. 18p. Planographed. 10c
   Vocational monograph number 22.

**Music as a career. Institute for Research. 1939. 29p. 75c
   Qualifications, preparation, opportunities, advantages, and disadvantages. Information concerning work of the pianist, accompanist, vocalist, orchestra player, orchestra conductor, organist, composer, music critic, piano teacher, radio musician, musicologist, music therapist, and school music supervisor. Seven illustrations. Bibliography.

Music as a vocation. Corcoran, J. P. Xavier University. 1938. 20p. Mimeographed. 50c
   Discussion of the occupational opportunities for Negro youth in the various branches of music. Bibliography.

MUSICIAN—*Continued*

Musician and music teacher. Prepared for the War Department. by the National Roster. Supt. of Documents, Washington 25, D.C. 1945. 5c
Occupational brief containing summary, earnings, outlook, qualifications, and training.

Popular music as a career. Institute for Research. 1940. 30p. 75c
Types of positions, qualifications, training, typical day's work, salaries, favorable and unfavorable features. Seven illustrations.

Preparing for music careers. Science Research Associates. No date. 4p. Planographed. 15c
Occupational reprint number 26. Two illustrations.

Susan Brown: wants to make music her life career. Science Research Associates. 1945. 4p. 15c
Guidance reprint number 190. Two illustrations.

The unashamed accompanist. Moore, Gerald. Macmillan Company. 1945. 84p. $1.50
Encourages amateur pianists to take up accompanying for their careers and suggests preparation and qualifications. Most useful, however, as advice to the beginning accompanist.

NAVAL ARCHITECT. *See* Engineer

NAVAL SERVICEMAN. *See* Sailor

NEMATOLOGIST   0-39.72

Description of the profession of parasitology. National Roster. 1945. 2p. Free
See p. 34 for description of series.

NURSE   0-33.

Description of profession of registered nurse. National Roster. 1946. Free
In preparation. See p. 34 for description of series.

Desirable qualifications of nurses appointed to public health nursing positions in industry. American Public Health Association, 1790 Broadway, New York 19, N.Y. 1939. 2p. Free

Educational funds available for student nurses and graduate registered nurses. Nursing Information Bureau of the American Nurses' Association, 1790 Broadway, New York 19, N.Y. 1944. 11p. Single copies free
Information about specific scholarships, loans, and fellowship funds.

Employment opportunities in public health. American Public Health Association, 1790 Broadway, New York 19, N.Y. 1945. 30p.
Information about the nurse in industry and in public health work.

Jobs in military service for women. Science Research Associates. 1943. 4p. 15c
Occupational brief number 3. Includes some information about nurses in the Army and Navy medical departments.

The nurse in industry.   Science Research Associates. 1942. 2p. 15c
    Occupational reprint number 114.   One illustration.

The nurse in the industrial field.   National Organization for Public
    Health Nursing, 1790 Broadway, New York 19, N.Y.   No date.
    8p. Free
    Duties, preparation, qualifications, salaries, and methods of securing
    positions in industrial nursing.   Bibliography.

The nurse in the orthopedic field.   Joint Orthopedic Nursing Ad-
    visory Service, 1790 Broadway, New York 19, N.Y. 1944. 12p.
    Free
    Preparation, types of opportunities, and sources of scholarships and
    grants-in-aid.

Nurse (registered).   Prepared for the War Department by the Na-
    tional Roster.   Supt. of Documents, Washington 25, D.C.   1945.
    5c
    Occupational brief containing summary, earnings, outlook, qualifications,
    and training.

Nurses at work.   Keliher, Alice, ed.   Hinds, Hayden and Eldredge,
    Inc. 1939. 57p. 80c
    See p. 28 for description of Picture Fact Books.

Nursing.   Davis, Anne S., ed.   Commonwealth Book Co. 1938. 23p.
    Mimeographed. 75c
    Information presented according to the NVGA outline.   See p. 26
    for description of series.   Information about public health, private duty,
    and institutional nursing fields.

Nursing.   Greenleaf, Walter J.   U. S. Office of Education. Supt.
    of Documents, Washington 25, D.C. 1932. 12p. 5c
    Guidance leaflet number 15.   Qualifications, training, and compensation.

* Nursing.   Revised edition.   Occupational Index. 1945. 6p. 25c
    Occupational abstract.   Duties, qualifications, preparation, entrance, ad-
    vancement, compensation, number and distribution of nurses, advantages,
    and disadvantages.   Annotated bibliography.

Nursing.   Quarrie Corporation. 1938. 7p. Planographed. 10c
    Vocational monograph number 23.

Nursing.   Schulz, Cecilia.   Bellman Publishing Co. 1941. 20p. 50c
    Requirements, training, opportunities, and advantages.   Description of
    the kinds of nursing courses.   Bibliography.

Nursing.   Shade, Chloris, ed.   2nd edition revised.   Morgan-Dillon
    & Co. 1939. 24p. 32c
    Description of work in institutional nursing, private duty, public health,
    Red Cross, and Federal government nursing services.   Qualifications, train-
    ing, and conditions of work.   Classified bibliography.

**Nursing—a profession for college women.   Nursing Information
    Bureau of the American Nurses' Association, 1790 Broadway,
    New York 19, N.Y. 1945. 35p. 25c
    Presents opportunities in nursing, requirements, working conditions,
    cost of preparation and discusses programs offered by various types of
    nursing schools.   A chart listing positions within various salary ranges in
    major nursing fields is included.   Bibliography.

NURSE—*Continued*

**Nursing and how to prepare for it. Nursing Information Bureau of the American Nurses' Association, 1790 Broadway, New York 19, N.Y. 1945. 22p. Single copies free

> Written primarily for high school students, it gives general information about the nursing school program, admission requirements and criteria for choosing the right school.

Nursing as a career. Institute for Research. 1940. 24p. 75c

> Temporarily out of print.

Nursing—books, pamphlets, films. Nursing Information Bureau of the American Nurses' Association, 1790 Broadway, New York 19, N.Y. 1943. 6p. 5c

> Annotated bibliography of fiction, biography, and occupational literature. A good list to give the girl considering nursing as a career.

Opportunities for men nurses. Science Research Associates. No date. 2p. Planographed. 15c

> Occupational reprint number 50. One illustration.

Our veterans need more nurses. Science Research Associates. 1944. 4p. 15c

> Occupational reprint number 177. Five illustrations.

**Professional nurses. Women's Bureau, U. S. Dept. of Labor. Supt. of Documents, Washington 25, D.C. 1945. 61p. Mimeographed. 10c

> Number 3 of series "The outlook for women in occupations in the medical services." Describes major fields of nursing activity, earnings, hours, advancement, and opportunities. Includes prewar number and distribution, wartime changes, and postwar outlook in major fields and in certain specialties. Requirements for entrance to a state-accredited school of nursing, for graduation, for licensure as a registered nurse, for membership in the American Nurses' Association and for Civil Service positions in Federal agencies. Bibliography.

Professional nurses are needed. U. S. Office of Education and Division of Nurse Education, U. S. Public Health Service. Supt. of Documents, Washington 25, D.C. 1944. 30p. 10c

> Suggestions to counselors for cooperating in the recruiting of prospective student nurses. Includes examples of personality summary report, personal data blank, and educational experience summary. An occupational brief presents nature of work in private practice, public health, nursing education, and hospital and other institutional nursing. Discussion of state licensing, admission requirements to schools of nursing, and selection of a program. List of motion pictures, film strips, and pamphlet references.

Professional nurses at work. Nursing Information Bureau of the American Nurses' Association, 1790 Broadway, New York 19, N.Y. 1945. 4p. Single copies free; 100 copies $1

> A folder of twelve small pictures showing nurses active in various fields.

The registered professional nurse. The Chronicle. 1943. 6p. 5c

> Guidepost to occupational information number 57. Annotated bibliography.

The trained nurse. Corcoran, J. P. Xavier University. 1937. 14p. Mimeographed. 50c
> Addressed to Negro youth, this pamphlet discusses educational and personal qualifications, legal requirements in the various states, training, and opportunity for Negro nurses. Bibliography.

Trained nurse. Science Research Associates. 1943. 4p. Planographed. 15c
> Occupational brief number 37. Two illustrations. Annotated bibliography.

—What tuberculosis nursing offers you. National Tuberculosis Association, 1790 Broadway, New York 19, N.Y. 1945. 6p. Free
> Recruiting leaflet presenting opportunities.

See also Practical nurse; Public health nurse

NURSERY SCHOOL TEACHER   0-30.02
Vocations for women in nursery education. National Federation of Business and Professional Women's Clubs. 1942. 4p. 10c
> Nature of work, opportunities, advantages, and disadvantages. Four illustrations. Bibliography.

NURSERYMAN   3-38.20
* Nursery and flower growing. Davis, Anne S., ed. Commonwealth Book Co. 1936 with 1939 supplement. 26p. Mimeographed. 75c
> Information presented according to the NVGA outline. See p. 26 for description of series. Describes the work of retail growing and selling.

NUTRITIONAL CHEMIST   0-07.02
Description of the profession of nutrition research. National Roster. 1945. 3p. Free
> See p. 34 for description of series.

Educational qualifications of nutritionists in health agencies. American Public Health Association, 1790 Broadway, New York 19, N.Y. 1941. 4p. Free
> *See also* Dietician

OCEANOGRAPHER   0-39.53
Description of the profession of oceanography. National Roster. 1945. 1p. Free
> See p. 34 for description of series.

OCCUPATIONAL THERAPIST   0-32.04
American Occupational Therapy Association—activities of the Association. The Association, 33 W. 42nd St., New York 18, N.Y. 1945. 10p. Free
> Includes a list of the twenty-one schools approved by the Council on Medical Education and Hospitals of the American Medical Association.

Description of profession of occupational therapist. National Roster. 1946. Free
> In preparation. See p. 34 for description of series.

OCCUPATIONAL THERAPIST—*Continued*

Minimum standards for training in occupational therapy. American Occupational Therapy Association, 33 W. 42nd St., New York 18, N.Y. 1945. 3p. Mimeographed. Free

Prerequisites for admission, curriculum, and technical training.

**Occupational therapists. Women's Bureau, U. S. Dept. of Labor. Supt. of Documents, Washington 25, D.C. 1945. 15p. 10c

Number 2 of series "The outlook for women in occupations in the medical services." Describes duties, earnings, hours, advancement, and opportunities. Includes prewar number and distribution of occupational therapists, wartime changes, and postwar outlook. Requirements for entrance to a school for training, for completion of training, for registration, and for beginning Federal Civil Service positions in occupational therapy. Two illustrations. Bibliography.

* Occupational therapy. Greene, Marjorie; Lythgoe, Dorothea; and Fish, Marjorie. Bellman Publishing Co. 1941. 20p. 50c

Qualifications, requirements, opportunities, and description of work in the treatment media used in occupational therapy: creative arts and crafts, educational programs, recreational activities, and pre-vocational training. Bibliography.

* Occupational therapy. Hansen, Borghild. Revised edition. Occupational Index. 1944. 6p. 25c

Occupational abstract. Description of work, abilities, training, earnings, advantages, disadvantages, and postwar prospects. Annotated bibliography.

Occupational therapy. Milwaukee-Downer College, Milwaukee, Wis. 1942. 20p. Free

A college bulletin describing what is expected of an occupational therapist and the required courses.

* Occupational therapy as a career. Institute for Research. 1940. 22p. 75c

Types of institutions which employ occupational therapists, personal qualifications, duties, typical day's work, advantages, disadvantages, educational requirements and description of recommended courses. List of twenty-one accredited schools. Four illustrations. Bibliography.

Occupational therapy as a vocation. Science Research Associates. 1942. 4p. Planographed. 15c

Occupational reprint number 117. Three illustrations.

Therapists. Science Research Associates. 1943. 4p. Planographed. 15c

Occupational brief number 62. Two illustrations. Annotated bibliography.

OCEAN LINER WORKER   2-28.

Blue highway—the way of life on an ocean liner. Haddock, Laura B. Row, Peterson and Co. 1940. 64p. 96c

Glimpses of work on an ocean liner are included in the story of a girl's trip to Europe. See p. 41 for description of series. Forty-one illustrations.

OFFICE MACHINE OPERATOR 1-25.

* The occupation of the office machine operator. Revised edition. Occupational Index. 1941. 6p. 25c
  Occupational abstract. Abilities essential to success, preparation, advancement, number and distribution of workers, compensation, advantages, and disadvantages. Annotated bibliography.

Office machine operation. Davis, Anne S., ed. Revised edition. Commonwealth Book Co. 1939. 24p. Mimeographed. 75c
  Information presented according to the NVGA outline. See p. 26 for description of series. Includes requirements and opportunities in calculating, dictating, bookkeeping, duplicating, and tabulating machine operation.

Office machine operators. Science Research Associates. 1943. 4p. Planographed. 15c
  Occupational brief number 7. Three illustrations. Annotated bibliography.

* Office machines. Agnew, Peter. Bellman Publishing Co. 1941. 16p. 50c
  Discussion of twenty-one positions that involve the use of office machines. Qualifications of office workers, working conditions, and a list of modern business office equipment. Bibliography.

Office machines. Shade, Chloris, ed. 2nd edition revised. Morgan-Dillon & Co. 1939. 24p. 32c
  Duties of operators of eight office machines. Qualifications, training, conditions of work, and trends. Bibliography.

OFFICE MANAGER 0-97.12

Office management as a career. Revised edition. Institute for Research. 1945. 22p. 75c
  Scope of the work, duties, typical day's work, personal qualifications, training, opportunities, salaries, attractive and unattractive features. Also routes of promotion to office management. One illustration.

Vocations for women—office management. National Federation of Business and Professional Women's Clubs. 1940. 4p. 10c
  Includes a summary of inquiry sent to fifty women office managers. Two illustrations.

OIL INDUSTRY WORKER. *See* Petroleum industry worker

OPHTHALMOLOGIST (EYE SPECIALIST). *See* Physician

OPTOMETRIST 0-53.10

Optometric education; a statement for individuals in the armed forces. American Optometric Association, 707 Jenkins Bldg., Pittsburgh 22, Pa. 1945. 7p. Free
  Nature of work and educational requirements with special reference to the education of the returned veteran-optometrist.

Optometrist. Prepared for the War Department by the National Roster. Supt. of Documents, Washington 25, D.C. 1945. 5c
  Occupational brief containing summary, earnings, outlook, qualifications, and training.

OPTOMETRIST—*Continued*

Optometrists. Science Research Associates. 1945. 4p. Planographed. 15c
> Occupational brief number 114. Two illustrations. Annotated bibliog-
> raphy.

**Optometry. American Optometric Association, 518 Wilmac Bldg.,
Minneapolis, Minn. 1945. 21p. Free
> Development of the profession, educational requirements, names of
> the eight schools approved by the American Optometric Association,
> standard minimum curriculum, and distribution of optometrists in states,
> regions, and large cities. Bibliography.

Optometry. Bellman Publishing Co. 1946. 32p. 75c
> In press.

Optometry. Davis, Anne S., ed. Commonwealth Book Co. 1938.
20p. Mimeographed. 75c
> Information presented according to the NVGA outline. See p. 26
> for description of series. Includes the number of licensed optometrists
> in each state.

Optometry. Greenleaf, Walter J. U. S. Office of Education. Supt.
of Documents, Washington 25, D.C. 1934. 11p. 5c
> Guidance leaflet number 22. Development of optometry, requirements,
> and training. Bibliography.

Optometry as a career. Institute for Research. 1937. 12p. 75c
> History and development, typical day's work, personal qualifications,
> educational requirements, types of positions, salaries, and license require-
> ments. Illustrated.

**Planning your professional career—optometry. Public Health Bu-
reau, American Optometric Association, 707 Jenkins Bldg., Pittsburgh 22, Pa. 1943. 11p. Free

> Illustrated booklet describing nature of work, educational requirements,
> and the fields of specialization within this profession.

ORDNANCEMAN　　　　　　　　　　　4-52.481

Ordnance workers. Science Research Associates. 1943. Planographed. 4p. 15c
> Occupational brief number 12. Two illustrations. Annotated bib-
> liography.

ORNITHOLOGIST　　　　　　　　　　0-39.67

Description of the profession of zoology including fish and wildlife
management. National Roster. 1945. 3p. Free
> See p. 34 for description of series.

OSTEOPATH　　　　　　　　　　　0-39.96

Description of profession of osteopath. National Roster. 1946.
Free
> In preparation. See p. 34 for description of series.

**Osteopathy. Greenleaf, Walter J. Revised Edition. U. S. Office of Education. Supt. of Documents, Washington 25, D.C. 1945. 11p. 5c

Guidance leaflet number 23. Discussion of osteopathy as a career, training, education required, and compensation. A chart shows state requirements for licensure of osteopathic physicians. Information is given concerning the six approved colleges of osteopathy. Bibliography.

Osteopathy. Shade, Chloris, ed. 2nd edition revised. Morgan-Dillon & Co. 1942. 24p. 32c

Development of osteopathy, nature of work, qualifications, preparation, compensation, trends, and code of ethics. Requirements for licensure and number of workers licensed in each state. Bibliography.

Osteopathy. Thorburn, Thomas R. Bellman Publishing Co. 1942. 24p. 50c

Training, requirements for license, income, and number of osteopathic physicians in each of the states. Information about the six approved colleges. Bibliography.

Osteopathy as a career. Institute for Research. 1940. 12p. 75c

Temporarily out of print.

**Osteopathy as a profession. American Osteopathic Association, 139 No. Clark St., Chicago 2, Ill. 1945. 23p. 10c

Origin and basis of osteopathy: physical, mental, and educational qualifications; training and requirements for licensure; list of the six colleges approved by the American Osteopathic Association; gives the standard minimum curriculum of approved colleges offering training in osteopathy.

Preosteopathic and osteopathic college requirements and courses. American Osteopathic Association, 139 No. Clark St., Chicago 2, Ill. 1944. 16p. 10c

Academic requirements for entrance, including preparatory college subjects required and recommended by each of the six approved osteopathic colleges.

Women in osteopathy. Osteopathic Women's National Association, 139 No. Clark St., Chicago 2, Ill. 1942. 29p. 15c

Discussion of growth of the profession, prominence of women in it, preparatory education and training, personal qualifications, and earnings. Illustrated. Bibliography.

OTOLOGIST (EAR SPECIALIST). *See* Physician

PAINTER   5-27.

An appraisal and abstract of available literature on painting as an occupation. Meyer, Herbert and Allen, Lillian D. Occupational Index. 1936. 12p. 25c

Duties, abilities, rewards, number employed, advantages, disadvantages, and union requirements. Annotated bibliography of forty-four references.

Building a national painting and decorating apprenticeship system. Federal Committee on Apprenticeship, U. S. Dept. of Labor. Supt. of Documents, Washington 25, D.C. 1939. 15p. 10c

Includes qualifications for apprenticeship applicants, term of apprenticeship, work experience, related school instruction, and an example of an apprentice agreement.

PAINTER—*Continued*

Establishing and operating a painting and decorating contracting business. U. S. Dept. of Commerce. Supt. of Documents, Washington 25, D.C. 1945
Industrial series. Intended as a practical guide to experienced skilled persons who are considering starting their own businesses. In preparation.

Paint and varnish workers. Science Research Associates. 1943. 4p. Planographed. 15c
Occupational brief number 78. Two illustrations. Annotated bibliography.

The paint, varnish and lacquer industry. Trigg, Ernest. Bellman Publishing Co. 1945. 24p. 75c
Includes description of opportunities in the industry in manufacturing, distribution, and application.

* Painter. Davis, Anne S., ed. Commonwealth Book Co. 1938. 27p. Mimeographed. 75c
Information presented according to the NVGA outline. See p. 26 for description of series. Includes duties of interior painter, exterior painter, maintenance painter, and spray painter.

Painters. Science Research Associates. 1945. 4p. 15c
Occupational brief number 109. Two illustrations. Annotated bibliography.

PALEONTOLOGIST 0-39.46

Description of the profession of geology. National Roster. 1945. 3p. Free
See p. 34 for description of series.

PAPER INDUSTRY WORKER 4-41. through 4-42.

How paper is made. Whiting Paper Company, 14th St. and 7th Ave., New York 11, N.Y. 1943. 32p. Free
A brief sketch of the paper industry, including thirteen photographs of workers such as the paper technologist, calender man, and paper sorter.

Planning a career in the paper industry. Science Research Associates. 1941. 2p. Planographed. 15c
Occupational reprint number 101. One illustration.

Post war market, sales and industrial progress survey of the paper products, stationery and allied lines. National Paper Box Manufacturers Association, Liberty Trust Bldg., Philadelphia 7, Pa. 1945. 24p. $2.50; $1 to schools and libraries.
One of a series of postwar industrial surveys, discussing employment, demand for products, and packaging problems.

* The pulp and paper industry. Cornell, John. Bellman Publishing Co. 1941. 16p. 50c
Description of paper-making and pulping operations. Number and locations of paper mills. Remuneration, training, and list of technical schools. Bibliography.

Pulp and pulp workers. Science Research Associates. 1943. 4p. Planographed. 15c
Occupational brief number 80. Two illustrations. Annotated bibliography.

PARASITOLOGIST   0-39.71

Description of the profession of parasitology. National Roster.
1945. 2p. Free
See p. 34 for description of series.

Zoologist, entomologist, and parasitologist. Prepared for the War
Department by the National Roster. Supt. of Documents, Washington 25, D.C. 1945. 5c
Occupational brief containing summary, earnings, outlook, qualifications, and training.

PASSENGER AGENT   1-44.27

Airline passenger agents—their training and duties. Science Research Associates. 1943. 2p. 15c
Occupational reprints number 128. One illustration.

PATHOLOGIST   0-26.10

Description of the profession of medical pathology. National Roster. 1945. 2p. Free
See p. 34 for description of series.

Description of the profession of speech pathology. National Roster.
1945. 3p. Free
See p. 34 for description of series.

PATROLMAN. *See* Watchman

PATTERNMAKER   5-17.

Patternmaker. Revised edition. Occupational Index. 1944. 6p.
25c
Occupational abstract. Duties, abilities, preparation, entrance and advancement, advantages, and disadvantages. Annotated bibliography.

* Patternmaking. Shade, Chloris. 2nd edition revised. Morgan-Dillon & Co. 1940. 24p. 32c
Duties of the metal patternmaker and the wood patternmaker. Qualifications, training, and conditions of work. Bibliography.

PENOLOGIST   0-39.99

Stone and steel—the way of life in a penitentiary. Lawes, Lewis.
Row, Peterson and Co. 1941. 64p. 96c
Contains some information about the work of the warden and correspondence censor. See p. 41 for description of series. Forty-four illustrations.

Vocations for women—penology. National Federation of Business
and Professional Women's Clubs. 1940. 4p. 10c
Includes brief biographical sketches of women who work in penal institutions.

PERSONAL SERVICE WORKER   2-21. through 2-48.

Job descriptions for domestic service and personal service occupations. Division of Occupational Analysis. Supt. of Documents, Washington 25, D.C. 1939. 261p. $1
See p. 58 for comment on National Job Descriptions. Describes occupations found in barber shops, beauty parlors, garment alteration and repair

PERSONAL SERVICE WORKER—*Continued*

shops, public baths, shoe shining shops, textile weaving and mending shops, and undertaking establishments; includes jobs, such as hat checker, that occur in a large number of establishments and involve services to or for a person.

PERSONAL SHOPPER   1-97.20

Career as a personal shopper. Institute for Research. 1937. 19p. 75c

> Describes shopping services of department stores, magazines, and newspapers. Discusses duties, typical day's work, qualifications, training, opportunities, salaries, advantages and disadvantages.

PERSONNEL COUNSELOR. *See* Employment manager

PERSONNEL INTERVIEWER. *See* Employment interviewer

PERSONNEL MANAGER   0-39.83

* Careers in labor relations. Peterson, Florence. Science Research Associates. 1943. 50p. 60c

> Discussion of labor relations work with unions, industry, national and state boards, and private enterprise. Requirements and opportunities. Twenty-one illustrations. Bibliography.

Current policies in personnel relations in banks. Industrial Relations Section, Princeton University, Princeton, N.J. 1940. 50p. $1

> Discussion of employment policies, promotional plans, employee rating, educational plans, financial security, health services, and group relations work. Gives a picture of the nature of work in personnel relations and the conditions of work in a bank. Bibliography.

Description of the profession of personnel administration. National Roster. 1945. 4p. Free

> See p. 34 for description of series.

* The fields of personnel work. Darley, John and Berdie, Ralph. Science Research Associates. 1945. 50p. 60c

> Description of personnel work in industry, government service, school, and college. Qualifications, training, opportunities, and salaries. Ten illustrations. Annotated bibliography.

* Guidance and personnel services. Strang, Ruth and Hoppock, Robert. Revised edition. Occupational Index. 1945. 6p. 25c

> Occupational abstract. Brief description of personnel work in educational institutions, social agencies, industry, and government. Preparation, entrance, advancement, earnings, number and distribution of workers, advantages, and disadvantages. Annotated bibliography.

Handbook of descriptions of specialized fields in personnel administration. National Roster. 1946

> In preparation.

More efficient use of women in industry. Trigg, Frances. Tennessee State Board for Vocational Education, Nashville 3, Tenn. 1944. 83p. Mimeographed. 50c

> Problems and duties of the industrial counselor are included in this report of five training conferences.

Personnel management. Davis, Anne S., ed.   Revised edition.
Commonwealth Book Co.   1939.   21p.   Mimeographed.   75c
  Information presented according to the NVGA outline.   See p. 26 for
  description of series.   Includes industrial, educational, and government personnel work.

* Personnel work in commerce and industry as a career.   Institute
  for Research.   1939.   16p.   75c
    Duties, typical day's work, personal qualifications, training, salaries, fav-
    orable and unfavorable features.   Describes the activities of personnel di-
    rector, employment manager, supervisor of training, supervisor of apprentice-
    ship, vocational counselor, safety engineer, supervisor of research, super-
    visor of insurance and benefits, and supervisor of compensation.   One illus-
    tration.   Bibliography.

Personnel worker.   Prepared for the War Department by the National Roster.   Supt. of Documents, Washington 25, D.C.   1945.
5c
  Occupational brief containing summary, earnings, outlook, qualifications,
  and training.

Personnel workers.   Science Research Associates.   1943.   4p.   Planographed.   15c
  Occupational brief number 54.   Two illustrations.   Annotated bibliography.

Qualifications of an industrial training director.   Science Research
Associates.   1944.   4p.   15c
  Occupational reprint number 180.   One illustration.

Trouble shooters.   Mademoiselle, 122 E. 42nd St., New York 17,
N.Y.   1944.   5p.   10c
  Duties of employee counselor, qualifications, training, salaries, and out-
  look.

Vocations for women—careers on the labor front.   National Federation of Business and Professional Women's Clubs.   1942.   4p.
10c
  Brief discussion of work for labor organizations.   Four illustrations.   Bibliography.

Vocations for women—personnel work.   National Federation of
Business and Professional Women's Clubs.   1941.   4p.   10c
  Discussion of four divisions of personnel work: industrial, educational,
  governmental, and social service.   One illustration.   Bibliography.

PETROLEUM ENGINEER   0-20.11

Description of the professions of petroleum and natural gas engineering.   National Roster.   1945.   3p.   Free
  See p. 34 for description of series.

So, you want to be a petroleum engineer?   Science Research Associates.   No date.   4p.   15c
  Occupational reprint number 112.   One illustration.

  See also Engineer

PETROLEUM INDUSTRY WORKER   5, 7, 9-20. and 4, 6, 8-55.
Careers in the petroleum industry. Institute for Research. 1935.
16p. 75c
> Temporarily out of print.

* Petroleum. Shade, Chloris, ed. 2nd edition revised. Morgan-
Dillon & Co. 1940. 24p. 32c
> Description of work in producing, distributing, refining, and selling petro-
> leum. Classified bibliography.

* The petroleum industry. Clevenger, Keith. Bellman Publishing
Co. 1941. 28p. 50c
> Description of production of petroleum and exploration methods: geology,
> geophysics, soil analysis, and core drill. Information about twenty schools
> of petroleum engineering. Bibliography.

Petroleum production and refining. Labor market information for
USES counseling—Industry Series. U. S. Dept. of Labor.
Washington 25, D.C. 1945. 11p. Mimeographed. Free
> Statement including a description and location of the industry, nature of
> work in exploration, drilling, refining, and crude petroleum production, train-
> ing, qualifications, and employment prospects. Bibliography.

Roughneck—the way of life in the oil fields. Cumley, Russell.
Row, Peterson and Co. 1941. 64p. 96c
> See p. 41 for description of series. Thirty-six illustrations.

PHARMACIST   0-25.10
An appraisal and abstract of available literature on pharmacy as an
occupation. Noall, Irvin. Occupational Index. 1937. 8p. 25c
> Duties, preparation, rewards, number employed, advantages, and disad-
> vantages. Annotated bibliography of forty-three references.

Careers ahead in pharmacy. National Federation of Business and
Professional Women's Clubs, 1819 Broadway, New York 23, N.Y.
1945. 4p. 15c
> Describes the need for more pharmacists, the training, opportunities, earn-
> ings, and future outlook. Four illustrations. Bibliography.

Description of profession of pharmacists. National Roster. 1946.
Free
> In preparation. See p. 34 for description of series.

**New horizons—pharmacy. American Foundation for Pharma-
ceutical Education, 330 W. 42nd St., New York 18, N.Y. 1945.
21p. Free
> Description of work, opportunities, earnings, and requirements. List of
> the sixty-six colleges of pharmacy.

Pharmacist. Prepared for the War Department by the National
Roster. Supt. of Documents, Washington 25, D.C. 1945. 5c
> Occupational brief containing summary, earnings, outlook, qualifications,
> and training.

Pharmacists. Science Research Associates. 1945. 4p. 15c
> Occupational brief number 101. Two illustrations. Annotated bibliogra-
> phy.

Pharmacy. Corcoran, J. P. Xavier University. 1937. 20p. Mimeographed. 50c
> Addressed to Negro youth, this pamphlet discusses requirements, training, income, and opportunities for Negro youth.

**Pharmacy. Greenleaf, Walter J. Revised edition. U. S. Office of Education. Supt. of Documents, Washington 25, D.C. 1945. 20p. 5c
> Guidance leaflet number 14. Requirements, opportunities, and salary. Chart showing the minimum state requirements for the practice of pharmacy and license. Expenses, enrollments, and number of degrees awarded in each of the sixty-six schools of pharmacy.

* Pharmacy. Guth, Earl P. Bellman Publishing Co. 1945. 24p. 50c
> History of pharmacy, qualifications, training, and remuneration. Vocational opportunities for pharmacists, pharmacologists, pharmaceutical chemists, pharmacognosists, and teachers of pharmacy. Bibliography.

* Pharmacy. Shade, Chloris, ed. Morgan-Dillon & Co. 1940. 24p. 32c
> History and development of pharmacy. Qualifications, training, and duties of registered pharmacist, manager, proprietor, and research worker. Describes work in drug store, pharmacies, hospital dispensaries, and government service. Information about schools of pharmacy and minimum state requirements for the practice of pharmacy. Bibliography.

Pharmacy as a career. American Foundation for Pharmaceutical Education, 330 W. 42nd St., New York 18, N.Y. No date. 13p. Single copies free; 10c each in quantity
> Illustrated booklet describing the varied opportunities and the outlook in pharmacy.

Pharmacy as a career. Revised edition. Institute for Research. 1946. 16p. 75c
> In press.

* Your future in pharmacy. American Foundation for Pharmaceutical Education, 330 W. 42nd St., New York 18, N.Y. 1944. 16p. Free
> Presents opportunities of pharmacy. Two editions, one for civilian use and the other for veterans.

PHARMACOLOGIST   0-25.19
Description of the profession of pharmacology. National Roster. 1945. 2p. Free
> See p. 34 for description of series.

See also Pharmacist

PHOTOGRAPHER   0-56.
An appraisal and abstract of available literature on photography as an occupation. Sandell, Maynard. Occupational Index. 1937. 12p. 25c
> Information concerning the cameraman, darkroom technician, retoucher, head printer, printer, and finisher. Annotated bibliography of one hundred and three references.

PHOTOGRAPHER—*Continued*

Career in photography. Science Research Associates. 1943. 2p.
15c
Occupational reprint number 137.

**If you are considering photography. Neblette, C. B. Rochester
Institute of Technology. 1944. 31p. 10c
Describes twenty-eight specialities such as aerial photography, photo-
copying, photomicrography, spectrography, police photography, and X-ray
photography. Appropriate readings are given after each section.

* Motion picture photography. Western Personnel Service. 1944.
16p. 25c
Describes nature of work of the director of photography, the operative
cameraman, the still cameraman, and specialists in miniature and other
types of process photography. Includes special requirements, earnings,
opportunities, and promotional steps. Bibliography.

Photo retouching as a career. Science Research Associates. 1944.
2p. 15c
Occupational reprint number 172.

Photographers. Science Research Associates. 1943. 4p. Planographed. 15c
Occupational brief number 50. Two illustrations. Annotated bibliography.

Photography. Davis, Anne S., ed. Commonwealth Book Co. 1936.
26p. Mimeographed. 75c
Information presented according to the NVGA outline. See p. 26
for description of series. Includes a chart listing various branches of
photography. Bibliography.

* Photography. Shade, Chloris, ed. 2nd edition revised. Morgan-
Dillon & Co. 1939. 24p. 32c
Description of work in industrial, mechanical, news, architectural, life,
legal, amateur finishing, aerial, and applied photography. Duties of workers
on a studio staff. Qualifications, training, and conditions of work. List
of twenty schools of photography. Classified bibliography.

Photography as a career. Institute for Research. 1941. 20p. 75c
Branches of photography, types of positions, qualifications, earnings,
attractive and unattractive features. List of seven special schools of photography. Four illustrations.

**Photography as a vocation. Hecht, Andrew and Berkowitz, George.
Science Research Associates. 1941. 50p. 60c
Table of contents: Photography comes of age, The man behind the
lens, Jobs related to photography, Requirements for success. The photographer at work, Getting a job in photography, and A snapshot of the
future. Includes list of thirty jobs in Civil Service for which photographers may take examinations. Twenty-six illustrations. Bibliography.

Photography—profession, adjunct, recreation. Institute of Women's
Professional Relations, Connecticut College, New London, Conn.
1940. 135p. Mimeographed. 75c
Proceedings of a conference at which talks by specialists in various
phases of photography such as aerial photography, theatrical photography,
and cinemanalysis.

Portrait and commercial photography. Bellman Publishing Co. 1946. 24p. 75c
> In press.

* Record photography in industry. Cornwell, Wallace. Bellman Publishing Co. 1945. 23p. 75c
> Qualifications, training, opportunities, and description of work of the microfilm camera operator, record copying camera and contact printer operator.

Success in photography. Science Research Associates. No date. 2p. Planographed. 15c
> Occupational reprint number 30. One illustration.

PHYSICAL INSTRUCTOR   0-57.41

Description of profession of physical educator. National Roster. 1946. Free
> In preparation. See p. 34 for description of series.

Institutions giving professional training in health and physical education. American Association for Health, Physical Education, and Recreation. 1201 16th St., N.W., Washington 6, D.C. 1945. 8p. Mimeographed. Free
> Lists by states the colleges and universities offering a bachelor's degree with physical education as a major subject.

Opportunities for the preparation of teachers in health education. Kleinschmidt, Earl. U. S. Office of Education. Supt. of Documents, Washington 25, D.C. 1942. 117p. 20c
> Titles and description of courses in twenty representative teacher-education institutions.

Physical education. Corcoran, J. P. Xavier University. 1938. 21p. Mimeographed. 50c
> Addressed to Negro youth, this pamphlet discusses qualifications, training, salaries, and opportunities for Negroes. Bibliography.

Physical education. Davis, Anne S., ed. Commonwealth Book Co. 1938. 29p. Mimeographed. 75c
> Information presented according to the NVGA outline. See p. 26 for description of series. Deals with physical education and recreation work in school, community center, public recreation, social, religious, and industrial organizations.

* Physical education. Shade, Chloris, ed. 2nd edition revised. Morgan-Dillon & Co. 1940. 24p. 32c
> Information about the work of community recreation leader, industrial recreation leader, teacher, playground director, recreational leader of clubs and organizations, camp director, and therapeutic specialist. Qualifications, preparation, and compensation. Classified bibliography.

* Physical education as a career. Institute for Research. 1940. 16p. 75c
> Qualifications, training, opportunities, salaries, advantages, and disadvantages. Includes description of recent developments in recreational activities, private camps, and physical therapy.

PHYSICAL INSTRUCTOR—*Continued*

Physical educator. Prepared for the War Department by the National Roster. Supt. of Documents, Washington 25, D.C. 1945. 5c

Occupational brief containing summary, earnings, outlook, qualifications, and training.

PHYSICAL THERAPIST　　　　　　　　　　　0-52.22

Description of profession of physical therapist. National Roster. 1946. Free

In preparation. See p. 34 for description of series.

One thousand scholarships available now. National Foundation for Infantile Paralysis, 120 Broadway, New York 5, N.Y. 1945. 2p. Free

Brief statement of scholarships for the training of physical therapists.

**Physical therapists. Women's Bureau. Supt. of Documents, Washington 25, D.C. 1944. 14p. 10c

Number 1 of series "The outlook for women in occupations in the medical services." Definitions, number and distribution of physical therapists, wartime changes, earnings, hours, advancement, opportunities for women, and postwar outlook. Minimum requirements for entrance and completion of training in a school for physical therapists approved by the American Medical Association. Also requirements for registration and active membership in the American Physiotherapy Association and for beginning Federal Civil Service positions. List of approved schools. Two illustrations. Bibliography.

* Physical therapy. Rome, Florence. Revised edition. Occupational Index. 1945. 6p. 25c

Occupational abstract. Nature of work, abilities, preparation, entrance, advancement, number and distribution of workers, earnings, and postwar prospects. Bibliography.

**Physical therapy—a service and a career. American Physiotherapy Association, 1790 Broadway, New York 19, N.Y. 1944. 16p. Free

Description of the work, questions to determine one's interest in this profession, training requirements, and suggestions to the prospective student.

* Physical therapy as a career. Institute for Research. 1941. 18p. 75c

History and development of work, types of institutions which employ physical therapy technicians, duties and a typical day's work, personal qualifications, training and usual course of instruction, opportunities, salaries, attractive and unattractive features. Also requirements for membership in the American Physiotherapy Association. Four illustrations. Bibliography.

Physical therapy training schools approved by the Council on Medical Education and Hospitals of the American Medical Association. American Physiotherapy Association, 1790 Broadway, New York 19, N.Y. 1944. 6p. Free

Information on length of course, tuition and living costs, and prerequisite requirements for each of the twenty-four approved physical therapy training schools, and eight U. S. Army hospitals selected for training courses.

Therapists.   Science Research Associates.   1943.   4p.   Planographed.   15c
> Occupational brief number 62.   Two illustrations.   Annotated bibliog-
> raphy.

PHYSICIAN   0-26.10

Description of the profession of medical physiology.   National
Roster.   1945.   2p.   Free
> See p. 34 for description of series.

Description of profession of physician.   National Roster.   1946.   Free
> In preparation.   See p. 34 for description of series.

Doctor Jad—the way of life of a physician.   Robinson, Victor.
Row, Peterson and Co.   1941.   64p.   96c
> See p. 41 for description of series.   Chapter headings: medical stu-
> dent, the interne, first patients, a doctor's day, and at the clinic.   Thirty-one
> illustrations.

Doctors at work.   Keliher, Alice, ed.   Hinds, Hayden and Eldredge,
Inc.   1941.   56p.   80c
> Nature of work and preparation.   See p. 28 for description of Pic-
> ture Fact Books.

Educational qualifications of school physicians.   American Public
Health Association, 1790 Broadway, New York 19, N.Y.   1944.
8p.   Free
> General scope of the field, duties, and classification of school physicians
> are included.

Eye, ear, nose, and throat specialists—careers.   Institute for Research.   1941.   16p.   75c
> History, development, and present status of work, typical day's work,
> personal qualifications, educational requirements, special training and cer-
> tification, opportunities, attractive and unattractive features.   Require-
> ments for fellowship in the American College of Surgeons.   Two illus-
> trations.

* Medicine.   Blank, Helen.   Revised edition.   Occupational Index.
1945.   6p.   25c
> Occupational abstract.   Duties, abilities, preparation, compensation,
> number and distribution of physicians and surgeons, advantages, disad-
> vantages, and postwar prospects.   Annotated bibliography.

**Medicine.   Greenleaf, Walter J.   Revised edition.   U. S. Office of
Education.   Supt. of Documents, Washington 25, D.C.   1941.
24p.   5c
> Guidance leaflet number 6.   Requirements, opportunities, and training.
> Names and addresses of the sixteen examining boards in medical special-
> ties.   Information about the seventy-seven approved medical schools.   Lists
> of approved schools, length of training, and enrollment are given for re-
> lated occupations: clinical laboratory technician, physical therapy technician,
> and occupational therapist.   Bibliography.

Medicine.   O'Hara, Dwight.   Bellman Publishing Co.   1940.   28p.
Vari-typed.   50c
> Includes discussion of choice of college and medical school and the
> cost of medical education.   List of recognized medical schools.   Bibliog-
> raphy.

PHYSICIAN—*Continued*

Medicine Revised edition. Quarrie Corporation. 1943. 11p.
Planographed. 10c
Vocational monograph number 20.

* Medicine. Shade, Chloris, ed. 2nd edition revised. Morgan-Dillon
& Co. 1939. 24p. 32c
Description of work in general practice, public health work, surgery,
laboratory work, medical teaching and research, and employment in industrial and commercial organizations. Qualifications, training, and compensation. List of thirty-six specialized fields of medicine and a list of
approved medical colleges. Bibliography.

Medicine. Union of American Hebrew Congregations, Cincinnati,
Ohio. 1937. 46p. Mimeographed. 25c
Discussion of requirements, advantages, disadvantages, and opportuni-
ties. The last half of booklet is addressed to Jewish youth. Bibliography.

Medicine as a career. Institute for Research. 1940. 24p. 75c
Qualifications, training, advantages, disadvantages, and distribution of
physicians by states. Describes work of the general practitioner and of
many of the thirty-one specialists listed. Two illustrations. Bibliography.

The Negro physician. Corcoran, J. P. Xavier University. 1937.
20p. Mimeographed. 50c
Addressed to Negro youth, this pamphlet discusses requirements, training, problems in competition, and income. Includes questions to be
answered by one considering medicine as a vocation. Bibliography.

Physician. Prepared for the War Department by the National
Roster. Supt. of Documents, Washington 25, D.C. 1945. 5c
Occupational brief containing summary, earnings, outlook, qualifications,
and training.

* Physicians and medical care. Brown, Esther. Russell Sage Foundation, 130 E. 22nd St., New York 10, N.Y. 1937. 202p. 75c
Detailed discussion of training, number and distribution of physicians,
income, and trends. Eleven tables including number of physicians and
population per physician in the United States, 1850 to 1930.

Physicians and surgeons. Science Research Associates. 1943. 4p.
Planographed. 15c
Occupational brief number 36. Two illustrations. Annotated bibliog-
raphy.

**Postwar outlook for physicians. Bureau of Labor Statistics, U. S.
Dept. of Labor. Supt. of Documents, Washington 25, D.C. 1945.
10c
Occupational Outlook Division series. Presents employment prospects,
training, and working conditions.

Women doctors. Science Research Associates. No date. 2p. Planographed. 15c
Occupational reprint number 22. One illustration.

**Women physicians. Women's Bureau, U. S. Dept. of Labor. Supt.
of Documents, Washington 25, D.C. 1945. 28p. 10c
Number 7 of the series "The outlook for women in occupations in the
medical services." Duties, number of women physicians certified by each
of eleven specialty boards, earnings, hours, and advancement. Discussion

of the prewar situation, wartime changes, and postwar outlook. Requirements for entrance to an approved medical school and for earning the M.D. degree. Requirements for a beginning position as a physician in the Federal government, Army, Navy, and U. S. Public Health Service. Five illustrations. Bibliography.

PHYSICIAN'S ASSISTANT   1-32.20

**Physicians' and dentists' assistants. Women's Bureau, U. S. Dept. of Labor. Supt. of Documents, Washington 25, D.C. 1945. 10c
> Number 11 of the series "The outlook for women in occupations in the medical and other health services." Duties, number and distribution of workers, qualifications, and postwar outlook. Bibliography.

PHYSICIST   0-39.48

Careers in physics. American Institute of Physics, 57 E. 55th St., New York 22, N.Y. 1945. 7p. Mimeographed. Free
> Description of work, opportunities, compensation, personal qualifications, and training. Includes list of seven professional organizations.

Description of the profession of physics. National Roster. 1945. 6p. Free
> See p. 34 for description of series.

Handbook of descriptions of specialized fields in physics. National Roster. 1946
> In preparation.

List of colleges and universities offering graduate instruction in physics. American Institute of Physics, 57 E. 55th St., New York 22, N.Y. 1942. Mimeographed. 3p. Free
> Number of Master's and Ph.D. degrees conferred in each of a hundred and eighteen colleges and universities during period 1937-1942.

Physicist. Prepared for the War Department by the National Roster. Supt. of Documents, Washington 25, D.C. 1945. 5c
> Occupational brief containing summary, earnings, outlook, qualifications, and training.

PLANNING ENGINEER. *See* City planning engineer

PLANT PATHOLOGIST   0-39.37

Botanist, plant pathologist and plant physiologist. Prepared for the War Department by the National Roster. Supt. of Documents, Washington 25, D.C. 1945. 5c
> Occupational brief containing summary, earnings, outlook, qualifications, and training.

Description of the professions of plant pathology and plant physiology. National Roster. 1945. 2p. Free
> See p. 34 for description of series.

Handbook of descriptions of specialized fields in plant pathology. National Roster. Supt. of Documents, Washington 25, D.C. 1945. 7p. Mimeographed. 5c
> Occupational summary, related fields, functional activities, fields of specialization, and related occupations.

PLANT PHYSIOLOGIST 0-39.38

Botanist, plant pathologist and plant physiologist. Prepared for the War Department by the National Roster. Supt. of Documents, Washington 25, D.C. 1945. 5c

Occupational brief containing summary, earnings, outlook, qualifications, and training.

Description of the professions of plant pathology and plant physiology. National Roster. 1945. 2p. Free

See p. 34 for description of series.

PLASTERER 5-29.100

* Plasterer. Davis, Anne S., ed. Commonwealth Book Co. 1938. 22p. Mimeographed. 75c

Information presented according to the NVGA outline. See p. 26 for description of series. Includes duties of finish work plasterer, ornamental plasterer, and stucco plasterer.

Plasterer. Revised edition. Occupational Index. 1944. 6p. 25c

Occupational abstract. Duties, abilities, preparation, entrance, advancement, compensation, advantages, and disadvantges. Annotated bibliography.

Plasterers. Science Research Associates. 1945. 4p. 15c

Occupational brief number 105. Two illustrations. Annotated bibliography.

PLASTICS INDUSTRY WORKER 5, 7, 9-10.

Job trends in the plastics industry. Science Research Associates. 1940. 4p. Planographed. 15c

Occupational reprint number 59. Two illustrations.

Plastic workers. Science Research Associates. 1943. 4p. Planographed. 15c

Occupational brief number 79. Two illustrations. Annotated bibliography.

* Plastics. Alpert, Max. Revised edition. Occupational Index. 1944. 6p. 25c

Occupational abstract. Description of work in the major divisions in the plastics industry: chemical, engineering, mechanical, and design. Abilities, preparation, entrance, advancement, earnings, number and distribution of workers. Annotated bibliography.

— Plastics products. Labor market information for USES counseling —Industry Series. U. S. Dept. of Labor, Washington 25, D.C. 1945. 8p. Mimeographed. Free

Statement including nature of work in production, tool room, professional, and office jobs in the industry, requirements, working conditions, and employment prospects. Chart shows distribution of workers by occupational groups. Bibliography.

—* Your opportunity in plastics. Lougee, E. F. Plastics Industries Technical Institute, 122 E. 42nd St., New York 17, N.Y. 1944. 14p. Free

Opportunities, training, and trends. Description of the major divisions of the plastics industry: chemical, engineering, mechanical, and design.

PLAYWRIGHT. *See* Actor and actress

PLUMBER 5-30.
* Careers in plumbing and plumbing contracting. Institute for Research. 1941. 24p. 75c
    History and development, personal qualifications, opportunities, earnings, apprenticeship, union training, and training in the non-union field. Includes work of journeyman and plumbing contractor.

Establishing and operating a heating and plumbing business. U. S. Dept. of Commerce. Supt. of Documents, Washington 25, D.C. 1945
    Industrial series. Intended as a practical guide to experienced skilled persons who are considering starting their own businesses. In preparation.

The plumber. Baltimore Department of Education. 1942. 7p. 10c
    Opportunities, requirements, training, remuneration, advantages, and disadvantages. Bibliography.

Plumber. Davis, Anne S., ed. Commonwealth Book Co. 1938. 22p. Mimeographed. 75c
    Information presented according to the NVGA outline. See p. 26 for description of series. Includes requirements and duties of apprentices.

Plumbers and steamfitters. Science Research Associates. 1943. 4p. Planographed. 15c
    Occupational brief number 44. Two illustrations. Annotated bibliography.

* Plumbing. Shade, Chloris, ed. 2nd edition revised. Morgan-Dillon & Co. 1940. 24p. 32c
    Nature of work of the journeyman plumber and the master plumber. Qualifications, apprenticeship requirements, earnings, and employment possibilities. Bibliography.

Putting national plumbing apprenticeship standards to work. Federal Committee on Apprenticeship. Supt. of Documents, Washington 25, D.C. 1941. 15p. 10c
    A manual of procedure for establishing local joint plumbing apprenticeship standards. Includes term of apprenticeship, qualifications, apprentices' wages, and a standard agreement.

Related instruction for plumber apprentices. Hambrook, Robert. U. S. Office of Education. Supt. of Documents, Washington 25, D.C. 1939. 87p. 15c
    Intended as a guide to employers and apprenticeship officials, information is presented about plumbing instruction courses and apprenticeship standards.

What it takes to be a plumber. Clarke, James M. Occupational Index. 1936. 8p. 25c
    License requirements, opportunities, and duties of apprentice, journeyman, and master plumber.

POLICE OFFICER 2-66.01
* Law enforcement, a profession for peace. Western Personnel Service. 1945. 47p. 50c
    Descriptions are given of the duties of the municipal policeman, the county sheriff and his deputies, state policeman, federal agent, private policeman,

POLICE OFFICER—*Continued*

and policewoman. Two tables are included: one showing number of policemen in twenty-four representative Western cities, salaries and hours of work required; the other showing police department trends as to number of employees and salaries received.

Police. Science Research Associates. 1946. 4p. 15c
Occupational brief number 127. Duties, requirements, and earnings. Three illustrations. Bibliography.

Police and fire protection. Shade, Chloris, ed. 2nd edition revised. Morgan-Dillon & Co. 1939. 24p. 32c
The first part of the booklet gives information about the work of the policeman, qualifications, training, and conditions of work. The second part describes workers in fire protection. Bibliography.

Recruitment of policemen. Stone, Donald. International Association of Chiefs of Police, 1313 E. 60th St., Chicago, Ill. 1938. 28p. Mimeographed. 50c (Out of print)
Discussion of qualifications, examination of applicants, training, and promotion. Presents an example of job specification for patrolman, check list of medical standards for examination of candidates for patrolman, suggested rating form for oral interview, and a typical application form. Although out of print, it may be examined in many municipal libraries.

Riders in scarlet—the way of life of the Mounties. Montague, Sydney. Row, Peterson and Co. 1941. 64p. 96c
Work of a mounted policeman in Canada. See p. 41 for description of series. Twenty-six illustrations.

* Police officer. Revised edition. Occupational Index. 1945. 6p. 25c
Occupational abstract. Nature of work, qualifications, preparation, advancement, earnings, number and distribution of workers, advantages, disadvantages, and postwar prospects. Also qualifications for position of policewoman. Annotated bibliography.

— Techniques of law enforcement in the use of policewomen with special reference to social protection. National Advisory Police Committee on Social Protection of the Federal Security Agency, Washington 25, D.C. 1945. 95p. Free
Includes description of the qualities and qualifications which women should have if they wish to take up the career of police officer. The manual also outlines the duties, responsibilities, and opportunities for service in the field of social protection. Bibliography.

See also Fireman

POLITICAL SCIENTIST　　　　　　　　　0-39.10

Description of the profession of political science. National Roster. 1945. 4p. Free
See p. 34 for description of series.

POLITICIAN　　　　　　　　　0-83.

Politicians. Science Research Associates. 1945. 4p. 15c
Occupational brief number 106. One illustration. Annotated bibliography.

POST OFFICE CLERKS   1-27

* Postal service. Davis, Anne S., ed. Commonwealth Book Co. 1936. 22p. Mimeographed. 75c

> Information presented according to the NVGA outline. See p. 26 for description of series. Describes work of the postal clerk, letter carrier, railway mail clerk, sea post clerk, motor vehicle service worker, air mail service worker, post-office inspector, and postmaster.

Postal workers. Science Research Associates. 1943. 4p. Planographed. 15c

> Occupational brief number 100. Two illustrations. Annotated bibliography.

POULTRY FARMER   3-08.

Poultry raising. Davis, Anne S., ed. Commonwealth Book Co. 1936. 26p. Mimeographed. 75c

> Information presented according to the NVGA outline. See p. 26 for description of series. Concerned chiefly with chicken raising.

Poultrymen and fruit farmer. Science Research Associates. 1943. 4p. Planographed. 15c

> Occupational brief number 34. Two illustrations. Annotated bibliography.

POULTRY HUSBANDMAN   0-68.04

Animal, dairy and poultry scientist. Prepared for the War Department by the National Roster. Supt. of Documents, Washington 25, D.C. 1945. 5c

> Occupational brief containing summary, earnings, outlook, qualifications, and training.

Description of the professional fields in the animal, dairy and poultry sciences. National Roster. 1945. 4p. Free

> See p. 34 for description of series.

PRACTICAL NURSE   2-38.20

— **Become a trained practical nurse. National Association for Practical Nurse Education, 250 W. 57th St., New York 19, N.Y. 1945. 12p. Free

> Illustrated folder giving information about student activities and graduate duties, giving list of the thirteen schools accredited by the New York State Department of Education which prepare for a state license in practical nursing.

Earn and serve—be a practical nurse. National Association for Practical Nurse Education, 250 W. 57th St., New York 19, N.Y. 1945. 4p. Free

> Illustrated leaflet giving information in question and answer form and including names of schools approved by State Boards of Nurse Examiners for training of practical nurses or licensed attendants in states which have released their lists for publication.

The practical nurse. The Chronicle. 1943. 6p. 5c

> Guidepost to occupational information number 59. Bibliography.

PRACTICAL NURSE—*Continued*

Practical nurses. Science Research Associates. 1943. 4p. Planographed. 15c
> Occupational brief number 98. Two illustrations. Annotated bibliog-
> raphy.

**Practical nurses and hospital attendants. Women's Bureau, U. S.
Dept. of Labor. Supt. of Documents, Washington 25, D.C.
1945. 20p. 10c
> Duties, earnings, hours, advancement, and opportunities. Prewar num-
> ber and distribution of practical nurses and hospital attendants, wartime
> changes, and postwar outlook. Usual requirements for license, for en-
> trance Civil Service positions, and for entrance to a course for training.
> List of the fifty approved schools for training of licensed attendants or
> practical nurses. Four illustrations. Bibliography.

PRINTING AND PUBLISHING INDUSTRY WORKER
4-44. through 4-49.

Bookbinders. Science Research Associates. 1945. 4p. 15c
> Occupational brief number 110. Two illustrations. Annotated bibliog-
> raphy.

* Employment trends in the printing trades. Andrews, E. W. Revised edition. Science Research Associates. 1945. 50p. 60c
> History of printing, description of work, opportunities, and future out-
> look. Includes standards for apprentices. Ten illustrations. Annotated
> bibliography.

**If you are considering publishing and printing. Rochester Institute
of Technology. 1944. 19p. 10c
> List of jobs in this field with discussion of qualifications, methods of
> entrance, and lines of promotion.

* Is there a job for me in lithography? Joint Lithographic Advisory Council, 70 Pine St., New York 5, N.Y. 1945. 33p. Free
> Future of the industry, nature of the work, opportunities, qualifications,
> and policy of the Amalgamated Lithographers of America. Information
> concerning jobs such as that of photolithographer, photomechanical plate-
> maker, pressman, hand transfer platemaker, and press operator. Illustrated.

Opportunities for young men in the mechanical departments of daily
newspapers. American Newspaper Publishers Association, 370
Lexington Ave., New York 17, N.Y. 1945. 3p. Mimeographed.
Free
> Information is given in question and answer form about a career in the
> printing trades.

The printer. Baltimore Department of Education. 1943. 11p.
10c
> Description of the composing room workers and the pressroom occupa-
> tions. Qualifications, earnings, advantages, and disadvantages. Bibliog-
> raphy.

Printer. Davis, Anne S., ed. Commonwealth Book Co. 1938. 29p.
Mimeographed. 75c
> Information presented according to the NVGA outline. See p. 26
> for description of series. Emphasis given to setting of type by hand.

* Printing trades. Shade, Chloris, ed. 2nd edition revised. Morgan-Dillon & Co. 1940. 24p. 32c
  Information about the work of the compositor and the pressman. Qualifications, training, and apprenticeship requirements. Classified bibliography.

Publishing. Bellman Publishing Co. 1945. 24p. 75c
  In press.

Publishing as a career. Institute for Research. 1936. 20p. 75c
  Qualifications, training, salaries, advantages, and disadvantages. Describes work in a book publishing firm and a newspaper. Information concerning workers in the business management, correspondence, editorial, art, accounting, advertising, sales, manufacturing, and shipping departments.

PROBATION OFFICER 0-27.20

—Probation—what it is, how it works. National Probation Association, 1790 Broadway, New York 19, N.Y. 1945. 15p. Free
  Two pages are devoted to qualifications of the probation officer.

—Standards for selection of probation and parole officers. National Probation Association, 1790 Broadway, New York 19, N.Y. 1945. 11p. Free
  Duties, qualifications, requirements, and methods of selection.

PSYCHIATRIC SOCIAL WORKER 0-27.01

—All in the day's work of Miss Morton, psychiatric social worker. Woodcock, Mary Ellen. American Association of Psychiatric Social Workers, 1711 Fitzwater St., Philadelphia 46, Pa. 1943. 12p. Free
  A recruiting leaflet for professional social workers describing the work of the psychiatric social worker.

— Psychiatric social work. American Association of Psychiatric Social Workers, 1711 Fitzwater St., Philadelphia 46, Pa. 1943. 4p. Free
  Brief statement concerning nature of work, preparation, and opportunities. List of the ten accredited graduate schools of social work which offer professional training for psychiatric social work.

You may want to consider professional training in psychiatric social work. American Association of Psychiatric Social Workers, 1711 Fitzwater St., Philadelphia 46, Pa. 1945. 4p. Free
  Includes list of thirteen recognized schools.

PSYCHIATRIST 0-26.10

Psychiatrist. Prepared for the War Department by the National Roster. Supt. of Documents, Washington 25, D.C. 1945. 5c
  Occupational brief containing summary, earnings, outlook, qualifications, and training.

**Psychiatry as a career. Institute for Research. 1941. 23p. 75c
  Personal qualifications, educational requirements, advantages, disadvantages, typical day's work in private practice, institutional work, and government services. Some information about the related fields of psychologist, occupational therapist, psychiatric social worker, and supervisor of recreation. Requirements for internship and certificate of the American Board of Psychiatry and Neurology. Four illustrations. Bibliography.

PSYCHIATRIST—*Continued*
Vocations for women in psychiatry. McMahon, Lucile N. National
Federation of Business and Professional Women's Clubs. 1942.
4p. 10c
Nature of work, opportunities, and salaries.

PSYCHOLOGIST 0-39.17
Description of the profession of psychology. National Roster.
1945. 5p. Free
See p. 34 for description of series.

Psychologist. Prepared for the War Department by the National
Roster. Supt. of Documents, Washington 25, D.C. 1945. 14p. 5c
Occupational brief containing summary, earnings, outlook, qualifications,
and training.

Psychologists. Science Research Associates. 1945. 4p. 15c
Occupational brief number 104. Two illustrations. Annotated bibliography.

PUBLIC ACCOUNTANT 0-01.30
* Career as a public accountant (C. P. A.). Institute for Research.
1940. 24p. 75c
Development and growth of public accounting, duties, a typical day's work
in six types of positions, personal qualifications, training, salaries, opportunities, attractive and unattractive features, and requirements for C. P. A.
certificate and state license. Description of services such as auditing, system
installation, special investigation, tax reports, cost accounting, consultation
and interpretation. Bibliography.

The public accountant. Science Research Associates. No date.
4p. Planographed. 15c
Occupational reprint number 32. Two illustrations.

See also Accountant

PUBLIC ADMINISTRATOR. *See* Public Official

PUBLIC HEALTH NURSE 0-33.42
* Public health nursing. Revised edition. Occupational Index. 1944.
6p. 25c
Occupational abstract. Duties, qualifications, preparation, entrance, advancement, earnings, advantages, disadvantages, and postwar prospects. Annotated bibliography.

Recommended qualifications for public health nursing personnel,
1940-1945. American Public Health Association, 1790 Broadway, New York 19, N.Y. 1945. 5p. Free

Your career—will it be public health nursing? National Organization for Public Health Nursing, 1790 Broadway, New York 19,
N.Y. No date. 8p. Free
An illustrated recruiting leaflet including brief statements on qualifications,
training, and opportunities.

Your postwar job. National Organization for Public Health Nursing, 1790 Broadway, New York 19, N.Y. 1945. 6p. Free
> Addressed to the returning veteran nurse. Points out the opportunities and advantages of public health nursing.

PUBLIC HEALTH OFFICER   0-26.10
Careers in public health. Dould, Adrian. Science Research Associates. 1943. 50p. 60c
> Description of work in Federal, state, local, and voluntary health organizations. Conditions of work, qualifications, training, and future outlook. Twenty-five illustrations. Bibliography.

Educational qualifications of health officers. American Public Health Association, 1790 Broadway, New York 19, N.Y. 1939. 2p. Free

The educational qualifications of medical administrators of specialized health activities. American Public Health Association, 1790 Broadway, New York 19, N.Y. 1944. 6p. Free
> Brief statement of desirable graduate training and experience for specialized health activities in maternal and child health, tuberculosis, venereal disease, cancer control, mental hygiene, and industrial hygiene.

**Employment opportunities in public health. American Public Health Association, 1790 Broadway, New York 19, N.Y. 1945. 30p. Free
> Description of work and employment outlook for the health officer, sanitary engineer, sanitarian, public health dentist, school physician, public health laboratory worker, health educator, industrial hygienist, nutritionist, public health nurse, nurse in industry, and public health statistician. List of sixteen institutions offering graduate degrees in public health in fields other than public health nursing and public health engineering, list of thirty schools offering programs of study in public health nursing for graduate nurses approved by the National Organization for Public Health Nursing, and list of twenty-seven schools offering courses in sanitary engineering.

PUBLIC OFFICIAL
Handbook of descriptions of specialized fields in public administration. National Roster. 1946
> In preparation.

PUBLIC RELATIONS MAN   0-60.97
* Careers for women in public relations work. Institute for Research. 1944. 24p. 75c
> Describes work of a public relations director and a publicity assistant in a national trade association, hospital, public library, youth organization, farm cooperative, dental society, public utility, medical association, air line, and public relations agency. Includes qualifications, training, and salaries. Four illustrations. Bibliography.

Description of profession of public relations man. National Roster. 1946. Free
> In preparation. See p. 34 for description of series.

**Public relations. Bernays, Edward L. Bellman Publishing Co. 1945. 23p. 75c
> Historical development, duties, personal qualifications, scholastic training, opportunities, remuneration, and ethics of the profession.

PUBLIC RELATIONS MAN—*Continued*

Public relations workers. Science Research Associates. 1943. 4p. Planographed. 15c
> Occupational brief number 88. Two illustrations. Annotated bibliography.

Vocations for women—public relations. Fleischman, Doris. National Federation of Business and Professional Women's Clubs. 1941. 4p. 10c
> Qualifications, training, salaries. Bibliography.

PUBLIC UTILITY WORKER   5-51. to 5-54.

Public utility workers. Science Research Associates. 1945. 4p. 15c
> Occupational brief number 102. Two illustrations. Annotated bibliography.

PUBLISHER. *See* Editor; Printing and publishing industry worker

PULP INDUSTRY WORKER. *See* Paper industry worker

PURCHASING AGENT. *See* Buyer

RADIO AND TELEVISION INDUSTRY WORKER
                    0-61. and 4, 6, 8-98.

Blind date with Mike. Mademoiselle, 122 E. 42nd St., New York 17, N.Y. 1945. 4p. 10c
> Reprint of article describing work in radio auditions.

Careers in radio. Institute for Research. 1935. 16p. 75c
> Temporarily out of print.

* Occupations in radio. Bartlett, Kenneth G. and Miller, Douglass. Revised edition. Science Research Associates. 1945. 50p. 60c
> Describes work with radio network organizations, service organizations, and radio stations. Discusses qualifications and training for production work, radio writing, announcing, time selling, research, and school workshops. Thirteen illustrations. Annotated bibliography.

Opportunities in radio and electronics. Sarnoff, David. Radio Corporation of America, 30 Rockefeller Plaza, New York 20, N.Y. 1945. 28p. Free
> Includes list of possibilities in the radio-electronic field. Addressed to the returning veteran. Bibliography.

Radio. Quarrie Corporation. 1942. 13p. Planographed. 10c
> Vocational monograph number 25.

Radio and radar equipment. Labor market information for USES counseling—Industry Series. U. S. Dept. of Labor, Washington 25, D.C. 1945. 10p. Mimeographed. Free
> Statement including nature and location of the industry of the production of radio and radar equipment, except military. Training, requirements, earnings, employment by states and by type of work performed. Bibliography.

Radio and television. Davis, Anne S., ed. Commonwealth Book Co. 1936. 31p. Mimeographed. 75c
Information presented according to the NVGA outline. See p. 26 for description of series. Sales of radio sets from 1922 to 1938 reflect trend of occupation.

* Radio and television. Shade, Chloris, ed. 2nd edition revised. Morgan-Dillon & Co. 1940. 24p. 32c
Information about workers in technical positions: radio engineer, radio technician, radio serviceman, television engineers, and television technicians. Qualifications, preparation, opportunities, and trends. Classified bibliography.

Radio jobs. Science Research Associates. 1943. 4p. Planographed. 15c
Occupational brief number 24. Two illustrations. Annotated bibliography.

Radio manufacturing. Science Research Associates. No date. 2p. Planographed. 15c
Occupational reprint number 51. One illustration.

Radio workers. Keliher, Alice, ed. Hinds, Hayden and Eldredge, Inc. 56p. 80c
See p. 28 for description of Picture Fact Books.

— Working for radio. National Association of Broadcasters, 1760 N St., N.W., Washington 6, D.C. 1944. 23p. Free
Advice to young people who are considering careers in broadcasting. Contents: acting for radio, staging a radio show, radio play writing, singing for radio, writing for radio, radio announcing, musicians in radio, radio operators and technicians, selling radio advertising, working for smaller stations, and advertising agency work.

RADIO ENGINEER   0-17.02
Description of the profession of electrical engineering including radio and communications engineering. National Roster. 1945. 5p. Free
See p. 34 for description of series.

RADIO PROGRAM DIRECTOR   0-97.75
The program side of radio. Jennings, George. Bellman Publishing Co. 1941. 16p. 50c
Describes work performed by the program directors and staffs of the nine hundred twelve radio stations and the directors of radio programs in schools and colleges. Bibliography.

RADIO REPAIRMAN   5-83.411
* Radio service. Revised edition. Occupational Index. 1944. 6p. 25c
Occupational abstract. Duties, qualifications, preparation, entrance and advancement, compensation, number and distribution of workers, and postwar prospects. Annotated bibliography.

* A vocational guide in radio and electronics. Valparaiso Technical Institute, Valparaiso, Ind. 1944. 23p. Free
Discussion of the radio-electronic field, including opportunities, personality requirements, salaries, training, Federal licenses requirements, and a list of positions for trained technicians.

RADIO TECHNICIAN. *See* Radio repairman

RAILROAD MECHANIC AND REPAIRMAN
                                                5-79.00 to 5-79.29
Maintenance of railroad track and structures.   Santa Fe System
Lines, Railway Exchange, Chicago 4, Ill. 1943. 23p. Free
> Describes track construction, rail laying operations, track maintenance,
> and bridge and building work. Illustrated.

Wheels keep 'em rolling. Atchison, Topeka and Santa Fe Railway
Co., 80 East Jackson Blvd., Chicago 4, Ill. 1943. 25p. Free
> Includes description of the apprentice school and system for training
> mechanics in locomotive and equipment maintenance. Profusely illustrated.

RAILROAD STATION AGENT.   *See* Station agent

RAILROAD TRAINMAN   5-38.
Sunday punch. Brotherhood of Railroad Trainmen, 1370 Ontario
St., Cleveland 13, Ohio. 1945. 20p. Free
> Written primarily to describe the work of the organization, some in-
> formation is included about the work of men in train service.

RAILROAD TRANSPORTATION WORKER
                            0-98.7 and 5, 7, 9-38. through 9-44.
Local transportation workers. Science Research Associates. 1945.
4p. Planographed. 15c
> Occupational brief number 116. Two illustrations. Annotated bibliog-
> raphy.

The outlook for the railroad industry. Williams, Ernest W. National Planning Association, 800 21st St., N.W., Washington 6,
D.C. 1943. 23p. 25c
> Background information for the counselor concerning the place of the
> railroad in postwar transportation, technical possibilities, obstacles in the
> way of rapid adjustment, and the postwar prospect.

The railroad. Santa Fe System Lines, Railway Exchange, Chicago
4, Ill. 1943. 36p. Free
> History and development of railway transportation and its part in the
> unification and growth of our nation. Includes duties of locomotive engi-
> neer, conductor, brakeman, and signal supervisors. Illustrated.

* The railroad industry. Young, Bernard E. Bellman Publishing Co.
1941. 20p. 75c
> Kinds of employment, qualifications, training, and possibilities for ad-
> vancement. Number of employees and average compensation in each of
> seven groups in which railroad workers are classified. Bibliography.

Railroad workers. Keliher, Alice, ed. Hinds, Hayden and Eldredge,
Inc. 1941. 56p. 80c
> See p. 28 for description of Picture Fact Books.

Railroad workers. Science Research Associates. 1943. 4p. Planographed. 15c
> Occupational brief number 22. Two illustrations. Annotated bibliog-
> raphy.

Railroading (commercial). Davis, Anne S., ed. Commonwealth
Book Co. 1936 with 1939 supplement. 28p. Mimeographed. 75c
> Information presented according to the NVGA outline. See p. 26
> for description of series. Includes a chart listing the number of jobs in
> commercial railroading with the average weekly wage for each.

Railroading (mechanical). Davis, Anne S., ed. Commonwealth
Book Co. 1936 with 1939 supplement. 26p. Mimeographed. 75c
> Information presented according to the NVGA outline. See p. 26
> for description of series. Discussion of occupations in railroad shops, in
> the maintenance of roadways, and in train operation. Number of workers
> in each of fifty-nine jobs and the average weekly wage in 1929, 1933, and
> 1938.

RANGER. *See* Forest ranger; Forester

REAL ESTATE SALESMAN   1-63.10
Establishing and operating a real estate and insurance brokerage
business. U. S. Dept. of Commerce. Supt. of Documents, Washington 25, D.C. 1945
> Industrial series. Intended as a practical guide to experienced persons
> who are considering starting their own businesses. In preparation.

Real estate. Aplin, Lawrence. Revised edition. Occupational
Index. 1944. 6p. 25c
> Occupational abstract. License requirements, advancement, number of
> workers, and earnings. Annotated bibliography.

Real estate. Revised edition. Quarrie Corporation. 1944. 10p.
Planographed. 10c
> Vocational monograph number 26.

Real estate and insurance. Davis, Anne S., ed. Commonwealth
Book Co. 1938. 24p. Mimeographed. 75c
> Information presented according to the NVGA outline. See p. 26
> for description of series. Emphasizes the real estate occupation, discussing
> insurance only as it enters the activity of the real estate and insurance office.

* Real estate management as a career. Institute for Research. 1941.
23p. 75c
> Qualifications, typical day's work, earnings, trends, advantages, and
> disadvantages. List of twelve universities offering courses in real estate.

   See also Insurance agent

RECREATION EXECUTIVE   0-27.07
Executive leadership in Boys' Clubs of America. Boys' Clubs of
America, Inc., 381 4th Ave., New York 16, N.Y. No date. 16p.
Free
> This booklet sets forth the desirable qualifications for executive direc-
> tors of a boys' club. Also describes the employment practices, opportuni-
> ties, and salaries.

* Recreation leadership as a career. Institute for Research. 1941.
20p. 75c
> Types of positions and compensation, qualifications, requirements, op-
> portunities, trends, attractive and unattractive features. Three illustrations.

RECREATION EXECUTIVE—*Continued*

* Recreation leadership as a field of work. National Recreation Association, 315 4th Ave., New York 10, N.Y. 1944. 6p. Mimeographed. 10c
> Types of positions, qualifications, college preparation, demand, salaries, and methods of securing positions.

Recreation leadership standards—standards of training, experience, and compensation for positions in community recreation. National Recreation Association, 315 4th Ave., New York 10, N.Y. 1944. 30p. 35c
> Information about nature of work, qualifications, and salaries in positions in the recreation field. Qualifications are given for twenty-two specific jobs such as playfield director, camp director, and supervisor of arts and crafts.

Recreation workers. Science Research Associates. 1943. 4p. Planographed. 15c
> Occupational brief number 90. Two illustrations. Annotated bibliography.

Some colleges and universities listing courses in recreation. American Association for Health, Physical Education, and Recreation, 1201 16th St., N.W., Washington 6, D.C. 1945. 2p. Mimeographed. Free
> Alphabetical list of eighty-four schools.

Vocations for women—recreation. Blackstock, Josephine. National Federation of Business and Professional Women's Clubs. 1944. 4p. 15c
> Discussion of the need for recreation leaders.

Why not be a recreation worker? National Recreation Association, 315 4th Ave., New York 10, N.Y. 1945. 8p. Free
> Brief statement of qualifications and experience necessary to become supervisor of special activities, playground director, community center director, supervisor of girls and women, and superintendent of a community recreation center.

RED CROSS WORKER   0-27.

* Careers in the American Red Cross. Institute for Research. 1945. 24p. 75c
> List of thirty-three peacetime paid positions in a representative metropolitan area with specifications for each. Five illustrations.

* Employment opportunities in the American Red Cross. National Headquarters, American Red Cross, 18th and E Sts., N.W., Washington 13, D.C. 1945. 6p. Mimeographed. Free
> Description of work and qualifications for overseas and domestic jobs in club service, camp service, hospital service, and miscellaneous service.

REFRIGERATING ENGINEER   5-72.310

Stationary engineers. Science Research Associates. 1945. 4p. 15c
> Occupational brief number 103. Two illustrations. Annotated bibliography.
> *See also* Engineer

RELIGIOUS WORKER 0-69.79
Church vocations for women. Board of Christian Education, Presbyterian Church in the U. S. A., 808 Witherspoon Bldg., Philadelphia 7, Pa. 1944. 11p. Free
> Duties, training, and requirements of twelve types of work.

* Religion. Nichols, James. Bellman Publishing Co. 1945. 24p. 50c
> Qualifications for success in religious work, advantages, disadvantages, remuneration, and description of positions held by religious workers. Selected list of one hundred seventy-seven schools of religion and description of twenty-one subjects included in courses of study. Bibliography.

Vocations in the church: the church calls you. National Council, Protestant Episcopal Church, 281 4th Ave., New York 10, N.Y. 1944. 16p. 15c
> Presentation of the need for Christian leaders today, opportunities for service through the church, and the basic preparation for church workers. The cover has a handy pocket in which to keep other pamphlets in this series:
> The church calls doctors and nurses. 8p. 3c
> The church calls for college workers. 16p. 3c
> The church calls for directors of religious education. 12p. 3c
> The church calls for Negro workers. 6p. 3c
> The church calls for workers in the U. S. 16p. 3c
> The church calls for workers overseas. 16p. 3c
> The church calls social workers. 12p. 3c
> The church calls teachers. 8p. 3c
> The ministry and you. 24p. 5c

See also Clergyman

REPORTER 0-06.71
Description of profession of reporter and editor. National Roster. 1946. Free
> In preparation. See p. 34 for description of series.

Reporter and editor. Prepared for the War Department by the National Roster. Supt. of Documents, Washington 25, D.C. 1945. 14p. 5c
> Occupational brief containing summary, earnings, outlook, qualifications, and training.

See also Editor; Writer; Journalist

RESEARCH WORKER 0-68.42
* Motion picture research. Western Personnel Service. 1941. 11p. 25c
> Describes motion picture research "from script to screen." Includes requirements, outlook, and salaries based on questionnaire responses from more than fifty per cent of the total number of research workers employed by the Hollywood industry. Bibliography.

RESTAURANT MANAGER 0-71.
Establishing and operating a restaurant. U. S. Dept. of Commerce. Supt. of Documents, Washington 25, D.C. 1945
> Industrial series. Intended as a practical guide to experienced persons who are considering starting their own businesses. In preparation.

RESTAURANT MANAGER—*Continued*

* Restaurant and tea room operation as a career. Revised edition. Institute for Research. 1945. 24p. 75c

>Advantages, disadvantages, typical day's work, training, and earnings. List of eighteen routine positions in restaurant work. Three illustrations. Bibliography.

Restaurant management. Davis, Anne S., ed. Commonwealth Book Co. 1936. 27p. Mimeographed. 75c

>Information presented according to the NVGA outline. See p. 26 for description of series. Includes related work such as that of caterer and pastry chef. Bibliography.

RESTAURANT WORKER   2-20. through 2-29.

The efficient waitress manual. Dahl, J. O. Revised edition. The Dahls, Haviland Road, Stamford, Conn. 1944. 64p. 35c

>Written as a manual for beginners, it describes waitresses' duties, rules of conduct, and qualifications. Illustrated.

Employment opportunities in the restaurant field. Pennsylvania Restaurant Association, 315 State Theatre Bldg., Harrisburg, Pa. No date. 8p. Free

>Sets forth the advantages of restaurant work, naming thirty-eight occupations typical of large restaurants.

* Restaurant and tea room work. Shade, Chloris, ed. 2nd edition revised. Morgan-Dillon & Co. 1940. 24p. 32c

>Growth of the restaurant industry, nature of work, qualifications, training, earnings, and a list of related occupations. Bibliography.

**Restaurant business. Voegele, Walter. Bellman Publishing Co. 1941. 32p. 50c

>Description of various types of commercial food service establishments. Duties of workers, qualifications, and earnings. List of schools and suggested questions to consider before selecting this field of work. Bibliography.

RETAIL MANAGER   0-72.

How to start in the hardware business. National Retail Hardware Association, 333 N. Pennsylvania St., Indianapolis 4, Ind. 1945. 8p. Free

>Points to consider before starting a hardware business. Information concerning capital required, location of store, and distribution methods. No other occupational information.

What does small business offer the veteran. Federation Employment Service, 67 West 47th St., New York 19, N.Y. 1945. 20p. 10c

>Information concerning ten small businesses in New York City, including number and type of firms, investment required, qualifications, working conditions, and outlook. Includes restaurants, dress manufacturing, dry cleaning stores, filling stations, and pest control industry.

Book store operation as a career. Institute for Research. 1935. 16p. 75c

>Temporarily out of print.

Bookstore workers. Science Research Associates. 1943. 4p. Planographed. 15c
> Occupational brief number 71. Two illustrations. Annotated bibliog-
> raphy.

* Chain store management. Davis, Anne S., ed. Revised edition.
Commonwealth Book Co. 1939. 24p. Mimeographed. 75c
> Information presented according to NVGA outline. See p. 26 for
> description of series. Includes earnings for managers of drug, department
> store, clothing, shoe, restaurant, insurance, and variety-price chain stores.

Gift and art shop operation as a career. Institute for Research.
1938. 16p. 75c
> Types of positions, typical day's work, qualifications, opportunities, at-
> tractive and unattractive features. Two illustrations.

Hazards of retailing. Twentieth Century Fund, 330 W. 42nd
St., New York 18, N.Y. 1940. 12p. 2c
> Presents brief facts, statistics and requirements to make a success of a
> retail store.

How to start in the hardware business. National Retail Hardware
Association, 333 No. Pennsylvania St., Indianapolis 4, Ind. 1945.
8p. Free
> Advice to persons who are considering opening a hardware store about
> capital needed, equipment, and management.

If you are considering retailing. Hogadone, Edwina B. Rochester
Institute of Technology. 1944. 15p. 10c
> Discussion of the major types of retail work: selling, buying, personnel,
> advertising, and small store management.

Job descriptions for the retail trade. Division of Occupational
Analysis. Supt. of Documents, Washington 25, D.C. 1938. 743p.
3 volumes. $1 each
> One of a series of National Job Descriptions. Describes occupations
> in retail store establishments, including both department stores and spe-
> cialty shops. Volume I includes merchandise handling, management and
> personnel jobs, maintenance and operation jobs, and accommodation serv-
> ices such as credit and adjustment. Volume II includes merchandising jobs
> and merchandise services. Volume III includes selling and sales promotion
> such as advertising and display. Illustrated.

* Men's furnishings store operation as a career. Revised edition.
Institute for Research. 1945. 20p. 75c
> Qualifications, training, typical day's work, attractive and unattractive
> features, and opportunities for operating an independent store and a chain
> store. Two illustrations. Bibliography.

Opportunities in retail trade for service men. Dun and Bradstreet,
Inc., 290 Broadway, New York 8, N.Y. 1945. 40p. Free
> Requirements for entering trade, rewards, hazards, value of training
> and a supplement on operating expenses of retail grocery stores.

Radio-music store operation as a career. Revised edition. Institute
for Research. 1945. 20p. 75c
> Qualifications, opportunities, typical day's work, attractive and unattrac-
> tive features. Information about work of radio salesman, record clerk,
> and radio serviceman. One illustration. Bibliography.

RETAIL MANAGER—*Continued*

Retail meat dealer. Davis, Anne S., ed. Revised edition. Commonwealth Book Co. 1939. 24p. Mimeographed. 75c

Information presented according to the NVGA outline. See p. 26 for description of series. Includes the retail meat dealer's working staff.

Retail merchandising. Davis, Anne S., ed. Commonwealth Book Co. 1936 with 1939 supplement. 30p. Mimeographed. 75c

Information presented according to the NVGA outline. See p. 26 for description of series. Includes positions in the department stores.

* Retailing. Chamberlain, Elsie and Cox, Muriel. Bellman Publishing Co. 1945. 24p. 50c

Brief descriptions of seven positions in merchandising, six in publicity, twelve in store operation, and three in finance. Factors making for success in department stores and specialty shops. List of nine schools of retailing and description of typical courses of study. Separate discussions of opportunities for men and women. Bibliography.

Standard ratios for retailing—guides to efficiency and profits in fifty trades. Dun and Bradstreet, Inc., 290 Broadway, New York 7, N.Y. 1940. 11p. Free

For thirty-nine retail trades, information is given concerning sales volume in dollars in 1936 and in 1939, gross margin, total expense, and profit or loss. Typical operating and merchandising characteristics of fifty retail trades in 1939.

Variety store workers. Science Research Associates. 1943. 4p. Planographed. 15c

Occupational brief number 77. Two illustrations. Annotated bibliography.

Vocations for women—retailing. Plant, George. National Federation of Business and Professional Women's Clubs. 1944. 4p. 15c

Includes suggestions concerning the major problems on which intelligent advance planning is necessary.

What it takes to be a retailer. Domestic Distribution Department, Chamber of Commerce of the United States, Washington 6, D.C. 1945. 21p. Free

Information addressed to servicemen on opportunities in retailing.

Women's apparel-shop management as a career. Institute for Research. 1935. 16p. 75c

Temporarily out of print.

RHINOLOGIST (Nose specialist). *See* Physician

RUBBER INDUSTRY WORKER   4, 6, 8-57.

* Occupations in rubber. Ufford, Charles. Science Research Associates. 1942. 50p. 60c

Description of work, requirements, opportunities, and trends. Includes a chart of occupations in the rubber industry. Thirty-two illustrations. Bibliography.

Rubber workers. Science Research Associates. 1943. 4p. Planographed. 15c
> Occupational brief number 17. Two illustrations. Annotated bibliog-
> raphy.

Synthetic rubber. Labor market information for USES counseling
—Industry Series. U. S. Dept. of Labor, Washington 25, D.C.
1945. 6p. Mimeographed. Free
> Statement including nature and location of the industry, requirements,
> working conditions, and employment prospects. Chart shows distribution
> of employment by occupational group. Bibliography.

SAFETY ENGINEER   0-18.03

Description of the profession of safety engineering. National
Roster. 1945. 2p. Free
> See p. 34 for description of series.

The safety man in industry. National Safety Council, 20 No.
Wacker Drive, Chicago 6, Ill. 1939. 8p. 35c
> Discussion of opportunities, the desired education, experience, and
> qualifications, and a description of twenty-five duties of safety men.

See also Engineer

SAILOR   2-68.20

Careers in the naval services of the United States. Institute for
Research. 1942. 30p. 75c
> History of the Navy and description of work in its various branches.
> Qualifications, attractive and unattractive features, and salaries and al-
> lowances for officers and enlisted men. Six illustrations. Bibliography.

Jobs in the Navy. Science Research Associates. 1943. 4p. 15c
> Occupational brief number 2. Annotated bibliography.

The Navy, Coast Guard and Merchant Marine. Niles, Palmer A.
Bellman Publishing Co. 1941. 24p. 50c
> Qualifications for entrance, information about the examinations, pay,
> and courses of study. Bibliography.

Warriors of the sea—the way of life in the U. S. Navy. Stirling,
Yates. Row, Peterson and Co. 1942. 64p. 96c
> See p. 41 for description of series. Thirty-one illustrations.

SALES MANAGER   0-97.61

Marketing, advertising and selling. Pace Institute, 225 Broadway,
New York 7, N.Y. 1945. 28p. Free
> Recruiting bulletin containing information about work in advertising,
> selling, market analysis, sales planning, and sales management.

* Professional opportunities in the general sales promotion field.
Henthorn, Ben H. National Council of Business Schools, 839
17th St., N.W., Washington 6, D.C. 1945. 18p. 10c
> Minimum training requirements and career opportunities within (1)
> the field of salesmanship and sales management, (2) the field of advertis-
> ing and sales promotion, and (3) the field of business correspondence.

SALESPERSON 1-75.

Automobile salesman. Occupational Index. 1944. 6p. 25c
Occupational abstract. Duties, abilities, preparation, earnings, advantages, disadvantages, number and distribution of workers. Annotated bibliography.

Commercial travelers. Science Research Associates. 1943. 4p. Planographed. 15c
Occupational brief number 74. Two illustrations. Annotated bibliography.

Food store workers. Science Research Associates. 1943. 4p. Planographed. 15c
Occupational brief number 70. Two illustrations. Annotated bibliography.

* The grocery store. Shade, Chloris, ed. 2nd edition revised. Morgan-Dillon & Co. 1940. 24p. 32c
Duties of clerks, managers, and proprietors. Number and distribution of workers, preparation, and conditions of work. Bibliography.

House-to-house canvassers. Science Research Associates. 1943. 4p. Planographed. 15c
Occupational brief number 75. Two illustrations. Annotated bibliography.

—The most interesting thing in business. Pace Institute, 225 Broadway, New York 7, N.Y. 1945. 12p. Free
A recruiting leaflet presenting advantages, opportunities, and postwar challenges.

Printing salesmanship. Davis, Anne S., ed. Commonwealth Book Co. 1938. 23p. Mimeographed. 75c
Information presented according to the NVGA outline. See p. 26 for description of series. Describes work of salesmen in the printing, publishing, and engraving industry.

* Retail sales workers. Keliher, Alice, ed. Hinds, Hayden and Eldredge, Inc. 1941. 56p. 80c
Discussion of over-the-counter selling in food, variety, and department stores. See p. 28 for description of Picture Fact Books.

* Salesmanship. Shade, Chloris, ed. 2nd edition revised. Morgan-Dillon & Co. 1940. 24p. 32c
Opportunities and duties in retail, wholesale, and direct selling. Qualifications, preparation, opportunities, and conditions of work. Number of stores engaged in retail distribution in sixty-seven kinds of business. Classified bibliography.

* Salesmanship as a career. Institute for Research. 1940. 20p. 75c
Importance of salesmanship, typical day's work, salaries, ways of getting started, advantages and disadvantages. Duties and qualifications for retail salesman and traveling specialty and commodity salesmen.

What makes a good industrial salesman? Science Research Associates. No date. 2p. Planographed. 15c
Occupational reprint number 11

SANITARY ENGINEER   **0-16.01**
Educational qualifications of personnel in environmental sanitation.
American Public Health Association, 1790 Broadway, New York
19, N.Y. 1938. 8p. Free
> Public health engineers, sanitarians, and sub-professional field personnel
> in sanitation.

* Sanitary engineering as a career. Institute for Research. 1938.
20p. 75c
> Advantages, disadvantages, qualifications, training, opportunities, and
> salaries. Typical work in government service, industry, manufacturing
> plant, and private office of a consulting engineer. Four illustrations.

SCHOOL ADMINISTRATOR. *See* Superintendent, Schools

SCIENTIST   **0-39.11 to 0-39.79**
Science. Revised edition. Quarrie Corporation. 1944. 19p. Planographed. 10c
> Vocational monograph number 28.

SECRETARY   **1-33.01**
The chemical secretary. Science Research Associates. No date.
2p. Planographed. 15c
> Occupational reprint number 19. One illustration.

Choose your position—practical suggestions for secretaries. Katharine Gibbs School, Boston 16, Mass. 1942. 46p. Free
> Summary of suggestions of business executives about the importance
> of vocational planning, an immediate employment plan, methods of con-
> ducting an interview, and an ultimate employment plan with suggestions
> for taking inventory of oneself and one's organization.

Commercial and trade association secretaryship as a career. Institute for Research. 1935. 16p. 75c
> Temporarily out of print.

Memo: how to be a super secretary. Remington Rand, Inc., 315
Fourth Ave., New York 10, N.Y. 1945. 20p. Free
> Gives the qualifications many business executives state are important
> for success in secretarial work. Includes a rating chart.

Private and social secretaryship as a career. Revised edition. Institute for Research. 1946. 16p. 75c
> In press.

The private secretary—qualifications and requirements. Katharine
Gibbs School, Boston 16, Mass. 1942. 20p. Free
> Embodies suggestions made by business executives concerning quali-
> fications considered most important in an applicant, technical proficiency,
> qualifications for holding a position, and requirements for continued
> value and growth. Section on business ethics.

* Secretarial science. Langston, Mildred. Bellman Publishing Co.
1945. 23p. 50c
> Qualifications, training, chances for advancement, and remuneration.
> Includes types of organizations employing secretaries. Bibliography.

* Secretarial work. Shade, Chloris, ed. 2nd edition revised. Morgan-Dillon & Co. 1939. 24p. 32c

    Duties, qualifications, training, and trends. Discussion of methods of finding a position and qualifications for holding it. Classified bibliography.

Secretaryship. Davis, Anne S., ed. Commonwealth Book Co. 1936. 21p. Mimeographed. 75c

    Information presented according to the NVGA outline. See p. 26 for description of series. Includes some information about the court reporter and the public stenographer.

**Secretaryship as a career—a handbook of vocational information. Purvis, Elgie G. National Council of Business Schools, 839 17th St., N.W., Washington 6, D.C. 1944. 23p. 10c

    Describes the duties, requirements, opportunities, rewards and the various types of secretarial positions for which students may prepare. Includes comparative salaries of secretarial positions in government service and in private business.

SEISMOLOGIST   0-39.56

Description of the profession of geophysics (geophysical prospecting, hydrology, seismology, geodesy). National Roster. 1945. 3p. Free

    See p. 34 for description of series.

SHIP STEWARD. *See* Ocean liner worker

SHIPBUILDER   5, 7, 9-05.50

Shipbuilders. Science Research Associates. 1943. 4p. Planographed. 15c

    Occupational brief number 13. Two illustrations. Annotated bibliography.

The training of shipyard personnel. Society of Naval Architects and Marine Engineers, 29 W. 39th St., New York 18, N.Y. 1941. 37p

    Descriptions of four apprenticeship systems in the shipbuilding industry. Qualifications and training desirable for supervisors, draftsmen, engineers, loftsmen, and welders. Outline of course in shipfitting. Bibliography.

SHOE REPAIRMAN   4-60.100

Establishing and operating a shoe repair business. U. S. Dept. of Commerce. Supt. of Documents, Washington 25, D.C. 1945. 41p. 35c

    Industrial series number 17. Intended as a practical guide for the perienced skilled shoe repairman who is considering opening his own shop. Includes discussion of operating costs and shop management. Twenty-seven illustrations.

Shoe repairmen. Science Research Associates. 1943. 4p. Planographed. 15c

    Occupational brief number 69. Two illustrations. Annotated bibliography.

* Shoemaking and repairing. Davis, Anne S., ed. Commonwealth
Book Co. 1938. 27p. Mimeographed. 75c
Information presented according to the NVGA outline. See p. 26
for description of series. Includes manufacturing, retail distribution, and
repairing.

SHOEMAKER. *See* Shoe repairman

SILVERSMITH   **4-71.310**
Silversmith. Davis, Anne S., ed. Commonwealth Book Co. 1938.
22p. Mimeographed. 75c
Information presented according to the NVGA outline. See p. 26
for description of series. Information pertains to small shops as well as
to mass production.

SKILLED TRADES WORKER   **4-01. through 5-99.**
* Careers in the skilled trades. Cohen, I. David. B'nai B'rith Vocational Service Bureau, 1746 M St., N.W., Washington 25, D.C.
1940. 48p. 10c
Discussion of work in the building, metal, printing, garment, shoe,
transportation, communication, and specialty trades. Bibliography at end
of each section. Illustrated.

SOCIAL WORKER   **0-27.20**
Build your career in social work. American Association of Schools
of Social Work, 1313 E. 60th St., Chicago 37, Ill. 1945. 6p.
Free
May be used as a poster. Brief information given under the head-
ing "Some questions you may ask."

Consider social work. Science Research Associates. 1944. 2p. 15c
Occupational reprint number 167. One illustration.

Description of the profession of social work. National Roster.
1945. 4p. Free
See p. 34 for description of series.

* Family case work, a good profession to choose. Family Welfare
Association of America, 122 E. 22nd St., New York 10, N.Y.
1945. 21p. 10c
Requirements, duties, and necessary basic training. Presents types of
situations with which family case workers offer help. List of forty-five
accredited schools of social work located in twenty-three states, Canada,
and Hawaii.

* Social service. Davis, Anne S., ed. Revised edition. Commonwealth Book Co. 1938. 29p. Mimeographed. 75c
Information presented according to the NVGA outline. See p. 26
for description of series. Includes description of various types of positions such as family case worker, child welfare worker, visiting teacher,
probation or parole officer, medical social worker, and community organization worker.

Social work. Revised edition. Quarrie Corporation. 1944. 9p.
Planographed. 10c
Vocational monograph number 29.

SOCIAL WORKER—*Continued*

* Social work. Rome, Florence L. Occupational Index. 1945. 6p. 25c

Occupational abstract. Summarizes work of the social case worker, social group worker, social research, social administration, and community organization worker. Discussion of preparation, earnings, number and distribution of workers, and postwar prospects. Annotated bibliography.

* Social work. Shade, Chloris, ed. Morgan-Dillon & Co. 1940. 24p. 32c

Discussion of social case work, group work, welfare planning, and administration of social agencies. Qualifications, training, working conditions, and qualifications for membership in three professional social work organizations. Classified bibliography.

* Social work. White, R. Clyde. Bellman Publishing Co. 1941. 28p. Vari-typed. 50c

Description of work in various types of social work agencies, qualifications, training, opportunities, and remuneration. Includes list of accredited schools and description of typical courses. Bibliography.

Social work and the Joneses. Lerigo, R. and Buell, B. Public Affairs Committee, Inc., 30 Rockefeller Plaza, New York 20, N.Y. 1944. 32p. 10c

Includes several case histories which describe the duties of modern social workers.

Social work as a career. Institute for Research. 1939. 24p. 75c

Typical day's work of a family welfare worker and a rural child welfare worker. Types of work in Federal positions, community organizations, and in local and state public welfare departments. Qualifications, preparation, salaries. List of schools approved by American Association of Schools of Social Work. Three illustrations. Bibliography.

Social work as a career. University of New Mexico, Albuquerque, N.M. 1946. 6p. Free

Recruiting bulletin describing nature of the work, personal qualifications, preparation, and opportunities.

**Social work as a profession. Revised edition. American Association of Schools of Social Work, 1313 E. 60th St., Chicago 37, Ill. 1945. 32p. 10c

Nature and scope of social work, personal requirements, employment opportunities, pre-social work education, and professional educational standards. The appendixes include lists of the forty-four member schools of the American Association of Schools of Social Work, professional associations, and selected references on social work as a profession.

**Social work as a profession. Brown, Esther. Russell Sage Foundation. 130 E. 22nd St., New York 10, N.Y. 1942. 232p. $1

Detailed discussion of the scope of social work, training, number of workers, salaries, and national associations. Eleven tables including distribution of social workers and of population in urban and rural areas by states.

Social work fellowships and scholarships. American Association of Social Workers, 130 E. 22d St., New York 10, N.Y. 1945. 14p. Free

An annual compilation of information about social work fellowships, scholarships, assistantships, loan funds, and work-study plans.

The social worker. Corcoran, J. P. Xavier University. 1937.
19p. Mimeographed. 50c
> Addressed to Negro youth, this pamphlet discusses personal and educational qualifications, training, salaries, and opportunities for Negro students. Bibliography.

Social worker. Prepared for the War Department by the National
Roster. Supt. of Documents, Washington 25, D.C. 1945. 5c
> Occupatoinal brief containing summary, earnings, outlook, qualifications, and training.

The social worker, who is he, what does he do, what preparation
does he need? American Association of Schools of Social Work,
1313 E. 60th St., Chicago 37, Ill. No date. 13p. 10c
> Includes a discussion of opportunities and salaries.

Social workers. Science Research Associates. 1943. 4p. Planographed. 15c
> Occupational brief number 38. Three illustrations. Annotated bibliography.

SOCIOLOGIST
0-39.18
Description of the profession of sociology. National Roster. 1945.
4p. Free
> See p. 34 for description of series.

**Sociologist. Prepared for the War Department by the National
Roster. Supt. of Documents, Washington 25, D.C. 1945. 5c.
> Occupational brief containing summary, earnings, outlook, qualifications, and training.

* Social anthropology. Mead, Margaret. Western Personnel Service.
1945. 25c
> Describes the need for more highly trained anthropologists for the understanding and communication between peoples of different cultures.

SOIL SCIENTIST. *See* Agronomist

SOLDIER
2-68.10
The armed forces of the United States. Ketchum, Elizabeth. Educational Research Bureau, 1217 13th St., N.W., Washington 5,
D.C. 1942. 31p. 15c
> The ranks, pay, and insignia of the Army, Navy, Marines, and Coast Guard. Duties and responsibilities of each unit or division.

Careers in the armored forces. Institute for Research. 1942. 20p.
75c
> History and division of modern armored might. Qualifications, attractive and unattractive features, and salaries and retirement pay of officers and enlisted men. Five illustrations. Bibliography.

Careers in the U. S. Army. Institute for Research. 1942. 34p.
75c
> History of the Army and description of work in its several services. Qualifications for men in the various branches, attractive and unattractive features, and salaries and allowances of enlisted men and officers. Five illustrations. Bibliography.

SOLDIER—*Continued*

Jobs in the Army. Science Research Associates. 1943. 4p. Plano-graphed. 15c
  Occupational brief number 1. Annotated bibliography.

To the colors!—the way of life of an army officer. Dupuy, Ernest and Dupuy, Trevor. Row, Peterson and Co. 1942. 64p. 96c
  See p. 41 for description of series. Twenty illustrations.

SOUND ENGINEER
0-17.01

* Motion picture sound technicians. Western Personnel Service. 1944. 8p. 25c
  Nature of work, related fields of employment, outlook, requirements, number of workers employed and the previous experience of the sound technicians in Hollywood.

  See also Engineer

SPEECH PATHOLOGIST. *See* Pathologist

STAINED GLASS INDUSTRY WORKER
4-65.

Standards and organization for apprenticeship in the stained glass industry. Apprentice-Training Service, U. S. Dept. of Labor, Washington 25, D.C. 1945. 12p. Free
  Includes schedule of wages in the apprentice program, training program, and an example of an apprenticeship agreement.

STATION AGENT
1-44.22

Meet John Santa Fe. Martin, Leo J. Santa Fe System Lines, Railway Exchange, Chicago 4, Ill. 1944. 24p. Free
  Describes duties of the local agent, qualifications, and advantages.

STATIONARY ENGINEER. *See* Refrigerating engineer

STATISTICIAN
0-28.10

Description of the profession of actuarial science. National Roster. 1945. 3p. Free
  See p. 34 for description of series.

Description of the profession of statistics. National Roster. 1945. 4p. Free
  See p. 34 for description of series.

The educational qualifications of public health statisticians. American Public Health Association, 1790 Broadway, New York 19, N.Y. 1938. 7p. Free

* Opportunities for statistical workers. Henderson, Donald. Science Research Associates. 1944. 52p. 60c
  Discussion of statistics in business, in research, and in the Federal government. Describes types of training and experience necessary to find employment as a statistician. Some information about the work of card-punch operators, field investigators, and statistical clerks. Six illustrations. Annotated bibliography.

Statistical work as a career. Institute for Research. 1940. 20p. 75c

> Qualifications, preparation, and salaries of statistical work in business and in the Federal government. Statement of U. S. Civil Service requirements. Includes description of statistical clerk, statistical draftsman, clerk coder, sorting machine operator, card punch operator, and tabulating machine operator. Three illustrations.

Statistician. Prepared for the War Department by the National Roster. Supt. of Documents, Washington 25, D.C. 1945. 5c

> Occupational brief containing summary, earnings, outlook, qualifications, and training.

Vocations for women—statistical work. National Federation of Business and Professional Women's Clubs. No date. 4p. 10c

> Nature of work, training, and opportunities. Bibliography.

> *See also* Actuarial statistician

STEAM FITTER 5-30.410

Suggested local standards for training steamfitting apprentices. Federal Committee on Apprenticeship. Supt. of Documents, Washington 25, D.C. 1940. 15p. 10c

> Includes qualifications for apprenticeship applicants, wages, skills in which experience and training shall be given, and an example of an apprenticeship agreement. Based on the national standards for steamfitting apprenticeship.

STEEL INDUSTRY WORKER. *See* Iron and steel industry worker

STENOGRAPHER 1-37.12

Shorthand and secretarial practice. Pace Institute, 225 Broadway, New York 7, N.Y. 1944. 34p. Free

> Recruiting bulletin containing factual information about the stenographer, private secretary, law stenographer, and shorthand reporter.

Shorthand reporting as a profession. Gregg College, 6 No. Michigan Ave., Chicago 2, Ill. 1945. 48p. Free

> College bulletin describing duties, requirements, training, and preparation for convention and court reporting.

Stenographers and typists. Science Research Associates. 1943. 4p. Planographed. 15c

> Occupational brief number 8. Three illustrations. Annotated bibliography.

* Stenographic work. Spiegler, Samuel. Revised edition. Occupational Index. 1945. 6p. 25c

> Occupational abstract. Duties, abilities, preparation, entrance, advancement, compensation, number and distribution of workers, and postwar prospects. Annotated bibliography.

> *See also* Secretary

SUPERINTENDENT, SCHOOLS   0-31.10

Public school administration as a career. Institute for Research.
1940. 29p. 75c

> General duties, typical day's work, typical week's work, types of positions,
> training, personal qualifications, attractive and unattractive features. Also
> brief information about the work of supervisor, business manager, and state
> supervisory officer.

SURGEON   0-26.10

Special bulletin of the American College of Surgeons. American
College of Surgeons, 40 E. Erie St., Chicago 11, Ill. 1945. 100p.
Free

> Information concerning graduate training in surgery. Includes a list of
> hospitals with approved plans for graduate training in general surgery and
> in the surgical specialties.

* Surgeon as a career. Institute for Research. 1940. 19p. 75c

> Historical background, training, a typical day's work, personal qualifica-
> tions, income, opportunities outside of private practice, attractive and un-
> attractive features. Also distribution and description of surgical specialists,
> and minimum standards for graduate training and for certification in surgery.
> Two illustrations. Bibliography.

See also Physician

TAILOR   4-26.

Tailoring. Davis, Anne S., ed. Commonwealth Book Co. 1938.
26p. Mimeographed. 75c

> Information presented according to the NVGA outline. See p. 26 for
> description of series. Emphasizes work in the making of men's clothing.

Tailors and dressmakers. Science Research Associates. 1943. 4p.
Planographed. 15c

> Occupational brief number 97. Two illustrations. Annotated bibliogra-
> phy.

TAXI DRIVER   7-36.040

* Taxi driver. Selina, Ruth. Revised edition. Occupational Index.
1945. 6p. 25c

> Occupational abstract. Duties, qualifications, preparation, earnings, ad-
> vantages, disadvantages, number and distribution of workers, and postwar
> prospects. Annotated bibliography.

TEACHER   0-30. through 0-32.

Adult education. Hallenbeck, Wilbur. Bellman Publishing Co.
1941. 24p. 50c

> Kinds of adult education, and description of jobs in administration, teach-
> ing, and teacher training. List of schools offering courses in adult education.
> Bibliography.

Career in teaching. Science Research Associates. 1943. 2p. 15c

> Occupational reprint number 145. One illustration.

City teachers: their preparation, salaries, and experience. National
Education Association, 1201 16th St., N.W., Washington 6, D.C.
1940. 48p. 25c

> Research study reporting on the preparation, experience, and salaries of
> classroom teachers in cities above 2500 in population.

College professors. Science Research Associates. 1943. 4p. Planographed. 15c
> Occupational brief number 66. Two illustrations. Annotated bibliogra-
phy.

Description of profession of educator (college teacher of professional education). National Roster. 1946. Free
> In preparation. See p. 34 for description of series.

Description of profession of high school teacher. National Roster.
1946. Free
> In preparation. See p. 34 for description of series.

Description of the professional occupations in foreign languages.
National Roster. 1945. 2p. Free
> See p. 34 for description of series.

Education. Union of American Hebrew Congregations, Cincinnati,
Ohio. 1937. 37p. Mimeographed. 25c
> Discussion of requirements, advantages, disadvantages, and opportunities.
The last half of the booklet is addressed to Jewish youth. Bibliography.

Education as a field of work. Corcoran, J. P. Xavier University.
1937. 19p. Mimeographed. 50c
> Addressed to Negro youth, this pamphlet discusses qualifications, training,
income, demand, and opportunities for Negro students. Bibliography.

Handbook of descriptions of specialized fields in professional education. National Roster. 1946
> In preparation.

Let us consider teaching. Bowers, Harold J. State Department of
Education, Columbus, Ohio. 1944. 26p. Free
> Qualifications, demand, opportunities, and advantages. List of the 45 Ohio
colleges and universities approved for the preparation of teachers, with the
specialized training offered by each. Bibliography.

Opportunities for the preparation of teachers in conservation education. Cook, Katherine and Reynolds, Florence. U. S. Office of
Education. Supt. of Documents, Washington 25, D.C. 1940. 13p.
5c
> Titles of courses and the institutions in which are offered courses con-
cerned with the conservation of our natural resources and designed for teachers in elementary and secondary schools. Includes courses in one hundred
and thirty-eight institutions in thirty-five states.

Opportunities in agricultural education. Dept. of Vocational Education, Virginia Polytechnic Institute, Blacksburg, Va. 1944.
10p. Free
> Duties, working conditions, opportunities, and qualifications for teachers
of vocational agriculture. Two illustrations.

* Rural teacher. Revised edition. Occupational Index. 1944. 6p. 25c
> Occupational abstract. Qualifications, preparation, entrance and advance-
ment, compensation, number employed, geographical distribution, advantages,
disadvantages, and postwar prospects. Also a report of a typical rural teacher. Bibliography.

TEACHER—*Continued*

Salaries of city-school employees, 1944-45. National Education Association, 1201 16th St., N.W., Washington 6, D.C. 1945. 24p. 25c

> Research study reporting on the range and distribution of salaries in 1944-45 and the trends in salaries from 1930 to 1945.

So you're going to teach. Evans, Eva. Julius Rosenwald Fund, 4901 Ellis Ave., Chicago 15, Ill. 1943. 52p. 10c

> A whimsical portrait of a teacher, nature of work, and qualifications. Twenty-three cartoons.

The status of the teaching profession. National Education Association, 1201 16th St., N.W., Washington 6, D.C. 1940. 28p. 25c

> Report of a research study on educational preparation, professional experience, salaries, provisions for tenure and retirement, and distribution in various types of schools.

Teacher, high school. Prepared for the War Department by the National Roster. Supt. of Documents, Washington 25, D.C. 1945. 5c

> Occupational brief containing summary, earnings, outlook, qualifications, and training.

Teacher, vocational schools. Perpared for the War Department by the National Roster. Supt. of Documents, Washington, D.C. 1945. 5c

> Occupational brief containing summary, earnings, outlook, qualifications, and training.

Teachers. Science Research Associates. 1943. 4p. Planographed. 15c

> Occupational brief number 65. Annotated bibliography. Two illustrations.

Teachers of the blind—their status and salaries. Lowenfeld, Berthold. American Foundation for the Blind, 15 W. 16th St., New York 11, N.Y. 1941. 44p. $1

> Summary of information received from seven hundred and three teachers in the fifty-five residential schools for the blind. Intended to give reliable information on conditions as they exist and to aid in improving inadequacies where they are found.

* Teaching. Burton, William H. Bellman Publishing Co. 1940. 40p. Vari-typed. 50c

> Number and types of positions available, activities and responsibilities of educational workers, advantages, disadvantages, and rewards. List of teachers colleges and a list of colleges accredited by the Association of American Universities which offer training for teaching. Bibliography.

* Teaching. Revised edition. Occupational Index. 1945. 6p. 25c

> Occupational abstract. Abilities, preparation, entrance, advancement, salaries, number and distribution of workers, advantages, disadvantages, and postwar prospects. Annotated bibliography.

Teaching. Revised edition. Quarrie Corporation. 1944. 10p. Planographed. 10c

> Vocational monograph number 30.

* Teaching as a career. Houle, Cyril. Science Research Associates. 1944. 50p. 60c
  Discussion of training, future outlook and the personal qualities that affect success. Ten illustrations. Bibliography.

Teaching as a career. Revised edition. Institute for Research. 1946. 36p. 75c
  In press.

**Teaching as a man's job. Lee, Edwin A., chairman. Phi Delta Kappa, 2034 Ridge Road, Homewood, Ill. 1939. 79p. 10c
  Presents the sacrifices and rewards of teaching. Annotated bibliography.

**Teaching as a profession. Frazier, Benjamin W. U. S. Office of Education. Supt. of Documents, Washington 25, D.C. 1944. 34p. 10c
  Contents: general nature of the profession; opportunities for specialization; teacher supply, demand, and placement; nature of the teacher's work; working conditions; requirements for becoming a teacher; opportunities for preparation; annotated bibliography. Six illustrations.

Teaching industrial arts. School of Education, New York University, New York 3, N.Y. 1945. 8p. Free
  Recruiting bulletin describing the nature of work, qualifications, training, opportunities, and advantages.

Teaching vocational agriculture as a career. Michigan State College, East Lansing, Mich. 1945. 16p. Free
  Duties, requirements, training, and opportunities. Twelve illustrations.

What is a nursery school? Association for Childhood Education, 1201 16th St., N.W., Washington 6, D.C. 1940. 25p. 35c
  A typical day, names of schools giving preparation for nursery school teaching, and description of typical nursery schools in a settlement house, a philanthropic nursery school, college of education, public health organization, hospital, tax-supported state university, state university, public school, and WPA nursery school.

  See also Kindergarten teacher; Nursery school teacher

TELEGRAPH OPERATOR   1-41.
Telephone and telegraph operators. Science Research Associates. 1943. 4p. Planographed. 15c
  Occupational brief number 9. Three illustrations. Annotated bibliography.

TELEPHONE AND TELEGRAPH INDUSTRY WORKER
5-51. through 5-54.

Talking wires—the way of life in the telegraph industry. Oslin, George. Row, Peterson and Co. 1942. 64p. 96c
See p. 41 for description of series. Forty-two illustrations.

The telegraph industry. Oslin, George. Bellman Publishing Co. 1941. 20p. 75c
  Description of jobs in the traffic plant, engineering, commercial, accounting, and other departments. Qualifications, training, chances for advancement advantages, and disadvantages.

TELEPHONE AND TELEGRAPH INDUSTRY—*Continued*

Telegraphy. Davis, Anne S., ed. Commonwealth Book Co. 1938. 25p. Mimeographed. 75c

> Information presented according to the NVGA outline. See p. 26 for description of series. Discussion of jobs in the telegraphic field which do not require a college education.

Telephone and telegraph linemen. Science Research Associates. 1943. 4p. Planographed. 15c

> Occupational brief number 45. Two illustrations. Annotated bibliography.

Telephone and telegraph service. Shade, Chloris, ed. 2nd edition revised. Morgan-Dillon & Co. 1939. 24p. 32c

> The first part of booklet gives information about nature of work, duties, number engaged, and opportunities in telegraph service. The last part discusses telephone service. Bibliography.

Telephone jobs for women. New England Telephone & Telegraph Company, 50 Oliver St., Boston 7, Mass. 1943. 9p. Free

> Description of work, qualifications, training, and opportunities for advancement for the telephone operator, office worker, typist-stenographer, cashier, and service representative.

Telephony. Davis, Anne S., ed. Commonwealth Book Co. 1938. 28p. Mimeographed. 75c

> Discussion of work in the operating and maintenance divisions. Includes cable splicer, conduit layer, lineman, installer, dial operator, and manual operator.

Work and opportunity in the Bell System. American Telephone and Telegraph Company, 195 Broadway, New York 7, N.Y. 1941. 40p. Free

> Illustrated booklet describing the work and opportunities for college graduates capable of advancing into staff, supervisory, or executive positions. Written primarily for men.

TELEPHONE OPERATOR   1-42.

Telephone and telegraph operators. Science Research Associates. 1943. 4p. Planographed. 15c

> Occupational brief number 9. Three illustrations. Annotated bibliography.

Telephone jobs for women. Illinois Bell Telephone Co., 212 W. Washington St., Chicago 6, Ill. No date. 16p. Free

> Description of working conditions, benefit plan, recreational activities, rates of pay, and training. Statement of qualifications, training, and opportunity for advancement for the various workers. List of positions requiring advanced training. Attractive format. Illustrated.

The telephone operator. Baltimore Department of Education. 1943. 8p. 10c

> Qualifications, opportunities, advantages, and disadvantages.

TELEVISION INDUSTRY WORKER   0-61. and 4, 6, 8-98.

Jobs and futures in television. Mademoiselle, 122 E. 42nd St., New York 17, N.Y. 1945. 4p. 10c

> Reprint of article discussing future jobs in television.

* Television. Crawford, John E. Revised edition. Occupational
   Index. 1944. 6p. 25c
   Occupational abstract. Description of occupations in the industry, training,
   advantages, disadvantages, and postwar prospects. Annotated bibliography.

Television and its post-war outlook. Lansing, Mort. U. S. Dept.
   of Commerce, Washington 25, D.C. 1945. 3p. Free
   Reprint from Domestic Commerce.

* Television as a career. McLean, James D. General Electric Company, 1 River Road, Schenectady 5, N.Y. 1945. 4p. Free
   Describes the work in a television station such as that of the television
   camera operator, lighting expert, and program director. Eight illustrations.
   Bibliography.

Television workers. Science Research Associates. 1945. 4p. 15c
   Occupational brief number 117. Description of both technical and creative
   work, requirements, and the future outlook. Two illustrations. Annotated
   bibliography.

TEXTILE DESIGNER. *See* Cloth designer

TEXTILE INDUSTRY WORKER   4, 6, 8-14. through 8-27.
Introduction to opportunities and jobs in the textile industries and
   to the training offered by textile schools. National Council of
   Textile School Deans, Washington, D.C. 1944. 4p. Free
   Brief information addressed to veterans.

Job descriptions for cotton textile industry. Division of Occupational Analysis. Supt. of Documents, Washington 25, D.C. 1939.
   323p. $1
   One of a series of National Job Descriptions. Describes occupations concerned with manufacturing cotton yarn from raw cotton and with weaving all-
   cotton cloth of twelve inches or greater width. Illustrated.

The Mohawk carpet and rug manual. Mohawk Carpet Mills, Inc.,
   Amsterdam, N.Y. No date. 96p. Free
   Contains sixty photographs of workers engaged in spinning and dyeing
   yarns, designing patterns, and weaving various types of fabrics. Description of processes but no other occupational information.

* Opportunities for trained men and women in the textile and related
   industries. Published for the National Council of Textile School
   Deans by the Textile Foundation, Kent, Conn. 1945. 13p. Free
   Thumb-nail biographies show the diversification of jobs available and
   the value of specialized training. Includes description of the six divisions
   of the textile industry, types of training, length of courses, and the location
   of the nine schools listed in order of their geographic location on the east-
   ern seaboard.

Post war market, sales and industrial progress survey of the textile
   industries. National Paper Box Manufacturers Association, Liberty Trust Bldg., Philadelphia 7, Pa. 1945. 24p. $2.50; $1 to
   schools and libraries.
   One of a series of postwar industrial surveys, discussing employment,
   demand for products, and packaging problems.

TEXTILE INDUSTRY WORKER—*Continued*
* Textile workers. Keliher, Alice, ed. Hinds, Hayden and Eldredge, Inc. 1939. 56p. 80c
  Discussion of workers in textile mills. See p. 28 for description of Picture Fact Books.

Textile workers. Science Research Associates. 1943. 4p. Planographed. 15c
  Occupational brief number 81. Two illustrations. Annotated bibliography.

Woolen and worsted textiles. Labor market information for USES counseling—Industry Series. U. S. Dept. of Labor, Washington 25, D.C. 1945. 10p. Mimeographed. Free
  Statement including a description of the nature and location of the industry; the industrial processes and occupational structure; wages, hours, conditions of work, union affiliation; training, requirements, and employment prospects. Bibliography.

THEATRE MANAGER. *See* Manager, Recreation Establishment

THEATRICAL MAN   0-39.99
**Careers in the theatre. Institute for Research. 1939. 24p. 75c
  Describes the development of various types of theatres and the work of producer, playwright, director, scene designer, radio actor, stage manager, stage hands, wardrobe attendant, company manager, press agent, advance agent, theatre manager, drama critic, and teachers of drama, play production, and stagecraft. Discusses qualifications, opportunities, and training. Five illustrations. Bibliography.

TOBACCO INDUSTRY WORKER   3-03.50; 4, 6, 8-12.
Golden harvest—the way of life in the tobacco industry. Flannagan, Roy. Row, Peterson and Co. 1941. 64p. 96c
  Describes work of planting, cultivating, harvesting, and marketing tobacco. See p. 41 for description of series. Thirty-five illustrations.

Tobacco workers. Science Research Associates. 1943. 4p. Planographed. 15c
  Occupational brief number 86. Three illustrations. Annotated bibliography.

TOOL AND DIE MAKER   4-76.
* The tool and die maker. Davis, Anne S., ed. Commonwealth Book Co. 1936 with 1939 supplement. 23p. Mimeographed. 75c
  Information presented according to the NVGA outline. See p. 26 for description of series. Includes a schedule of the apprentice's duties.

Tool and die makers. Science Research Associates. 1943. 4p. Planographed. 15c
  Occupational brief number 39. Two illustrations. Annotated bibliography.

TRAFFIC ENGINEER. *See* Engineer

TRAFFIC MANAGER   0-97.66

* The carrier traffic manager—a transportation specialist. Western Personnel Service. 1944. 28p. 25c

> Describes nature of work in transportation over railway tracks, highways, waterways, pipe lines, and the air lanes. Presents educational requirements, opportunities for employment, and methods of entering this field of work. The suggested readings pertain to technical aspects of the subject.

Pipe line traffic management. Western Personnel Service. 1944. 15p. 25c

> Discussion of the pipe lines of the nation, nature of pipe line traffic management, qualifications, requirements, possibilities for employment, salaries, and opportunities in foreign fields. The suggested references pertain to technical aspects of the subject.

Traffic management as a career. Institute for Research. 1935. 16p. 75c

> Temporarily out of print.

TRANSPORTATION EQUIPMENT WORKER
5, 7, 9-02.000 through 9-05.99

Men of the mold loft. Science Research Associates. 1944. 2p. 15c
> Occupational reprint number 169. One illustration.

Transportation equipment workers. Science Research Associates. 1943. 4p. Planographed. 15c
> Occupational brief number 85. Two illustrations. Annotated bibliography.

TRANSPORTATION WORKER   7, 9-35. through 9-49.

Getting into the trucking business. American Trucking Associations, Inc., 1424 16th St., N.W., Washington 6, D.C. 1945. 63p. Free
> A guide for veterans who are thinking of going into the trucking business.

Opportunities for women in transportation. Science Research Associates. 1943. 2p. 15c
> Occupational reprint number 134. One illustration.

Streamliner—the way of life on a passenger train. Murphy, Ruby. Row, Peterson and Co. 1941. 64p. 96c
> Includes duties of the engineer, fireman, conductor, steward, brakeman, and train crew. See p. 41 for description of series. Forty-eight illustrations.

TRAVEL BUREAU SALESPERSON   1-87.69

Travel bureau. Davis, Anne S., ed. Commonwealth Book Co. 1938. 22p. Mimeographed. 75c
> Information presented according to the NVGA outline. See p. 26 for description of series. Includes duties of itinerary man, manager, tour conductor, courier and guide.

TREE SURGEON   0-68.13

The Bartlett School of tree surgery for the training of dendricians. F. A. Bartlett Tree Expert Co., Stamford, Conn.
> Illustrated recruiting booklet containing description of preliminary and laboratory training, nature of work, and advancement.

TREE SURGEON—*Continued*

Training and work of Davey tree experts. Davey Tree Expert Co.,
Kent, Ohio. No date. 16p. Free
> Pictures and brief captions concerning training activities in tree sur-
> gery, pruning, tree feeding, spraying, tree trimming for public utilities,
> diagnosis, and tree moving.

TRUCK DRIVER   5-36.010; 7-36.250; 7-36.260

Truck and bus drivers. Science Research Associates. 1943. 4p.
Planographed. 15c
> Occupational brief number 46. Two illustrations. Annotated bibliog-
> raphy.

TRUCK FARMER   3-09.10

Market gardening. Shade, Chloris, ed. 2nd edition revised. Morgan-Dillon & Co. 1939. 24p. 32c
> Description of work, qualifications, training, and future outlook. Bib-
> liography.

* Market gardening and truck farming. Davis, Anne S., ed. Commonwealth Book Co. 1937 with 1939 supplement. 29p. Mimeographed. 75c
> Information presented according to the NVGA outline. See p. 26
> for description of series. Includes number of truck gardens in each state.

Truck farmer. Science Research Associates. 1943. 4p. Planographed. 15c
> Occupational brief number 31. Two illustrations. Annotated bibliog-
> raphy.

TUBERCULOSIS ASSOCIATION WORKER   0-27.

An invitation. National Tuberculosis Association, 1790 Broadway,
New York 19, N.Y. 1944. 8p. Free
> Duties, qualifications, and opportunities in the various professional fields
> in national, state, and local tuberculosis associations: executive secretary,
> health educator, field secretary, rehabilitation consultant, social worker, sta-
> tistician, and public relations worker. Bibliography.

See also Public health worker

UNDERTAKER   0-65.20

* Funeral director. Revised edition. Occupational Index. 1945.
6p. 25c
> Occupational abstract. Types of work, abilities, training, entrance and
> advancement, number and distribution of workers, earnings, advantages,
> disadvantages, and postwar prospects. Annotated bibliography.

Funeral directors and embalmers. Science Research Associates.
1943. 4p. Planographed. 15c
> Occupational brief number 99. Two illustrations. Annotated bibliog-
> raphy.

**Funeral service as a vocation. National Funeral Directors Associa-
tion, 111 W. Washington St., Chicago 2, Ill. 1945. 24p. 10c
> Historical background, functions of funeral service, typical duties of
> the embalmer-funeral director, opportunities, qualifications, list of twenty-
> four schools and colleges of embalming and mortuary science, and require-
> ments for embalmer license and for funeral director's license in each of
> the states.

**Jobs in funeral service. National Selected Morticians, 520 No. Michigan Ave., Chicago 11, Ill. 1945. 31p. Free
  Information about work of manager, funeral director-embalmer, and apprentice. State board requirements for each of the states. List of twenty-five schools offering professional training.

The mortician. Davis, Anne S., ed. Revised edition. Commonwealth Book Co. 1939. 25p. Mimeographed. 75c
  Information presented according to the NVGA outline. See p. 26 for description of series. Includes summary of legislation regulating apprenticeship and practice of embalmers in the various states.

The mortician. Science Research Associates. No date. 2p. Planographed. 15c
  Occupational reprint number 46. One illustration.

Mortuary operation as a career. Institute for Research. 1938. 24p. 75c
  Temporarily out of print.

Mortuary service. Cincinnati College of Embalming, Cincinnati 29, Ohio. 1945. 29p. Mimeographed. Free
  Describes service to society, duties, personal qualifications, physical requirements, training, opportunities, and the minimum length of training and minimum length of apprenticeship required by each of the forty-eight states.

VETERINARIAN   0-34.10

Veterinarian. Prepared for the War Department by the National Roster. Supt. of Documents, Washington 25, D.C. 1945. 5c
  Occupational brief containing summary, earnings, outlook, qualifications, and training.

* Veterinarian. Revised edition. Occupational Index. 1945. 6p. 25c
  Occupational abstract. Duties, kinds of practice, abilities required, training, entrance, advancement, earnings, number and distribution of workers, advantages, disadvantages, and postwar prospects. Bibliography.

* Veterinary medicine. Greenleaf, Walter J. Revised edition. U. S. Office of Education. Supt. of Documents, Washington 25, D.C. 1940. 15p. 5c
  Guidance leaflet number 18. License requirements, incomes, and opportunities in the U. S. Bureau of Animal Industry, in the government service, and in the Veterinary Corps of the Army. Information about the twelve accredited schools. Bibliography.

* Veterinary medicine as a career. American Veterinary Medical Association, 600 So. Michigan Ave., Chicago 5, Ill. 1945. 12p. Free
  Nature of work, qualifications, opportunities, and rewards. List of twelve schools recognized by the American Veterinary Medical Association.

Veterinary medicine as a career. Institute for Research. 1936. 19p. 75c
  Licensing requirements, opportunities, earnings, typical day's work, advantages, and disadvantages. Includes description of work in the Bureau of Animal Industry. List of twelve schools recognized by the American Veterinary Medical Association. Three illustrations.

VOCATIONAL ADVISER. *See* Vocational counselor

VOCATIONAL COUNSELOR   0-39.84

Description of the profession of personnel administration. National
Roster. 1945. 4p. Free
  See p. 34 for description of series.

Everybody's business—vocational counseling. Mademoiselle, 122 E.
42nd St., New York 17, N.Y. 1945. 4p. 10c
  Nature of work, qualifications, and opportunities.

**Job of the vocational counselor. Prepared for the War Department
by the National Roster. Supt. of Documents, Washington 25,
D.C. 1945. 14p. 5c
  Occupational brief containing summary, earnings, outlook, qualifications,
  and training.

* The training of vocational counselors. Bureau of Training, War
Manpower Commission. Supt. of Documents, Washington 25,
D.C. 1944. 77p. 15c
  Designed primarily for those who are responsible for the training and
  placement of vocational counselors, the booklet includes an occupational
  description and an outline of the various professional training units. Bibliography at end of each section.

Veterans' counselor. Selina, Ruth. Revised edition. Occupational
Index. 1945. 6p. 25c
  Occupational abstract. Nature of work, qualifications, preparation,
  entrance, and earnings. Annotated bibliography.

Vocational and educational counseling as a career. Institute for
Research. 1937. 23p. 75c
  Temporarily out of print.

VOCATIONAL REHABILITATION WORKER   0-27.

Vocational rehabilitation. Revised edition. Occupational Index.
1944. 6p. 25c
  Occupational abstract. Duties, abilities and qualifications needed, preparation, entrance, advancement, earnings, advantages, disadvantages, and
  postwar prospects. Annotated bibliography.

Vocational rehabilitation workers. Science Research Associates.
1943. 4p. Planographed. 15c
  Occupational brief number 53. Two illustrations. Annotated bibliography.

WAREHOUSE AND STORAGE WORKER   5, 7-88.

Warehouse and storage. Davis, Anne S., ed. Commonwealth Book
Co. 1938. 23p. Mimeographed. 75c
  Information presented according to the NVGA outline. See p. 26
  for description of series. Discussion of work of providing public facilities
  for storage for commercial gain.

WATCHMAKER   4-71.510
Watchmaking and watch repairing. Davis, Anne S., ed. Revised
edition. Commonwealth Book Co. 1939. 29p. Mimeographed.
75c
> Information presented according to the NVGA outline. See p. 26
> for description of series. Emphasis on skilled workers who make watches
> in factories or repair them in jewelry stores and shops.

Watchmaking as a vocation for you. Elgin Watchmakers College,
Elgin, Ill. 1945. 17p. Free
> Recruiting bulletin describing work and training.

WATCHMAN   2-61.01 ; 2-61.03
They guard the gates—the way of life on the American borders.
Rak, Mary K. Row, Peterson and Co. 1941. 64p. 96c
> Describes work of the U. S. Immigration Border Patrol, the Customs
> Patrol, the Coast Guard, and the Plant Quarantine inspectors. See p. 41
> for description of series. Forty-seven illustrations.

WELDER   4, 6-85.
* An appraisal and abstract of available literature on the occupation
of the welder. Spiegler, Samuel. Occupational Index. 1938.
11p. 25c
> Information concerning electric welding, electric arc welding, resistance
> welding, thermit welding, and oxyacetylene welding. Annotated biblio-
> raphy of eleven references.

* Electric arc welding. Shade, Chloris, ed. 2nd edition revised. Morgan-Dillon & Co. 1940. 24p. 32c
> Duties, qualifications, training, conditions of work, and trends. Bib-
> liography.

**Employment opportunities for welders. Bureau of Labor Statistics,
U. S. Dept. of Labor. Supt. of Documents, Washington 25, D.C.
1945. 19p. 10c
> Occupational Outlook Division series. Nature of the occupation, train-
> ing, earnings, hours, other working conditions, and employment prospects.

Jobs for young workers in welding occupations. Science Research
Associates. No date. 2p.
> Occupational reprint number 146. One illustration.

Welders. Science Research Associates. 1943. 4p. Planographed.
15c
> Occupational brief number 42. Two illustrations. Annotated bibliog-
> raphy.

Welding. Davis, Anne S., ed. Commonwealth Book Co. 1936.
15p. Mimeographed. 75c
> Information presented according to the NVGA outline. See p. 26
> for description of series. Emphasis given to autogenous welding, electric
> welding, and oxyacetylene welding.

Welding in a steel mill. Science Research Associates. No date. 2p.
Planographed. 15c
> Occupational brief number 27. One illustration.

WILDLIFE WORKER 0-94.99

* Careers in wildlife management. Elliott, Charles N. Science Research Associates. 1942. 50p. 60c

Discussion of private, state, and Federal jobs, including qualifications and earnings. List of ten colleges which offer degrees and graduate work in wildlife management. Twenty illustrations. Bibliography.

* Employment possibilities in the fish and wildlife service. Fish and Wildlife Service, Chicago 54, Ill. 1945. 13p. Mimeographed. Free

Description of work, qualifications, and opportunities for a career in the conservation of the Nation's natural resources in the field of wildlife, including the land and water mammals and birds, the fishes, reptiles, mollusks, amphibians, and crustaceans. List of schools that offer a full wildlife curriculum, a partial wildlife course in connection with forestry, agriculture, and biology.

See also Animal farmer

WINDOW TRIMMER 0-43.30

Window display. Revised edition. Occupational Index. 1940. 6p. 25c

Occupational abstract. Duties, abilities essential to success, preparation, entrance, advancement, earnings, number and distribution of workers, advantages, disadvantages, and probable future trends. Annotated bibliography.

WRITER 0-06.19

Free-lance writer. Revised edition. Occupational Index. 1944. 6p. 25c

Occupational abstract. Abilities, preparation, entrance, advancement, compensation, number and distribution of workers, advantages, disadvantages, and future trend of employment. Annotated bibliography.

Free-lance writers. Science Research Associates. 1945. 4p. 15c

Occupational brief number 121. Discussion of qualifications, earnings, advantages, disadvantages, and future outlook. Includes opportunities in radio. Two illustrations. Annotated bibliography.

Writer. Prepared for the War Department by the National Roster. Supt. of Documents, Washington 25, D.C. 1945. 5c

Occupational brief containing summary, earnings, outlook, qualifications, and training.

See also Editor ; Journalist

X-RAY TECHNICIAN 0-50.04

Approved schools for X-ray technicians. Council on Medical Education and Hospitals of the American Medical Association, 535 N. Dearborn St., Chicago 10, Ill. 1945. 4p. Free

Tabulated information concerning a hundred and fifteen approved schools.

**Career as an X-ray technician. Institute for Research. 1945. 24p. 75c

Duties, qualifications, educational requirements, typical day's work, pleasant and unpleasant features. Describes work of the X-ray technician in hospital, industry, and in U. S. Civil Service. Requirements for registration with the American Registry of X-Ray Technicians. Six illustrations.

Description of the sub-profession of X-ray technicians. National Roster. 1945. 3p. Free
See p. 34 for description of series.

**Training of X-ray technicians. American Registry of X-Ray Technicians, 2900 E. Minnehaha Parkway, Minneapolis 6, Minn. 1945. 11p. Free
General qualifications of trainees, training course curricula, classification of X-ray technicians, and rules and regulations governing registration of X-ray technicians.

The X-ray technician. The Chronicle. No date. 6p. 5c
Guidepost to occupational information number 10. Bibliography.

X-ray technician. Davis, Anne S., ed. Commonwealth Book Co. 1938. 26p. Mimeographed. 75c
Information presented according to the NVGA outline. See p. 26 for description of series. Discusses work of the X-ray film technician and the X-ray therapeutic technician. List of tweny-nine training schools approved by the American Registry of X-Ray Technicians.

**X-ray technicians. Women's Bureau, U. S. Dept. of Labor. Supt. of Documents, Washington 25, D.C. 1945. 14p. 10c
Number 8 of series "The outlook for women in occupations in the medical services." Duties, number of workers, earnings, hours, and advancement. Discusses the prewar situation, the wartime changes, and the postwar outlook. Minimum requirements for entrance to an approved school and for completion of approved course. Minimum requirements for registration by the American Registry of X-ray Technicians and for membership in the American Society of X-ray Technicians. Minimum requirements for beginning Federal Civil Service position as assistant medical technician. Two illustrations. Bibliography.

Y. M. C. A. SECRETARY   0-27.

* Qualifications and training for the secretaryship of the Young Men's Christian Association. The Association Press, 347 Madison Ave., New York 17, N.Y. 1945. 4p. 10c
A statement of professional and personal qualifications and what are considered adequate training requirements.

Professional opportunities in the Y. M. C. A. National Council of Young Men's Christian Association, 347 Madison Ave., New York 17, N.Y. No date. 11p. 10c
Duties, qualifications, education and training of secretaries, and methods of entering the profession.

Y. W. C. A. SECRETARY   0-27.

A handbook of personnel policy. Walser, Olive H. Woman's Press, 600 Lexington Ave., New York 22, N.Y. 1941. 32p. 35c
Used by the Personnel Bureau of the National Board of the Y. W. C. A. Includes some discussion of selection of candidates, qualifications, opportunities, and work in the Y. W. C. A. as a profession. Bibliography.

* Going our way? National Board, Young Women's Christian Association, 600 Lexington Ave., New York 22, N.Y. 1945. 32p. Free
Information about professional work in the Y. W. C. A., including requirements and personnel policies.

Y. W. C. A. SECRETARY—*Continued*

Salaries and qualifications of YWCA professional workers. Hurlin, Ralph G. Russell Sage Foundation. Available from the Woman's Press, 600 Lexington Ave., New York 22, N.Y. 1943. 24p. 30c

> Includes many statistical reports such as: Distribution of associations and of professional workers by region and state; number of workers in each of thirty-two positions classified by full or part-time status; classification of workers by race, position, age, extent of college and university education, specialized training, and length of service. The studies of salaries include median, quartile, and extreme salaries of workers in each of thirty-one positions.

The Y is calling. National Board of Y. W. C. A., 600 Lexington Ave., New York 22, N.Y. 1945. 2p. Free

> Recruiting poster listing types of available positions and brief statements of qualifications. Three illustrations.

ZOOLOGIST   0-39.64

Animal kingdom—the way of life in a zoo. Ditmars, Raymond. Row, Peterson and Co. 1941. 64p. 96c

> Includes duties of several workers in a zoo. See p. 41 for description of series. Fifty-four illustrations.

Description of the profession of zoology including fish and wildlife management. National Roster. 1945. 3p. Free

> See p. 34 for description of series.

* Handbook of descriptions of specialized fields in zoology and parasitology. National Roster. Supt. of Documents, Washington 25, D.C. 1945. 14p. 10c

> Occupational summary, related fields, functional activities, fields of specialization, and related occupations.

* Zoologist, entomologist, and parasitologist. Prepared for the War Department by the National Roster. Supt. of Documents, Washington 25, D.C. 1945. 14p. 5c

> Occupational brief containing summary, earnings, outlook, qualifications, and training.

B. INFORMATION ABOUT SEVERAL OCCUPATIONS

Accredited higher institutions. Ratcliffe, Ella B. U. S. Office of Education. Supt. of Documents, Washington 25, D.C. 1944. 144p. 25c

> Part two names the professional and technical schools accredited by national organizations for architecture, business, chemistry, chemical engineering, dentistry, forestry, journalism, law, library science, medicine, music, nursing, occupational therapy, optometry, osteopathy, pharmacy, physical therapy, social work, theology, veterinary medicine, and engineering.

Approved technical institutes. National Council of Technical Schools, Washington 6, D.C. 1945. 35p. 15c
Lists of schools in forty-two fields which offer training for positions supplementary to professional engineering. Included are aeronautics, radio, chemistry, construction, refrigeration, and watchmaking. For each school there is given information concerning courses, entrance requirements, job opportunities, and recognition.

Careers for women. Syracuse University, Syracuse, N.Y. 1945. 80p. Free
Descriptions of the various fields, the opportunities they offer, and the training given in each by the colleges and schools of Syracuse University. Nature of work, qualifications, opportunities, and preparation for each of fifty-five vocations. The discussion on preparation includes the recommended high school courses and lists of subjects in each of the four years of college study.

Careers in New York state government. New York State Department of Civil Service, Albany, N.Y. 1942. 62p. Free
Description of position, specifications, and sample examination questions for each of the following: accounting, budgeting, dietetics, drafting, civil engineering, sanitary engineering, institution education, laboratory, law, library, medicine, nursing, occupational therapy, personnel, physiotherapy, psychology, social work, and statistics.

The door to opportunity swings open. Allis-Chalmers Manufacturing Co., Milwaukee 1, Wis. 1945. 43p. Free
Describes the employee training program. One page is devoted to each of twenty-five kinds of work such as blueprint reading, shop sketching, brass molding, and mechanical drafting. Thirty-six illustrations.

Employment of United States citizens in Latin America. Pan American Union, Washington, D.C. 1945. 18p. Mimeographed. Free
Indicates general and fundamental considerations that should be kept in mind by those who are looking to Latin America for possibilities for earning a living rather than information on specific job opportunities. Presents requisites for employment in Latin America, some wage and salary information, and highlights of the restrictive legislation of each of the twenty Latin American countries.

Employment opportunities in characteristic industrial occupations of women. Women's Bureau, U. S. Dept. of Labor. Supt. of Documents, Washington 25, D.C. 1944. 50p. 10c
Description of jobs which are likely to present future employment opportunities for women such as operation of machines, inspection, assembly, packing, wrapping, tool-crib and storeroom work. Discussion of probable opportunities in the electrical industry, professional and scientific instruments, transportation equipment, small metal products, and fabricated plastic products.

Guide to elective courses according to educational and vocational interests and objectives. College of Liberal Arts and Sciences, College of the City of New York, Convent Ave. and 139th St., New York 31, N.Y. 1945. 96p. 25c; free to schools and libraries
For eighty-one vocational possibilities, there are suggested background courses, essential or especially relevant elective courses, other desirable elective courses, graduate training required, specific fields of possible em-

ployment, and sources of information or readings about the field of interest. List of Civil Service positions for which graduates of colleges of liberal arts and sciences are eligible.

Home study blue book and directory of private home study schools and courses approved by the National Home Study Council. The Council, Washington 6, D.C. 1945. 32p. Free

For a hundred and twenty-four vocations, there are listed the approved home study and correspondence courses.

List of various technical courses approved by the Council. National Council of Technical Schools, 839 17th St., N.W., Washington 6, D.C. 1945. 4p. Mimeographed. Free

For forty-two occupations, names of approved technical institutes whose courses have been approved by the Council.

The 1941 student career conference. Alabama College, Montevallo, Ala. 1941. 76p. Free

Reports from the occupational round tables on thirty-four vocations include qualifications, necessary training, approximate income, conditions of work, disadvantages, future outlook, opportunities in Alabama, and number engaged in the vocation in Alabama. Also includes four talks presented by the general conference leader. Good example of a summary of career conference discussions.

Occupational data for counselors—a handbook of census information selected for use in guidance. Prepared by the Occupational Outlook Division of the Bureau of Labor Statistics in cooperation with the Occupational Information and Guidance Service of the U. S. Office of Education. Supt. of Documents, Washington 25, D.C. 1945. 36p. 10c

Statistics showing the number of workers in two hundred and twenty-five occupations from 1910 to 1940. Useful for comparing the number of workers in given occupations over a period of thirty years to find occupations that are growing; those that are diminishing in importance; new occupations; trends in women's activities, racial groups, age groups; and trends in various geographical areas.

Occupations for college women. Bulletin of the University of Wisconsin, Madison, Wis. 1944. 50p. Free

Survey of the twenty-eight fields of work and professions for which the University prepares women. Description of the kinds of work, opportunities, and educational preparation. The pamphlet indicates what general course of studies prepares for each field and, where high school training is important or extra-curricular activity is significant, what the best high school preparation is.

**The outlook for women in occupations in the medical and other health services. Women's Bureau, U. S. Dept. of Labor, Washington 25, D.C. 1945.

Comparison of the occupations discussed in the eleven pamphlets in the series of the same title containing a discussion of the supply and demand trends. In press.

Occupations of employed persons in each industry, for the United States: March 1940. Bureau of the Census, U. S. Dept. of Commerce, Washington 25, D.C. 1943. 37p. Free

For each of one hundred and thirty-two industries there is given the number of men employed in each of one hundred and sixteen occupations and the number of women employed in each of fifty-two occupations, providing both an industrial distribution for each of these occupations and an occupational distribution of each industry.

School courses and related careers. Bacher, Otto R. and Berkowitz, George J. Science Research Associates. 1941. 98p. $1
Includes list of school subjects and related vocations. There also is an index of occupations followed by required school subjects.

The situation and the challenge. Corcoran, J. P. Xavier University. 1937. 18p. 50c
Distribution of Negro workers in fields of occupations, trends, and outlook.

A social-economic grouping of the nation's labor force, 1910-1940. Bureau of the Census, U. S. Dept. of Commerce, Washington 25, D.C. 1943. 32p. Free
Useful information concerning the number of men and women engaged in two hundred and seventeen occupations classified into six social-economic groups.

Special aids for placing military personnel in civilian jobs—enlisted Army personnel. Supt. of Documents, Washington 25, D.C. 1944. 490p. $1
Consists of a series of job families, each of which lists civilian jobs related to a military occupational specialty. Indicates how military experience and training may be utilized in the return of servicemen and women to civilian life. The information is in tabular form. For each military occupational specialty four factors are shown: (1) Related civilian occupations listed by dictionary code and title; (2) additional training required; (3) physical activities; and (4) workng conditions. Helpful to counselors who are advising discharged servicemen and women.

Special aids for placing military personnel in civilian jobs—enlisted Naval personnel. Supt. of Documents, Washington 25, D.C. 1945. $1
Consists of a series of job families, each of which lists civilian jobs related to a naval rating. Indicates how naval experience and training may be utilized in the return of servicemen and women to civilian life. The information is in tabular form. For each naval rating, four factors are shown: (1) Related civilian occupations listed by dictionary code and title; (2) additional training required; (3) physical activities; and (4) working conditions. Of value to counselors who are advising returning naval veterans. Helps to utilize the veteran's naval experience and build upon it.

Steps to a career—a guidance handbook for career planning. Bates College, Lewiston, Me. 1945. 34p. Free
Programs of study leading to twenty-five specific careers open to college men. Brief statement concerning qualifications. Twenty-four illustrations.

Steps to a career—a guidance handbook for young women looking ahead to college. Bates College, Lewiston, Me. 1945. 34p. Free
Qualifications and programs of study leading to twenty-five specific careers open to college women. Includes careers such as language translation, medical technology, personnel and industrial relations, radio and dramatics. Twenty-five illustrations.

War emergency and career training for women. Bulletin of the Carnegie Institute of Technology, Schenley Park, Pittsburgh, Pa. 1943. 13p. Free

> Descriptive material concerning the programs of study offered by the departments of general science; home economics; teacher training; foods, nutrition, and management; art, clothing, and textiles; secretarial studies, and social work. Contains fourteen illustrations unusually well adapted to bulletin board display.

What kind of college for you? Union College, Schenectady 8, N.Y. 1945. 32p. Free

> Written for the student prepared to enter college and "desirous of finding the kind of institution that will help to make him what he wants to be." Some of the alternatives discussed are: a large or a small college, a man's college or a coeducational college, a new college or an old college, a "sports college" or not, a tax-supported college or a privately supported college, and a liberal or professional college.

What to do in the world's work. Hunter College of the City of New York, 695 Park Ave., New York 21, N.Y. 1941. 152p. 25c

> Preparation for each of three hundred and fifty vocations or fields of employment for women is indicated under courses of instruction at Hunter College which are considered essential for the vocation named. Also included are courses of instruction which are considered desirable or helpful though not essential, advanced professional or technical training required, fields of employment or specific vocations, sources of information concerning entry into the vocation, and bibliography of vocational literature.

What vocation? Corcoran, J. P. Xavier University. 1937. 23p. 50c

> Discussion of the opportunities for Negroes in several professions.

Where do we go from here? New York University, Washington Square, New York 3, N.Y. 1944. 40p. Free

> A bulletin of information addressed to servicemen and women. Includes a list of one hundred and ninety vocations and professions for which the University offers preparation. A chart shows four hundred and fourteen military or naval occupations opposite the comparable or related civilian activities and indicates which of the forty-one fields of study offer training.

Which jobs for young workers? Children's Bureau, U. S. Department of Labor, Washington 25, D.C. 1944-1945. 8p. each. Free

> Description of jobs which are comparatively safe and those which are too hazardous for sixteen and seventeen year old workers. Guide to placement officers and employers. Titles are:
> 9. Advisory standards for the pulp and paper industries
> 10. Advisory standards for the textile industries
> 11. Advisory standards for the railroad industry
> 12. Advisory standards for the foundries
> 13. Advisory standards for the brick and tile industry
> 15. Advisory standards for the slaughtering and meat-packing industry

Wilson and your career. Wilson College, Chambersburg, Pa. 1942. 34p. Free

> About one page is devoted to discussion of each of thirty-one vocations, including basic and related Wilson College courses, helpful extracurricular activities, and types of jobs. Twenty-four illustrations.

A young man's chances in the Latin American field. Carson, J. S. Pan American Union, Washington, D.C. 1944. 8p. Free
Discussion of opportunities in inter-American commercial relations by the chairman of the education committee, National Foreign Trade Council, Inc.

Your job is your future. The Board of Public Education, Philadelphia, Pa. 1941. 80p. 25c
Description of courses offered in the vocational schools of Philadelphia. Each of the thirty-one course descriptions considers the character of the work, the school program, probable line of promotion, special qualifications, if any, and working conditions in the trade. Ninety excellent illustrations.

Your job is your life pattern. Vol. I. London Free Press, London, Ontario, Canada. 1944. 16p. 15c
Sixteen occupational studies, prepared under the direction of the Department of Vocational Guidance of the London Board of Education, published weekly by the Free Press. Assembled and bound in booklet form, each article follows a uniform outline including: Importance of the occupation, conditions of work, personal qualifications, training required, rewards, advantages, disadvantages, and trends. Volume I includes accountant, advertiser, artist, chemist, engineer, farmer, home economist, lawyer, musician, nurse, office worker, popular musician, railroader, social welfare worker, teacher, and tradesman. In newspaper print, the booklets are 11½ by 17 inches in size. Illustrated.

Your job is your life pattern. Vol. II. London Free Press, London, Ontario, Canada. 1945. 43p. 25c
The second series of articles published weekly from March 1944 to May 1945. The occupations discussed include architecture, aviation, beauty culture, biology, dairying, dentistry, electrical engineering, fire fighting, forestry, geology, homemaking, hospital work, journalism, laundry work, library work, lithography, machinist, medicine, meteorology, ministry, motor mechanic, occupational therapy, optometry, pharmacy, photography, physical education, physiotherapy, police work, printing, radio repairing, radio technician, railway carman, salesmanship, telephony, watchmaking, and work with the Y. M. C. A. and Y. W. C. A. In newspaper print, the booklets are 11½ by 17 inches in size. Illustrated.

Your place in life and how to find it. McDonnell, John B., ed. The Trailblazers, 119 W. Park Ave., Champaign, Ill. 1938. 128p. 25c
About four pages are devoted to each of twenty-two skilled trades, such as tool and die making, welding, radio servicing, and upholstering. Includes information about qualifications, training, and apprenticeship. Bibliography for each section includes technical books, associations, and magazines.

C. APPRENTICESHIP

Apprentice training for veterans. Apprentice-Training Service, U. S. Dept. of Labor, Washington 25, D.C. 1945. 12p. Free
Explanation of apprentice training, qualifications required, career opportunities offered, and where to apply for apprentice training.

Apprentices. Science Research Associates. 1943. 4p. Planographed. 15c

> Occupational brief number 20. Two illustrations. Annotated bibliography.

Looking ahead by way of apprenticeship. Apprentice-Training Service, U. S. Dept. of Labor, Washington 25, D.C. No date. 8p. Free

> Suggestions for selecting an apprenticeship that is up to standard. An explanation of apprentice training and its advantages to young men in equipping them for careers as craftsmen in the skilled trades.

The national apprenticeship program. Apprentice-Training Service, U. S. Dept. of Labor, Washington 25, D.C. 1945. 9p. Free

> Includes a list of apprenticeable trades followed by the number of years' training customarily required in each trade.

There's work to be done. Allis-Chalmers Manufacturing Co., Milwaukee, Wis. 1941. 22p. Free

> Describes the apprentice training program of twelve trades. The four-year apprentice courses are offered for blacksmith, brass molder, electrical mechanic, iron molder, machinist, pattern maker, plate worker, sheet metal worker, toolmaker, and woodworker. Three year courses are offered for mechanical drafting and welding. Twenty illustrations.

D. CHARTS AND POSTERS

Accreditation requirements for junior colleges. American Association of Junior Colleges, 730 Jackson Place, Washington 6, D.C. 1941. 50c

> Wall chart, 38" by 38", showing entrance requirements for thirty-eight junior colleges.

Arts on the job. Mademoiselle. 122 E. 42nd St., New York 17, N.Y. 1944. 12" by 22½". 10c

> Mademoiselle's job chart no. 9. Horizontal columns contain information about art and photography, dance, acting, music, and writing and editing. Vertical columns are headed: radio and television; books, magazines, newspapers; stage and screen; brief biographical notes of young women "on their way."

Best Federal job opportunities. U. S. Civil Service Commission, Washington 25, D.C. 1945. Free

> Bulletin board announcement presenting names of positions, salaries, and brief statement of duties. The positions are grouped under the following headings: administrative, clerical and office machine, economics and business, engineering, library, medical, scientific, social and educational, and trades.

Brewer's vocational chart. Supt. of Documents, Washington 25, D.C. 1945. 2p. 5c

> Vocational opportunities for men are listed on reverse side of vocational opportunities for women. 16" by 21". Alongside each occupation is a figure denoting the number of thousands of workers in the field according to the U. S. Census of 1940. Useful for presenting a panoramic view of America's most common occupations.

Business as a career. New York University, Washington Square, New York 3, N.Y. 1945. 48p. Free

> The university bulletin contains a two-page chart of business opportunities, listing eighty-two typical positions in fourteen basic activities in business.

Career chart. Careers for you. Drexel Institute of Technology, 32nd and Chestnut Sts., Philadelphia 4, Pa. 1945. 22″ by 33″. Free

> Shows relationship existing between college courses and careers. Compilation of the resulting opportunities, estimated initial salary, qualifications for positions, and advantages of profession for each of the twenty vocations for which training is available at Drexel Institute. Six illustrations.

Career charts. Institute for Research. 537 S. Dearborn St., Chicago.

> Thirty charts, 22 by 17 inches, showing graphically the routes of promotion and relationships between jobs in a number of fields.

The Champaign guidance charts. Faculty of Champaign Senior High School, Champaign, Ill. 1939. 28p. $1.05; on bristol board $3.75

> Twenty-five charts designed to show the relationship between school subjects and vocations. Good for bulletin board use. The last edition contains suggestions for using these charts. Size 12″ by 18″.

Class to career posters. Science Research Associates. 1945. 17″ by 24″. Yearly subscription $1

> Indicates relationship between school subjects and careers. One poster published each month during school year 1945-1946.

Food: the way to the world's heart. Mademoiselle, 122 E. 42nd St., New York 17, N.Y. 1945. 10c

> Tabulated information on duties, earnings, education, and training for positions concerned with food. Groups positions requiring administrative, scientific, and journalistic abilities.

Forbes post-war job chart. Prepared by Science Research Associates. 1945. 4p. 15c

> Opposite the titles of military jobs are numbers referring to civilian jobs for which the military training is related. For each of sixty-eight civilian occupations, a brief job description and the name of a reference book or pamphlet are given.

Medical jobs for today and tomorrow. Mademoiselle, 122 E. 42nd St., New York 17, N.Y. 1945. 11½″ by 29″. 10c

> Mademoiselle's job chart no. 10. For thirteen medical occupations brief information is presented concerning requirements, getting started, practice, and outlook. Includes medical secretary, dental hygienist, occupational therapist, and medical librarian.

Poster entitled "Don't be a job hopper." U. S. Employment Service, Dept. of Labor, Washington 25, D.C. 1945. 1p. Free

> Colored picture by Walt Disney useful to combine with a caption such as "Have a definite study schedule."

Vocational slide rule. Northeastern University, Boston, Mass. No date. Circular. Free

> Lists of vocations leading from the study of each of eighteen college courses.

Vocational training chart for young women. Stephens College, Columbia, Mo. 1944. 33" by 22". Free

Compilation of the duties, estimated earnings, and necessary training prerequisites for each of the thirty-two vocations for which the college is equipped to offer training. A recommended schedule of courses which will qualify the student for employment is arranged for four semesters.

What you can do with your Army training as a civilian. B'nai B'rith Vocational Service Bureau, 1746 M St., N.W., Washington 6, D.C. 1944. 38" by 50". 20c

Based on information contained in *Special aids for the placement of military, personnel in civilian jobs.*

What you can do with your Navy training in a civilian job. B'nai B'rith Vocational Service Bureau, 1746 M St., N.W., Washington 6, D.C. 1945. 38" by 40". 20c

Titles and insignia are given for fifty-two Navy and Coast Guard ratings. In the three columns opposite each are titles and duties of related civilian jobs that may be done with (1) little or no additional training, (2) with more training, and (3) with extensive training. Based on the publication *Special aids for the placement of naval personnel in civilian jobs.*

Where do we go from here? New York University, Washington Square, New York 3, N.Y. 1944. 40p. Free

The booklet includes a fourteen page chart entitled "Fields of study for war veterans suggested by their military or naval occupations." Suggests forty-one fields of study related to the four hundred and fourteen military or naval occupations.

Where does your talent lie? Endicott Junior College, Beverly, Mass. 1945. Free

A single sheet 8½" by 11" listing the vocations that utilize each of fourteen school courses.

Your high school record—does it count? Revised edition. South Dakota Press, Vermillion, S.D. 1945. 18" x 22". Complete with glassed frame $13.50; without frame $11

Poster set adapted from book of same title proving to students that the records they are making in high school will count for or against them in later life.

E. CHOOSING A CAREER

Choosing a life work. Zubin, Joseph. Union of American Hebrew Congregations, Cincinnati, Ohio. 1937. 69p. Mimeographed. 25c

Discussion of factors determining success in occupational adjustment and the personal and economic factors involved in the choice of an occupation. The last half of booklet is addressed to Jewish youth. Bibliography.

Choosing your life work. B'nai B'rith Vocational Service Bureau, 1746 M St., N.W., Washington 6, D.C. 1945. 7p. 10c

Nine cartoon-like illustrations on a page grouped according to the topics: discovering yourself, discovering occupations, and discriminations.

The graduate looks to the future. Erickson, Clifford E. and Mc-
Colloch, Lois. McKnight and McKnight, Bloomington, Ill. 1940.
112p. 48c
>Discussion of topics such as surveying employment opportunities, choosing
a college, continuing one's schooling during spare time, continuing to grow
on the job, and how to get a job.

How to choose a career. Humphreys, J. Anthony. Science Research Associates. 1940. 50p. 60c
>Table of contents: Introduction, How to store facts about careers, What
to learn about occupations, What to learn about yourself, How to relate
analysis of occupation to self-analysis, and a few final words. Nine illustrations. Annotated bibliography.

Information for prospective college students. Partch, C. E. Rutgers University, New Brunswick, N.J. 1935. 48p. Free
>Discussion of choice of a vocation and choice of a college. Bibliography.

Investing in yourself. Strang, Ruth. National Association of Secondary-School Principals, 1201 16th St., N.W., Washington 6,
D.C. 1945. 90p. 25c
>Encouragement to the young person to use his resources effectively in
securing an education, investing in personal development, and getting a start
in his career. Bibliography at end of each section.

Job exploration workbook for occupational laboratory students.
Hahn, Milton E. and Brayfield, Arthur. Science Research Associates. 1945. 112p. 96c
>Consists of fourteen projects planned to help the students find answers to
questions about how to choose a career, how to get a job, what training is
needed, and how to succeed on the job.

Looking ahead—choosing and preparing for a vocation. Andrews,
E. W. Row, Peterson and Co. 1941. 48p. 20c
>Chapters on getting ready for tomorrow, career economics, knowing your-
self, and the road ahead urge youth to look ahead and plan a career. Forty-
two illustrations.

My life work. Davis, Anne S., ed. Revised edition. Commonwealth Book Co. 1939. 15p. Mimeographed. 75c
>A plea to youth to survey the occupational opportunities and formulate a
goal. Bibliography.

A post-war career for APO Joe. Cutler, Leon and Yura, Stephen.
Leon Cutler, 20 E. 35th Street, New York 16, N.Y. 1945. 96p
>A series of cartoons about entering the hobbycraft business.

Practice book on selecting an occupation. Prosser, C. A. McKnight
and McKnight, Bloomington, Ill. 1945. 72p. 20c
>Exercises and check lists to be used with *Selecting on occupation* by the
same author.

Preparing for industrial work. Revised edition. National Association of Manufacturers, 14 W. 49th St., New York 20, N.Y.
1945. 47p. Free
>Subtitle: Occupations you can choose from—what you want to do and
are qualified to do—what training is necessary to prepare you for a job. Includes list of a hundred and fifty major occupations in which three quarters
of all workers earn their living. Good suggestions on getting information
about occupations that appeal to one.

Selecting a career—decision based on information. Kitson, H. D. Institute for Research. 1931. 13p. 75c
Introduction to series of monographs. Youth is advised to look over the fields of work and become acquainted with their scope and variety.

Selecting an occupation—nine major occupational fields. Prosser, C. A. Revised edition. McKnight and McKnight, Bloomington, Ill. 1945. 155p. 60c
Suggestions and directions for finding the demands and opportunities of occupations, for checking individual assets against such demands, and for selecting a suitable occupation. Practice book for pupil's use is listed above. Bibliography.

Today's choice of tomorrow's job. Chicago Board of Education, Bureau of Occupational Research, 228 N. LaSalle St., Chicago, Ill. 1944. 35p. 25c
Suggestions to help the student recognize the important factors in the choice of an occupation, the sources of occupational information, and methods of observing occupational trends.

Time on your hands—choosing and using recreation. National Association of Secondary-School Principals, 1201 16th St., N.W., Washington, D.C. 1945. 122p. 25c
Includes some suggestions for choosing an avocation which would be helpful to young persons in planning a career. Bibliography.

Today and tomorrow—how will you serve? Milwaukee-Downer College, Milwaukee, Wis., 1942. 16p. Free
Description of nature of work and training for careers in education, social services, recreation, and nutrition. Illustrated.

The "which?" book—a guide indicating the vocational relationship of school subjects. B'nai B'rith Vocational Service Bureau, 1746 M St., N.W., Washington 6, D.C. 1937. 19p. 10c
Contains lists of occupations to which an ability or interest in seventeen specific school subjects may lead. Material originally prepared by the Guidance Department of the Samuel J. Tilden High School, Brooklyn, N. Y.

F. Occupations for the Handicapped

Blind persons employed in war industries in the U. S. as of January 1943. National Society for the Blind, Woodward Bldg., Washington 5, D.C. 1943. 33p. Free
Compilation of reports in chart form prepared by agencies for the blind. Positions held and wages earned in specific industries are given.

Blind workers in U. S. industries. Lewis, L. O. National Society for the Blind, Woodward Bldg., Washington 5, D.C. 1943. 170p. $1
Includes photographs and letters from employers of the blind attesting to their usefulness in many types of industrial jobs. Seventy-five illustrations.

Employment problems of the hard of hearing. American Society for the Hard of Hearing, 1537 35th St., N.W., Washington 7, D.C. 1941. 11p. Free
> Includes suggestions for meeting the employment problems of the hard of hearing.

Insurance underwriting—a study of the business in its relation to blind agents. Brown, Lela T. American Foundation for the Blind, 15 W. 16th St., New York 11, N.Y. 1928. 52p. 50c
> Discussion of opportunities, qualifications, and training facilities and suggestions drawn from the experience of thirty-five blind insurance agents. Requirements which seem essential to success include adjustment to the world of seeing people, both psychologically and socially; adequate guide and clerical assistance; systematic training, and the means of keeping informed as to developments in the business.

Jobs for the hard of hearing. American Association to Promote the Teaching of Speech to the Deaf, 1537 35th St., N.W., Washington 7, D.C. 1939. 4p. 3c
> Suggestions for the job seeker and brief biographical sketches of hard of hearing individuals who are earning their living as employees of the Federal government: an office manager, librarian, statistician, accountant, plant physiologist, and a chart corrector.

The kind of work disabled veterans can do. The Trundle Engineering Co., 1501 Euclid Ave., Cleveland 15, Ohio. 1945. 14p. Free
> Table showing a hundred and seventy-one occupations in which handicapped people are successfully employed as reported by fourteen companies with the following types of disablement: amputation of one arm, one hand, one leg; deaf in one ear or hard of hearing; completely deaf; blind in one eye; totally blind, serious speech impediment; and amputation of toes or fingers.

National physical demands information series: Number I—Apprenticeable occupations. Apprentice-Training Service, U. S. Dept. of Labor. 1944. 112p. Free
> Provides physical demands information which is typical of apprenticeable occupations. Occupations included are those in which persons with handicaps are generally found to be serving formal apprenticeships.

Occupations for those with heart disease. American Heart Association, Inc., 1790 Broadway, New York 19, N.Y. 1941. 10p. Free
> Although the selection of an occupation must depend primarily upon the mental equipment, education, and previous training of the individual, each patient should engage in an occupation which demands less than he is well able to perform. In this way he will avoid the probability of frequently overtaxing his endurance. A list of suitable occupations, compiled through the cooperation of the New York State Bureau of Rehabilitation, consists of thirty skilled occupations for men ad boys, seventeen skilled occupations for women and girls, fifteen unskilled and semi-skilled occupations for men and boys, and twenty-two unskilled and semi-skilled occupations for women and girls.

Open letter to my newly blinded friend in the armed forces. Clunk, Joseph. National Society for the Blind, Woodward Building, Washington 5, D.C. 1945. 36p. 10c
> The section on employment states that man's field of opportunity is limited by his mentality and not by physical imperfection. List of state agencies for the blind and a list of occupations in which blind persons have successfully engaged.

Operations manual for the placement of the physically handicapped. U. S. Civil Service Commission. Supt. of Documents, Washington 25, D.C. 1944. 473p. 60c

Each job has a code number to indicate type of disability acceptable for placement. There also is supplementary information on minimum requirements for more than five hundred jobs. A useful chart is included. The list has been compiled by the U. S. Civil Service Commission to show the occupations which the orthopedically disabled can undertake in Government industrial establishments and in private industries holding Government contracts: aircraft manufacture, repair, and inspection; ammunition, explosives, and firearms; inspection and fabrication of textile and leather goods; maintenance and reclamation activities; Post Office department positions; and ship building and repair. The functional and environmental factors of each job were studied and related to various abilities of handicapped persons.

Opportunities for the deaf in industry. American Association to Promote the Teaching of Speech to the Deaf, 1537 35th St., N.W., Washington 7, D.C. 1938. 2p. 3c

Brief discussion of opportunities in the building trades and the metal working industries.

Osteopathy—opportunities for the blind in training and practice. Brown, Lela T. American Foundation for the Blind, 15 W. 16th St., New York 11, N.Y. 1929. 50p. 50c

The requirements, rewards, training and licensure, income and the practice of fifty blind osteopathic physicians are discussed. The fact that thirty-seven blind osteopathic physicians reported annual incomes from $500 to $9000 with a median of $3000 indicates that this field of work is at least a possibility for one with the requirements and qualifications.

Professional writing—opportunities for the blind in journalism and allied fields. Lathrop, Gordon. American Foundation for the Blind. 1933. 42p. 50c

The difficulties and discouragements of sightless writers are described as well as the successes sometimes achieved. Twenty-three blind writers contributed information about their experiences and offered advice to sightless writers. Concluding that the field of professional writing does hold opportunities which those without sight can make their own, the warning is given that they must possess an adequate education, an objective point of view, and a limitless capacity for hard work.

Stand concessions—as operated by the blind in the United States and Canada. Brown, Lela T. American Foundation for the Blind, 15 W. 16th St., New York 11, N.Y. 1930. 72p. 50c

Information was obtained by interviews with fifty blind operators and twelve placement agents. The factors of success are discussed as well as the methods of securing the concessions and operating the stands.

A study of occupations of partially sighted boys and girls. Kastrup, Marguerite. National Society for the Prevention of Blindness, 1790 Broadway, New York 19, N.Y. 1935. 8p. 5c

Summary of inquiry sent to former sight-saving class pupils in Ohio public schools. List of eighty occupations with asterisks indicating those which may be satisfactory for myopes and others having low vision.

Untapped manpower. U. S. Civil Service Commission, Washington 25, D.C. 1943. 15p. Free

Facts and figures on employment of the physically handicapped. Brief summary of jobs in which handicapped are especially adept. Eight photographs.

Workshops for the blind. National Industries for the Blind, 15 W. 16th St., New York 11, N.Y. 1944. 11p. Free
> Purpose and principles of workshops. Includes brief discussion of selection of staff members, working conditions, and the work of training and placing blind workers.

G. Seeking the Job

How to get a job and win promotion. Prosser, C. A. and Sahlin, W. F. McKnight & McKnight, Bloomington, Ill. 1945. 101p. 50c
> Information, suggestions, and directions regarding the steps and successful ways of selecting a job, locating prospective employers, getting contact with the employer, applying for a job, and securing employment.

How to get THE job. Dreese, Mitchell. Science Research Associates. 1944. 50p. 60c
> Discussion of planning the job campaign, six ways to approach the job market, and methods of improving the interview. Fourteen illustrations. Annotated bibliography.

The job finding forum. Advertising Club of New York, 23 Park Ave., New York 16, N.Y. 1945. 10c
> Describes the forum conducted by the club and presents eight points as a "sales manual of man power."

Pick your job and land it! Edlund, Sidney W. Business Education World, 270 Madison Ave., New York 16, N.Y. 1940. 33p. 20c
> A reprint of a series of articles on such topics as: Know what you want to do, Dig out your hidden assets, Plan for each interview, and Offer a service instead of asking for a job.

Your job—how to find it, how to hold it. B'nai B'rith Vocational Service Bureau and the Chicago Jewish Vocational Service, 1746 M St., N.W., Washington 6, D.C. 1940. 31p. 10c
> Includes points to consider before an interview with an employer and a discussion of what employers want.

PART VII

Publishers' Directory

Advisory Board on Industrial Education, Board of Education, 110 Livingston St., Brooklyn 2, N.Y.

Advertising Club of New York, 23 Park Ave., New York 16

Air-Age Education Research, 100 E. 42nd St., New York 17

American Airlines Inc., 100 E. 42nd St., New York 17

American Association for Health, Physical Education, and Recreation, 1201 16th St., N.W., Washington 6, D.C.

American Association of Junior Colleges, 730 Jackson Place, Washington 6, D.C.

American Association of Medical Record Librarians, 18 E. Division St., Chicago 10

American Association of Nurse Anesthetists, 18 E. Division St., Chicago 10

American Association of Psychiatric Social Workers, 1711 Fitzwater St., Philadelphia 46

American Association of Schools and Departments of Journalism, Ohio State University, Columbus 10, Ohio

American Association of Schools of Social Work, 1313 E. 60th St., Chicago 37

American Association of Social Workers, 130 E. 22nd St., New York 10

American Association to Promote the Teaching of Speech to the Deaf, 1537 35th St., N.W., Washington 7, D.C.

American Bankers Association, 22 E. 40th St., New York 16

American Bar Association, 1140 No. Dearborn St., Chicago 10

American Chemical Society, 1155 16th St., N.W., Washington 6, D.C.

American College of Surgeons, 40 E. Erie St., Chicago 11

American Dental Association, 222 E. Superior St., Chicago 11

American Dental Hygienists' Association, 1704 No. Troy St., Arlington, Va.

American Dietetic Association, 620 No. Michigan Ave., Chicago 11

American Foundation for Pharmaceutical Education, 330 W. 42nd St., New York 18

American Foundation for the Blind, Inc., 15 W. 16th St., New York 11

American Heart Association, Inc., 1790 Broadway, New York 19

American Home Economics Association, 620 Mills Bldg., Washington 6, D.C.

American Hotel Association, 221 W. 57th St., New York 19

American Institute of Architects, 1741 New York Ave., N.W., Washington 6, D.C.

American Institute of Banking, 22 E. 40th St., New York 16

American Institute of Electrical Engineers, 33 W. 39th St., New York 18

American Institute of Laundering, Joliet, Ill.

American Institute of Mining and Metallurgical Engineers, 29 W. 39th St., New York 18

American Institute of Physics, 57 E. 55th St., New York 22

American Library Association, 520 No. Michigan Ave., Chicago 11

American Medical Association, Council on Medical Education and Hospitals, 535 No. Dearborn St., Chicago 10

American Meteorological Society, 5727 University Ave., Chicago 37

American Newspaper Publishers Association, 370 Lexington Ave., New York 17

American Occupational Therapy Association, 33 W. 42nd St., New York 18

American Optometric Association, 518 Wilmac Bldg., Minneapolis, Minn.

American Optometric Association, Public Health Bureau, 707 Jenkins Bldg., Pittsburgh 22, Pa.

American Osteopathic Association, 139 No. Clark Street, Chicago 2

American Physiotherapy Association, 1790 Broadway, New York 19

American Public Health Association, 1790 Broadway, New York 19

American Red Cross, National Headquarters, 18th and E St., N.W., Washington 13, D.C.

American Registry of X-Ray Technicians, 2900 E. Minnehaha Parkway, Minneapolis 6, Minn.

American Society for the Hard of Hearing, 1537 35th St., N.W., Washington 7, D.C.

American Society of Agricultural Engineers, St. Joseph, Mich.

American Society of Clinical Pathologists, Ball Memorial Hospital, Muncie, Ind.

American Telephone and Telegraph Company, 195 Broadway, New York 7

American Trucking Associations, Inc., 1424 16th St., N.W., Washington 6, D.C.

American Veterinary Medical Association, 600 So. Michigan Ave., Chicago 5

Apprentice-Training Service, U. S. Dept. of Labor, Washington 25, D.C.

Association for Childhood Education, 1201 16th St., N.W., Washington 6, D.C.

Association of Bank Women, Research Committee, (Miss Catherine Pepper, Chairman), National City Bank of New York, 55 Wall St., New York 15

Association of Business Institutes of the State of New York, 225 Broadway, New York 7

Association Press, 347 Madison Ave., New York 17

Atchison, Topeka and Santa Fe Railway Company, 80 E. Jackson Blvd., Chicago 4

Baltimore Department of Education, Division of Vocational Education, Vocational Guidance, 3 E. 25th St., Baltimore 18, Md.

Barbizon Studio of Fashion Modeling, 576 5th Ave., New York 19

F. A. Bartlett Tree Expert Company, Stamford, Conn.

Bates College, Lewiston, Me.

Bellman Publishing Company, 6 Park St., Boston 8

Bentley School of Accounting and Finance, 921 Boylston St., Boston 15

Bethlehem Steel Company, Bethlehem, Pa.

B'nai B'rith Vocational Service Bureau, 1746 M St., N.W., Washington 6, D.C.

Board of Christian Education, Presbyterian Church in the U. S. A., 808 Witherspoon Bldg., Philadelphia 7

Boys' Clubs of America, Inc., 381 4th Ave., New York 16

Brotherhood of Railroad Trainmen, 1370 Ontario St., Cleveland 13, Ohio

Building America, 2 W. 45th St., New York 19

Bureau of Foreign and Domestic Commerce, Washington 25, D.C.

Bureau of Labor Statistics, U. S. Dept. of Labor, Washington 25, D.C.

Burgess Publishing Company, 426 So. 6th St., Minneapolis 15, Minn.

Business Education World, 270 Madison Ave., New York 16

Caterpillar Tractor Company, Peoria 8, Ill.

Chamber of Commerce of the U. S., Domestic Distribution Department, Washington 6, D.C.

Chicago Board of Education, Bureau of Occupational Research, 228 N. LaSalle St., Chicago

The Chronicle, Port Byron, N.Y.

Cincinnati College of Embalming, Cincinnati 29, Ohio

Civil Aeronautics Administration, Dept. of Commerce, Washington 25, D.C.

College of the City of New York, College of Liberal Arts and Sciences, Convent Ave. and 139th St., New York 30

Commonwealth Book Company, 80 E. Jackson Blvd., Chicago 4

Connecticut Mutual Life Insurance Company, 140 Garden St., Hartford, Conn.

Cooperative League of the U. S. A., 343 So. Dearborn St., Chicago 4

Cutler, Leon, 20 E. 35th St., New York 16

The Dahls, Haviland Road, Stamford, Conn.

Davey Tree Expert Company, Kent, Ohio

Diesel Engine Manufacturers Association, 1 No. LaSalle St., Chicago 2

Drexel Institute of Technology, 32nd and Chestnut Sts., Philadelphia 4

Dun and Bradstreet, Inc., 290 Broadway, New York 8

Educational Research Bureau, 1217 13th St., N.W., Washington 5, D.C.

Elgin Watchmakers College, Elgin, Ill.

Endicott Junior College, Beverly, Mass.

Engineers' Council for Professional Development, 29 W. 39th St., New York 18

Family Welfare Association of America, 122 E. 22nd St., New York 10

Fashion Institute of Technology and Design, 225 W. 24th St., New York 11

Federal Bureau of Investigation, United States Department of Justice, Washington 25, D.C.

Federation Employment Service, 67 West 47th St., New York 19

Fish and Wildlife Service, Chicago 54

Florida, University of. Bureau of Economic and Business Research, Gainesville, Fla.

Franklin Institute, Rochester, N.Y.

General Electric Company, 1 River Road, Schenectady 5, N.Y.

General Motors Corporation, Clearing Point Activity, 3044 W. Grand Blvd., Detroit 2, Mich.

Girl Scouts, 155 E. 44th St., New York 17

Gregg College, 6 No. Michigan Ave., Chicago 2

Harian Publications, 270 Lafayette St., New York 12

Harper & Brothers, 49 E. 33rd St., New York 16

Hartford Accident and Indemnity Company, Hartford 15, Conn.

Hinds, Hayden and Eldredge, Inc., 105 5th Ave., New York 3

Hospital for Joint Diseases, 1919 Madison Ave., New York 35

Horse and Mule Association of America, Inc., 407 So. Dearborn St., Chicago 5

Hunter College of the City of New York, 695 Park Ave., New York 21

Illinois Bell Telephone Company, 212 W. Washington St., Chicago 6

Illinois Ceramic Institute, Urbana, Ill.

Indiana University, Bloomington, Ind.

Institute for Research, 537 So. Dearborn St., Chicago 5

Institute of Meat Packing, University of Chicago, Chicago 37

Institute of Women's Professional Relations, Connecticut College, New London, Conn.

International Association of Chiefs of Police, 1313 East 60th St., Chicago, Ill.

International Association of Ice Cream Manufacturers, 1105 Barr Bldg., Washington 6, D.C.

Investment Bankers Association of America, 33 South Clark St., Chicago 3

Iowa State College Press, Ames, Iowa

John Hancock Life Insurance Company, Boston, Mass.

Johns-Manville Corporation, 22 E. 40th St., New York 16

Joint Lithographic Advisory Council, 70 Pine St., New York 5

Joint Orthopedic Nursing Advisory Service, 1790 Broadway, New York 19

Julius Rosenwald Fund, 4901 Ellis Ave., Chicago 15

Katharine Gibbs School, 90 Marlboro St., Boston 16

Kraft Cheese Company, 500 Peshtigo Court, Chicago 90

Lehigh University, Bethlehem, Pa.

Life Insurance Sales Research Bureau, 115 Broad St., Hartford 5, Conn.

J. Gordon Lippincott and Company, 500 5th Ave., New York 18

McKnight and McKnight, Bloomington, Ill.

The Macmillan Company, 60 5th Ave., New York 11

Mademoiselle, The Magazine for Smart Young Women, 122 E. 42nd St., New York 17

Michigan, University of. Ann Arbor, Mich.

Milwaukee-Downer College, Milwaukee, Wis.

Minnesota, University of. Library. Minneapolis 14, Minn.

Modern Language Journal, 284 Hoyt St., Buffalo 13, N.Y.

Mohawk Carpet Mills, Inc., Amsterdam, N.Y.

Morgan-Dillon & Company, 6433 Ravenswood Ave., Chicago

Music Educators National Conference, 80 E. Jackson Blvd., Chicago 4

National Association of Broadcasters, 1760 N St., N.W., Washington 6, D.C.

National Association of Chiropodists, 3500 14th St., N.W., Washington 10, D.C.

National Association of Manufacturers, 14 W. 49th St., New York 20

National Association of Secondary-School Principals, 1201 16th St., N.W., Washington 6, D.C.

National Association for Practical Nurse Education, 250 W. 57th St., New York 19

National Chiropractic Association, Inc., 92 Norton St., New Haven, Conn.

National Council of Business Schools, 839 17th St., N.W., Washington 6, D.C.

National Council of Technical Schools, 839 17th St., N.W., Washington 6, D.C.

National Council of Textile School Deans. Edward T. Pickard, Secretary, Kent, Conn.

National Council, Protestant Episcopal Church, 281 4th Ave., New York 10

National Dairy Council, 111 No. Canal St., Chicago 6

National Education Association, 1201 16th St., N.W., Washington 6, D.C.

National Federation of Business and Professional Women's Clubs, Inc., 1819 Broadway, New York 23

National Foreign Trade Council Inc., Foreign Trade Education Committee, 26 Beaver St., New York 4

National Foundation for Infantile Paralysis, 120 Broadway, New York 5

National Funeral Directors Association, 111 W. Washington St., Chicago 2

National Home Study Council, 839 17th St., N.W., Washington 6, D.C.

National Institute of Public Affairs, 400 Investment Bldg., Washington 5, D.C.

National Organization for Public Health Nursing, Inc., 1790 Broadway, New York 19

National Paper Box Manufacturers Association, Liberty Trust Bldg., Philadelphia 7, Pa.

National Park Service, U. S. Dept. of the Interior, Chicago 54

National Planning Association, 800 21st St., N.W., Washington 6, D.C.

National Probation Association, 1790 Broadway, New York 19

National Recreation Association, 315 4th Ave., New York 10

National Retail Hardware Association, 333 No. Pennsylvania St., Indianapolis 4, Ind.

National Roster of Scientific and Specialized Personnel, U. S. Employment Service, Dept. of Labor, Washington 25, D.C.

National Safety Council, 20 No. Wacker Drive, Chicago 6

National Selected Morticians, 520 No. Michigan Ave., Chicago 11

National Society for the Blind, Woodward Bldg., Washington 5, D.C.

National Society for the Prevention of Blindness, 1790 Broadway, New York 19

National Tuberculosis Association, 1790 Broadway, New York 19

National Vocational Guidance Association, 82 Beaver St., New York 5

New England Telephone & Telegraph Company, 50 Oliver St., Boston 7

New Mexico, University of. Albuquerque, N.M.

New York Library Association, Public Library, Brooklyn, N.Y.

New York State Department of Civil Service, Albany, N.Y.

New York University, Washington Square, New York 3

Northeastern University, Boston, Mass.

Northwestern University, Lake Shore Drive, Chicago, Ill.

Nursing Information Bureau of the American Nurses' Association, 1790 Broadway, New York 19

Occupational Index, Inc., New York University, 80 Washington Square E., New York 3

Ohio Leather Company, 1052 No. State St., Girard, Ohio

Ohio State Department of Education, Columbus 15, Ohio

Osteopathic Women's National Association, 139 No. Clark St., Chicago 2

Pace Institute, 225 Broadway, New York 7

Pacific Northwest Loggers Association, Joint Committee on Forest Conservation, 364 Stuart Bldg., Seattle 1, Wash.

Pan American Union, 17th St. and Constitution Ave., N.W., Washington, D.C.

Park Publishing House, 4141 W. Vliet St., Milwaukee, Wis.

Pennsylvania Restaurant Association, 315 State Theatre Bldg., Harrisburg, Pa.

Pennsylvania State College, Bureau of Business Research, State College, Pa.

Pennsylvania State College, School of Mineral Industries, State College, Pa.

Phi Delta Kappa, 2034 Ridge Road, Homewood, Ill.

Plastics Industries Technical Institute, 122 E. 42nd St., New York 17
Princeton University, Industrial Relations Section, Princeton, N.J.
Printers' Ink Publishing Company, 205 E. 42nd St., New York 17
Procter and Gamble Company, Cincinnati 1, Ohio
Public Affairs Committee, Inc., 30 Rockefeller Plaza, New York 20

The Quarrie Corporation, 35 E. Wacker Drive, Chicago

Radio Corporation of America, 30 Rockefeller Plaza, New York 20
Radio Replies Press, 500 Robert St., St. Paul 1, Minn.
Registry of Medical Technologists of the American Society of Clinical
    Pathologist, Ball Memorial Hospital, Muncie, Ind.
Related Arts Service, 511 5th Ave., New York 17
Remington Rand, Inc., 315 4th Ave., New York 10
Rochester Institute of Technology, 65 Plymouth Ave., Rochester 8,
    N.Y.
Row, Peterson and Company, 1911 Ridge Ave., Evanston, Ill.
Rutgers University, New Brunswick, N.J.
Russell Sage Foundation, 130 E. 22nd St., New York 10

Santa Fe System Lines, Railway Exchange, Chicago 4
Science Research Associates, 228 So. Wabash Ave., Chicago 3
Social Protection Division, Office of Community War Services, Fed-
    eral Security Agency, Washington 25, D.C.
Society of American Foresters, 825 Mills Bldg., Washington 6, D.C.
Society of Naval Architects and Marine Engineers, 29 W. 39th St.,
    New York 18
South Dakota Press, Vermillion, S.D.
Special Libraries Association, 31 E. 10th St., New York 3
Stevens College, Columbia, Mo.
Superintendent of Documents, U. S. Government Printing Office,
    Washington 25, D.C.
Syracuse University, Syracuse, N.Y.

Tennessee State Board for Vocational Education, Nashville 3, Tenn.
The Textile Foundation, National Bureau of Standards, Washington
    25, D.C.
Transcontienntal and Western Air, Inc., Kansas City 6, Mo.
Twentieth Century Fund, 330 W. 42nd St., New York 18
The Trailblazers, 119 W. Park Ave., Champaign, Ill.

Union Central Life Insurance Company, 3d and Vine Sts., Cincin-
    nati 1, Ohio

Union of American Hebrew Congregations, Cincinnati, Ohio

United Air Lines, Dept. of School and College Service, 23 E. Monroe St., Chicago 3

U. S. Dept. of Commerce, Bureau of the Census, Washington 25, D.C.

U. S. Maritime Commission, Educational Section, Commerce Building, Washington 25, D.C.

U. S. Office of Education, Occupational Information and Guidance Service, Washington 25, D.C.

Union College, Schenectady 8, N.Y.

Valparaiso Technical Institute, Valparaiso, Ind.

Virginia Polytechnic Institute, Dept. of Vocational Education, Blacksburg, Va.

Vocational Guidance Manuals, Inc., 45 W. 45th St., New York 19

Western Personnel Service, 30 No. Raymond Ave., Pasadena 1, Calif.

Whiting Paper Company, 14th St., and 7th Ave., New York 11

Wisconsin, University of. Madison, Wis.

Women's Bureau, U. S. Dept. of Labor. (Publications available from Supt. of Documents, Washington 25, D.C.)

Woman's Press, 600 Lexington Ave., New York 22

Young Men's Christian Association, National Council, 347 Madison Ave., New York 17

Young Women's Christian Association, National Board, 600 Lexington Ave., New York 22

Index